The Renaissance

VOLUME 4

Other titles in the
World History by Era series:

WORLD HISTORY BY ERA

The Renaissance

VOLUME 4

Jeff Hay, *Book Editor*

Daniel Leone, *President*
Bonnie Szumski, *Publisher*
Scott Barbour, *Managing Editor*

Greenhaven Press, Inc., San Diego, California

Every effort has been made to trace the owners of copy-
righted material. The articles in this volume may have been
edited for content, length, and/or reading level. The titles
have been changed to enhance the editorial purpose.

No part of this book may be reproduced or used in any form
or by any means, electrical, mechanical, or otherwise, including, but not limited to, photocopy, recording, or any information storage and retrieval system, without prior permission
from the publisher.

Library of Congress Cataloging-in-Publication Data

The Renaissance / Jeff Hay, book editor.
　　p. cm. — (World history by era; vol. 4)
　Includes bibliographical references and index.
　ISBN 0-7377-0764-X (pbk. : alk. paper) —
ISBN 0-7377-0765-8 (lib. bdg. : alk. paper)
　1. Renaissance. 2. Italy—Civilization—1268–1559.
3. Civilization, Islamic. 4. Europe—Civilization—16th
century. 5. Turkey—History—1288–1453. 6. Indians.
7. Discoveries in geography. I. Hay, Jeff. II. Series.

CB361 .R372 2002
940.2'1—dc21　　　　　　　　　　　　　　　2001023842
　　　　　　　　　　　　　　　　　　　　　　　　CIP

Copyright © 2002 by Greenhaven Press, Inc.
P.O. Box 289009 San Diego, CA 92198-9009

Printed in the USA

CONTENTS

Chapter 4: An Era of Global Conquest: 1520–1540

Chapter 6: The International Exchange of People, Ideas, Products, and Diseases

Chapter 7: The Renaissance Closes with an Era of Great Leaders

indecisiveness, and an abiding interest in Renaissance secular culture.

6. Shakespeare Commemorates Elizabeth's Reign

FOREWORD

The late 1980s were a time of dramatic events worldwide. Tragedies such as the explosions of the space shuttle *Challenger* and the Chernobyl nuclear power plant shocked the world out of its complacent belief that humankind had mastered nature and firmly controlled its technological creations. In U.S. politics, scandal rocked the White House when several high-ranking officials in the Ronald Reagan administration were convicted of selling arms to Iran and aiding the Nicaraguan contra rebels. In global politics, U.S. president Ronald Reagan and Soviet president Mikhail Gorbachev signed a landmark treaty banning intermediate-range nuclear forces, marking the beginning of an era of arms control. In several parts of the world—including Beijing, China, the West Bank and Gaza Strip, and several nations of Eastern Europe—people rose up to resist oppressive governments, with varying degrees of success. In American culture, crack cocaine and inner-city poverty contributed to the development of a new and controversial music genre: gangsta rap.

Many of these events were unrelated to one another except for the fact that they occurred at about the same time. Others were linked to global developments. Greenhaven Press's World History by Era series provides students with a unique tool for examining global history in a way that allows them to appreciate the seemingly random occurrences as well as the general trends of human progress. This series divides world history—from the time of ancient Greece and Rome to the end of the second millennium—into ten discrete periods. Each volume then presents a collection of both primary and secondary documents that describe the major events of the period in chronological order. This structure provides students with a snapshot of events occurring simultaneously in all parts of the world. The reader can then see the connections between events in far-flung corners of the world. For example, the Palestinian uprising (*intifada*) of December 1987 was near in time—if not in character and location—to similar protests in Beijing, China; Berlin, Germany; Prague, Czechoslovakia; and Bucharest, Romania. While these events were different in many ways, they all involved ordinary citizens striving for self-autonomy and democracy against governments that were attempting to impose strict controls on their civil liberties. By making the connections between these events, students can see that they comprised a global movement for democracy and human rights that profoundly impacted social and political systems worldwide.

Each volume in this series offers features to enhance students' understanding of the era of world history under discussion. An introductory essay provides an overview of the period, supplying essential context for the readings that follow. An annotated table of contents highlights the main point of each selection. A more in-depth introduction precedes each document, placing it in its particular historical context and offering biographical information about the author. A thorough chronology and index allow students to quickly reference specific events and dates. Finally, a bibliography opens up additional avenues of research. These features help to make the World History by Era series an extremely valuable tool for students researching the rise and fall of civilizations, social and political revolutions, cultural movements, scientific and technological advancements, and other events that mark the unfolding of human history throughout the world.

The Renaissance, the name given to the historical period from 1454 to 1610, was an era of great cultural and political change. New empires emerged in such ancient centers of civilization as India, the Middle East, West Africa, and Mexico. While China continued to dominate East Asia, its ruling Ming dynasty turned in response to new challenges from Japan and from European explorers. Within Europe, aggressive national monarchies engaged in intense competition with one another that was to take many forms and last for centuries. Meanwhile, European culture was reinvigorated by the development of mechanized printing and a rebirth of appreciation for classical learning.

Perhaps the greatest transformation of this age, however, was effected by unprecedented global exploration by European powers. By 1610, almost the entire world had been drawn together into a single network of trade connected by ships from Portugal, Spain, England, France, and the Netherlands. In the process, Europe's aggressive sailors and merchants connected the New World of North and South America to the Old World of Europe, Asia, and Africa. The result was an expanding exchange of goods, ideas, peoples, and even diseases which completely transformed global civilization and helped establish European society as one of the most creative and dynamic on earth.

THE MING DYNASTY BUILDS ITS MONUMENTS

The most energetic civilizations of the Middle Ages, from 476 to 1453, had been China and the Islamic Middle East. Both remained important throughout the Renaissance. China, however, under the control of the Ming dynasty, from 1368 until 1644, turned inward after a brief period of overseas exploration of its own in the early 1400s. Following traditional Confucian ideals, Ming leaders sought to cultivate China from within rather than deal with foreign "barbarians." In many ways they were successful, as China remained among the wealthiest civilizations on earth, as well as the most populous.

One important reflection of this focus on inward cultivation was in foreign policy. Ming China conducted relations with foreign powers only according to an intricate system of tribute relationships. Foreign nations had to acknowledge the superiority of Chinese civilization with gifts and rituals; only then would China's emperors or officials allow outside trade or cultural exchange. Through such measures the Chinese believed they could control outside influences.

The Ming dynasty's suspicion of foreign interference as well as its inward focus resulted in the construction of some of the greatest monuments to China ever constructed. These include the Great Wall of China, built to keep marauding Central Asian nomads out. Earlier versions of a wall along China's northern border had been constructed, but only the Ming emperors could muster the resources to create this huge structure, which remains one of China's greatest landmarks. The wall rarely served its purpose, however, as gatekeepers often traded or accepted bribes from potential invaders. In other instances, nomadic warriors simply avoided the wall by going around it. Nonetheless, Ming leaders adhered to the claim that true civilization lay inside the Great Wall; outside was only barbarism.

Ming leaders also constructed the Forbidden City in the capital of Beijing. One of the great architectural wonders of the age, it is a self-sufficient network of cities-within-cities meant to reflect the Chinese emperor's status as the Son of Heaven. Oriented entirely on a north-south axis to demonstrate alignment with astrological principles, the Forbidden City was surrounded by fifteen miles of forty-foot-high walls. At its very center, restricted to high officials, were ceremonial halls and the emperor's quarters.

The structure, although intended to reflect the greatness of the Ming emperors, also had the effect of isolating them from their subjects. Common people were not allowed through the gates, and emperors, for their part, rarely left their comfortable palace quarters. By the end of the Renaissance, the isolation of the Ming emperors helped to leave China vulnerable to attacks from Japanese pirates as well as from Central Asian and Manchurian nomads.

THE MILITARY PROWESS OF THE OTTOMAN EMPIRE

If China, despite the isolation of its leaders, remained the great power in eastern Asia during the Renaissance, the Turkish Ottoman Empire grew to dominate western Asia. The Ottomans acquired their reputation as a military power in the early 1300s by taking territory from the Christian Byzantine Empire. In 1453, the Ottoman sultan Mehmed II conquered Constantinople, the capital of the Byzantine Empire and one of the great cities of the Middle Ages. The conquest of Constantinople, which soon became the Ottoman capital, gave the Turks command of the trade routes connecting Europe with Asia as well as freedom to pursue further conquests in southeastern Europe. In the decades following 1453 the Ottomans marched deeply into Europe, establishing control over Greece, the Balkans, and many of the islands of the eastern Mediterranean.

Although Turkish warriors suffered the occasional setback, the Ottoman Empire quickly expanded to include most of the Middle East, southeastern Europe, and North Africa, as well as the great Arab cities of Baghdad, Cairo, and Mecca. It reached its greatest geographical extent during the reign of Suleiman the Magnificent, who reigned from 1520 to 1566. Suleiman aggressively pursued expansion. His armies took the important Christian city of Belgrade in 1521, then defeated Hungary (and killed its king) at the Battle of Mohacs in 1526. Furthermore, the Ottomans built a huge navy and took command of the eastern Mediterranean and its lucrative trade.

The victory over the Hungarians left the way open to Vienna, a great central European city and, by common assent at the time, the gateway to Germany, Italy, France, and Spain in western Europe. Seeking to weaken in particular the Hapsburg Empire, which included Austria and Germany, Suleiman mounted a siege of Vienna in 1529. The siege lasted for weeks, but ultimately a coalition of Christian kings forced Suleiman to return his army to Budapest, the Hungarian capital. Western Europe had been saved from the Turkish onslaught, but the Ottoman Empire remained a major influence in European as well as Middle Eastern affairs until its dissolution in 1920.

DOMINANT EMPIRES IN AFRICA AND THE AMERICAS

Another major Islamic power emerged in West Africa in the late 1400s: the Empire of Songhay. From their base at the important trade city of Gao on the Niger River, Songhay tribal warriors rejected the rulership of Mali, which had controlled the region in the Late Middle Ages. They then established a prosperous and powerful kingdom of their own. Songhay, which lasted until 1591, controlled the trade routes that linked West Africa with the ports of North Africa as well as the trans-Saharan trade with the Islamic heartland of the Middle East.

Although few among the common folk converted, the ruling elites in Songhay were all Muslim and actively supported Islamic learning. They constructed an Islamic university in Timbuktu and encouraged the building of mosques throughout their territory. In recognition for his support of Islam, the Songhay king Muhammad Ture Askiya, reigning from 1493 to 1528, was named "Caliph of the Sudan," the head of Islam in all Central and West Africa.

Across the Atlantic in the Americas, other empires consolidated their hold over huge populations by the late 1400s. The Inca Empire of Peru controlled a region that stretched two thousand miles along the Pacific coast of South America. Based in the city of Cuzco high in the Andes Mountains, the Inca Empire was extremely well organized under the religious authority of its emperor, also known as the Inca, who was revered as a connection between this world and that of the gods. Its population enjoyed an extensive system of social welfare in return for demanding labor. In addition, a wide network of roads, traversed by both the Inca armies and a courier service, maintained communication and facilitated trade.

To the north in Mexico, the Aztecs had established a powerful state based in Tenochtitlán, which was one of the largest cities on earth. At its height in the late 1400s, the population of Tenochtitlán exceeded two hundred thousand, and the city served as a market center for almost all of Central and North America. Moreover, Tenochtitlán reflected the power of the Aztec tribe, who since 1325 had been engaged in conquest over numerous other native Mexican tribes. The great ceremonial centers and temple pyramids that dominated the Aztec skyline awed conquered peoples, who were sometimes brought to Tenochtitlán as human sacrifices. Such practices, however, worked against the stability of the empire, and Aztec kings and warriors fought almost constantly with enemy tribes. Nonetheless, the Aztec Empire was one of the great kingdoms of the world in the late 1400s and early 1500s. It dominated the huge populations and rich agriculture of Mexico and stretched from the Caribbean Sea to the Pacific Ocean.

Like the Inca Empire, however, the Aztec Empire ultimately fell to the European kingdom of Spain, which also emerged as a major power in the late 1400s. During the Middle Ages, Spain did not exist. Instead, the Iberian Peninsula was divided into numerous independent kingdoms, several of which were Arabic and Islamic. In 1454 the most important Iberian kingdoms were Christian Portugal, which was already carving a niche in overseas exploration; Granada, the last of the Islamic kingdoms of Spain; and the two largest Christian realms, Aragon and Castile.

Spain Unites Under Ferdinand and Isabella

In 1469 King Ferdinand of Aragon and Queen Isabella of Castile set the course for Spain's future by marrying. Their two kingdoms remained independent, but they practiced a common foreign policy directed at removing the Arabs from Granada and limiting the power of France. Moreover, Ferdinand and Isabella's heirs were to rule over a united Spain that aggressively pursued territorial expansion in defense of the Roman Catholic Church.

Spain cemented its position as the most powerful European monarchy when, in 1494, Ferdinand and Isabella's daughter Joanna married Philip, the son of the Holy Roman Emperor, who was in effect the Hapsburg king of Germany and Austria. Their eldest son was Charles I, the first king of a unified Spain. In 1519, Charles I was named Charles V, Holy Roman Emperor. His empire was to include not only huge portions of Europe but also much of North and South America. For most of the remainder of the Renaissance, Spanish ships dominated the Atlantic, Spanish armies were feared throughout Europe, and members of the Spanish royal family could be found in virtually every European court.

Spain (ca. 1450)

Among the great targets of Spanish expansion was Italy, a loose confederation of city-states from which Europe's cultural revival emerged. Rich Italian cities such as Florence, Venice, and Milan provided the setting for an intellectual and artistic movement that, indeed, gave the entire period a name: the rebirth, or Renaissance.

At the most basic level, what was reborn in Europe was an appreciation for classical antiquity: the literature, art, and thought of ancient Greece and Rome. In the 1300s, Italian writers, scholars, and artists began imitating the classics, which had mostly been ignored during the Middle Ages when Europe was dominated by the Roman Catholic Church. Interest in classical antiquity spread quickly as scholars unearthed increasing numbers of Greek and Roman manuscripts.

These men came to be known as humanists: students and teachers of humane studies or the liberal arts. During the Renaissance, the liberal arts included grammar, rhetoric, poetry, history, and moral philosophy. Following the lead of the Roman writer and orater Cicero, who was one of their great models, humanists claimed that those educated in the liberal arts were best able to communicate knowledge and wisdom.

Humanists, who frequently worked as tutors and advisers to the powerful, argued that the liberal arts celebrated the dignity of the individual. Moreover, they helped to educate the individual to lead an active life and be an example of virtuous behavior. Among the intellectual habits that humanism helped to introduce into Europe were curiosity about the world, the need for rational inquiry and examination, and the desirability of finding the original sources of knowledge. In all, Renaissance humanism helped to create a more secular culture, freed from the restrictions of Roman Catholic theology and focused upon human life and the things of this world.

Among the greatest of the humanists was Niccolò Machiavelli, a Florentine political philosopher. After retiring from the civil service, Machiavelli wrote prolifically. He combined an expertise in the Latin language and Roman history with intimate knowledge of the problems of Renaissance-era politics. Machiavelli's best-known work is *The Prince*, published in Italian in 1513. *The Prince* is a guidebook on how to acquire and maintain political power, and to make his points Machiavelli uses examples from both Roman history and Renaissance Europe. Since Machiavelli completely ignored moral considerations, claiming that the pursuit of power justifies any means, he has been vilified ever since the book appeared.

THE PRINTING PRESS TRANSFORMS EUROPE

Renaissance humanism was given a great boost by the invention of the printing press in the 1450s. The Chinese had actually produced block-printed books as early as the ninth century, although the huge number of Chinese characters necessarily limited the efficiency of the craft. During the Middle Ages, printed items from China such as paper money and playing cards trickled into Europe via merchants and adventurers. Intrigued by the potential of printing in both commerce and scholarship, craftsmen in the commercial centers of Italy and Germany competed in the early 1400s to develop an efficient printing press. Johann Gutenberg, a German goldsmith, won the competition: In 1455 he printed two hundred editions of a section of the Bible using moveable type made from metal molds.

Printing spread rapidly throughout Europe. By the early 1500s, European towns supported more than a thousand print shops, and perhaps a half-million printed books were in circulation. Printing technology, however, was not restricted to books. It facilitated commercial transactions by making record keeping more accurate, improved and speeded government and religious communication, and encouraged intellectual debate through the mass production of posters and pamphlets. The new printed books were far cheaper and easier to carry than the hand-copied books of the Middle Ages. As printing spread, it created a demand for literacy and education, and thanks to the introduction of this new technology, Europe's scholars, geographers, explorers, and religious reformers enjoyed a wide and curious audience.

Europe's cultural renaissance was characterized by more than humanist scholarship. It was also one of the great eras of artistic accomplishment in world history. From sculpture to architecture to painting, Renaissance masters produced works whose excellence is still considered unsurpassed.

Renaissance art reflected the increasingly worldly spirit of the era. Artists were concerned with observations and depictions of nature as well as with the expression of emotion. Their subject matter included not only religious or biblical themes, but also stories from classical history and myth. Moreover, certain Renaissance artists took it upon themselves to record the history of their day through portraiture or by including elements of the European setting in their works. Technical changes, such as the discovery of linear perspective and chiaroscuro (shading from light to dark), helped Renaissance art achieve a symmetry, richness, and depth unknown in earlier ages.

Great artists include the painter Masaccio and the sculptor Donatello, both of whom worked in the early 1400s. But new artistic heights were reached during the so-called High Renaissance, from approximately 1490 to 1520. Michelangelo, Raphael, and Leonardo da Vinci, perhaps the greatest Renaissance artists, created their most well known works in that relatively brief period. Michelangelo, for his part, was an accomplished sculptor and architect as well as painter. His greatest works include an eighteen-foot-high statue of David, currently housed in Florence, as well as the paintings on the ceiling of the Sistine Chapel in Rome. Michelangelo also contributed to the design of St. Peter's Basilica, under the guidance of Pope Julius II beginning in 1506.

Raphael's paintings are remarkable for their warmth, richness, and vitality. Among his favorite subjects were the Virgin Mary and the Madonna and Child, of whom he painted dozens of canvases. His work, however, reflected the Renaissance spirit in

Raphael's love of beauty is reflected in the warmth and richness of his painting **Madonna of the Goldfinch.**

more direct ways. One of his most famous frescoes is *The School of Athens*, which combines portraits of the great scholars and artists of Greece and Rome with those of his own day, including Michelangelo and Leonardo.

THE RENAISSANCE MAN

Michelangelo and Raphael were good examples of the "universal man," one who was capable of great accomplishments in a number of fields. Perhaps the greatest example of such a "Renaissance man" was Leonardo da Vinci, the painter whose *Mona Lisa* and *Last Supper* are among the finest and most well known works of art in the world. Leonardo was, however, also an accomplished scientist and engineer. His sketchbooks contained detailed anatomical studies derived from actual dissection and designs for such modern devices as machine guns and airplanes. A man of action as well, Leonardo designed military structures such as fortifications, catapults, and a cannon, for, among others, the king of France.

These three geniuses came from different parts of Italy, but all were associated at one time or another with Florence, the greatest center of Renaissance art and humanist scholarship as well as major banking and textile center. Located in the central Italian region of Tuscany, Florence was controlled by the Medici family for much of the Renaissance. Cosimo de Medici, who governed the city from 1434 to 1469, turned the city into a European power. His grandson, Lorenzo the Magnificent, was in power from 1478 to 1492. Lorenzo could be a brutal tyrant, but he was also an enthusiastic supporter of scholarship and art. He helped maintain a philosophical academy, the Florentine Platonic Academy, that drew to the city many of Europe's greatest thinkers. Michelangelo was a frequent visitor. Moreover, Lorenzo acted as Leonardo's patron, supporting him early in his career. Raphael was drawn to Florence from his native Urbino to perfect his art, sustained by Medici wealth and patronage.

The Renaissance spirit of curiosity and openness about the world was greatly reinforced by reports coming into Europe from sailors and adventurers whose voyages were increasingly wide ranging. The reports spoke of unknown lands, foreign peoples and customs, and exotic trade goods. Knowledge of and access to these new worlds would transform both Europe and the rest of the world.

EUROPEAN SHIPS SET SAIL

Europe's age of exploration began in the early 1400s when Prince Henry of Portugal began sending fleets of ships south along

Renaissance Italy

Africa's west coast in search of gold. By the 1450s, Portuguese ships had established regular trade with African coastal merchants, and not only gold but also ivory and slaves could be found in the markets of Lisbon, Portugal's capital. In the course of the voyages, the Portuguese first landed in the Canaries, Madeiras, and Azores, island groups in the central Atlantic. Europeans had known of their existence, but never before did such island groups seem to suggest that the Atlantic might be neither as wide nor as mysterious as many Europeans believed.

In the late 1400s, however, the goal of the Portuguese was neither to travel west across the Atlantic nor to simply secure a sliver of African trade. Instead, they hoped to enter into the rich trade of Asia, especially the trade in spices. Their motivation for finding new routes for the spice trade increased after 1453, when the Ottoman Empire conquered Constantinople and restricted European access to the markets of the Middle East. Understanding the opportunity for wealth and power the discovery of new trade routes offered, Portuguese captains pushed farther south along the coast of Africa in search of its southern tip and the entrance into the Indian Ocean.

The first Portuguese captain to lead a fleet into the Indian

Ocean was Bartolomeu Dias. In 1487, Dias's ships were caught in a storm. When the skies cleared and the navigators were able to perform their astronomical readings, Dias discovered that he had indeed rounded the tip of southern Africa, later known as the Cape of Good Hope. His sailors, however, were fearful of what lay ahead and forced Dias to return to Lisbon.

News of Christopher Columbus's successful voyage across the Atlantic in 1492 for Spain increased the pressure on the Portuguese to be the first to reach the Indies, as Europeans referred to the (to them) mysterious and rich lands of Asia. In 1497 Vasco da Gama led four ships around the Cape of Good Hope and up the east coast of Africa, anchoring in some of its ancient trade ports for information (and sometimes provoking violent conflict). There he learned of the south Indian city of Calicut, one of the major ports of the Indian Ocean. Vasco da Gama arrived there in 1498, and with difficulty he obtained a cargo of pepper and cinnamon. He returned to Portugal in 1499, where his cargo sold for sixty times the cost of the entire voyage. Now convinced of the wealth to be earned from global trade, Portugal began sending fleet after fleet into the Indian Ocean.

CHRISTIANS AND SPICES

Wealth, however, was never the sole motivation for exploration. Christian kings and mariners wanted to serve the faith as well. Prince Henry and later Portuguese leaders hoped to convert Africans to Christianity and check the spread of Islam. In addition, sailors believed they might find lost communities of Christians whom they could then bring under the authority of the pope. Indeed, financial and religious motivations worked hand in hand. When da Gama was asked upon arrival in Calicut what he was looking for, he replied, "Christians and spices."

By 1550 the Portuguese, who did not hesitate to use armed force in negotiations, had wrested control of the Indian Ocean trade from the Arabs and Indians who had dominated it for centuries. They maintained a network of trading posts stretching from Mozambique in East Africa to Goa in southern India to Macao in China and Nagasaki in Japan. In addition, the Portuguese controlled two strategic waterways by establishing colonies at Hormuz near the Persian Gulf and at Malacca on the straits that connect the Indian Ocean with the South China Sea. Their interests were truly global, as the potentially rich coast of Brazil lay in their hands as well.

The kingdom of Spain, however, dominated the Americas by 1550. The Spanish came late to exploration. Ferdinand and Isabella were more interested in the reconquest of Spain from the

Muslims and in European power than they were in vague promises of overseas wealth. What changed their mind about overseas adventures was, of course, the exploits of Christopher Columbus.

Columbus, an Italian from the ancient port of Genoa, was intrigued by navigation, geography, and the idea of contact with China and Japan. By studying ancient texts as well as talking to sailors and making journeys of his own to Africa and Ireland, Columbus became convinced that Asia lay only three thousand miles directly west across the Atlantic from Spain. Like most educated Europeans, as well as the Arabs and ancient Greeks, he also knew the earth was not flat but round.

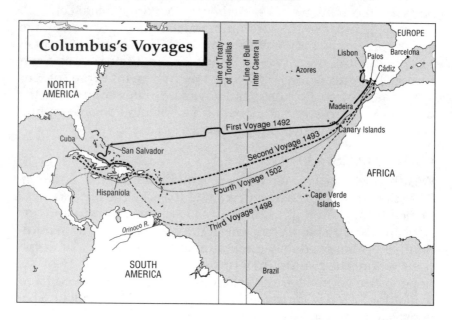

Hoping to mount an expedition to test his theory, Columbus sought support from various European monarchs. After being turned down in both Portugal and France, Columbus, through powerful friends, was finally able to convince Isabella to sponsor him with three ships, the *Nina,* the *Pinta,* and the *Santa Maria,* and sailed from the Spanish port of Palos in August 1492.

COLUMBUS ARRIVES IN THE NEW WORLD

On October 12, 1492, Columbus made landfall on an island in what is now the Bahamas. He claimed the territory he found for Spain and christened the local population Indians, since he believed that he had reached the eastern fringe of Asia, or the Indies. Indeed, Columbus was slow to accept the idea that the islands of the Caribbean were not in fact part of Asia. The mariners who followed him, however, soon learned that they had chanced upon a hemisphere previously unknown to Europeans.

Even after Columbus died in 1506 the search continued for a fast route to Asia. In 1513, while searching for gold in Central America, the Spanish officer Nunez de Balboa sighted the vast Pacific Ocean. It remained for Ferdinand Magellan, however, to test the width of the ocean. In so doing, Magellan's fleet became the first to circumnavigate the globe.

Magellan was a Portuguese sailor, and in Portuguese service he had traveled widely in the Indian Ocean. He believed that the ports of Asia lay a short distance west across the ocean that Balboa had sighted. Few Portuguese, however, were interested in sponsoring him, content to follow their established route around Africa. Magellan turned then, as Columbus had done, to the Spanish monarch. In 1519 Charles V authorized a fleet of five ships to test Magellan's theory and, Charles hoped, to give Spain a back door into the Asian trade.

Magellan's fleet experienced numerous difficulties sailing first around the southern tip of South America and then across the wide Pacific. Nonetheless, Magellan finally reached the western Pacific islands of Guam and the Philippines, where he was killed in a political dispute. Under the junior officer Juan Sebastian d'Elcano, one of Magellan's original five ships finally made it back to Spain in 1522 with a cargo of cloves, sailing the relatively familiar route through the Indian Ocean and thus circumnavigating the globe. Although the Spanish later returned to colonize the Philippines, Magellan's voyage proved that the Pacific Ocean was too wide to permit regular traffic given the shipping of the day.

The Spanish, in any case, were busy with their conquest of North and South America, which had given them control of most of the Western Hemisphere. By 1519, the Spanish had taken command of much of the Caribbean and Central America. But Spanish conquistadors found little of the gold they sought. Local tribes had spoken of a rich empire to the west, which might offer more in the way of precious metals. Consequently, in 1519 the conquistador Hernán Cortés landed on the Mexican mainland with a small force of about 450 Europeans and a few Indian guides. His target was the mighty Aztec Empire.

CONQUISTADORS AND DISEASES CONQUER THE AMERICAS

At first, the Aztecs were curious about the mysterious white men who brought horses and gunpowder weapons, both unknown in America. But Cortés soon displayed his aggressive and violent intentions, claiming that he had come "to seek gold, not plow the

earth like a peasant." Following an attack, the Spanish seized the
Aztec king Moctezuma II, who later died in captivity. Cortés then
built a small fleet of boats and lay siege to Tenochtitlán, aided by
several local tribes who had grown weary of the constant Aztec
demands for tribute and human sacrifice.

Tenochtitlán held out for months, but the population suffered
greatly from both starvation and diseases introduced by the Europeans. In 1521, Moctezuma's successor Cuahtemoc surren-
dered the city to Cortés. The Spanish proceeded to loot Tenochtitlán, then destroy it. Before 1525 they began to erect their own
capital, Mexico City, atop the ruins of the Aztec city.

**Routes of the
Conquistadors**

----- Cortés 1519
.... Pizarro 1531

European diseases, not surprisingly, were not confined to besieged Tenochtitlán. Smallpox and malaria, in particular, spread
rapidly in the densely populated regions of Central Mexico. Millions died, and the Aztec Empire could no longer function as
many of its administrators and producers fell to the epidemic. It
was within this context that the Spanish, who themselves had acquired resistance to smallpox, took control of Aztec territory.

The conquest of the Aztecs was quickly followed by a conquest of the Inca Empire in Peru. Francisco Pizarro led a force of
about six hundred Europeans equipped with horses, armor, and

firearms into Inca lands in 1530. They were fortunate in that at that moment Inca rulership was divided among competing factions; Pizarro played leaders against one another and took control of Cuzco in 1533. Finally Pizarro arranged a meeting with most of the important leaders, during which he had them killed. He temporarily spared the final Inca king, Atahualpa, so that he could ransom the king for a roomful of gold.

As in Mexico, the Spanish conquest of the Incas was hastened by local tribes who hated their Inca rulers as well as by smallpox. The disease had entered Peru in the 1520s, even before the Spanish arrived, and its effects were as devastating as they had been in Mexico. For Native American peoples, indeed, European diseases proved worse than the Spanish conquest itself. Some historians claim that disease killed seven of every eight people who lived in the Americas in the sixteenth century.

Spanish conquests in the period between 1520 and 1540 were not limited to the Americas. Charles V, the king of Spain as well as Holy Roman Emperor, sought to expand his influence in Europe as well. His major opponent was the king of France, and the major battleground, Renaissance Italy. The French had long sought to counter the growing power of Spain by conquering the rich city-states of Italy. In 1515 the French king Francis I launched an invasion of Italy, inspiring a Spanish counterinvasion. Northern Italy remained a battleground for years. Among the most dramatic events was the sack of Rome by troops from the Holy Roman Empire in 1527. Soon after, much of Italy lay under the domination of Charles V. His status as the most powerful Christian monarch was confirmed.

THE ONGOING EXPANSION OF ISLAMIC EMPIRES

Islamic empires aggressively expanded as well in the period. The Ottoman Empire continued to spread throughout the Middle East, North Africa, and southeastern Europe. The Ottomans conquered Hungary in 1526 and, again, besieged Vienna in 1529. Moreover, they added Baghdad and the rich, historic Tigris-Euphrates Valley to their possessions in 1534. Their domination of trade in the Persian Gulf and Red Sea was confirmed with the conquests of Yemen and Aden, in southern Arabia, during the same period.

Meanwhile, another Islamic empire, that of the Mughals, emerged in India. The Mughals were warriors from Central Asia who claimed to be descended from earlier conquerors such as Genghis Khan and Tamerlane. In 1523, under the leadership of Babur ("the Tiger"), they began to make plundering raids into India from their base in Afghanistan. Their timing, like that of the

Spanish in the New World, proved auspicious.

India in the 1520s was chaotic and disordered, divided among numerous small Hindu and Muslim kingdoms. Babur's highly disciplined troops, who had mastered gunpowder weapons, found it reasonably easy to defeat their disorganized Indian opponents. They took the north Indian city of Delhi in 1526 and established it as their capital. Although he disliked India, Babur decided that the wealthy and vibrant region provided an effective base from which to realize his dream of a huge Asian empire. Under Babur the Mughals ultimately took control of most of northern India. Babur's descendants were to extend those conquests to much of the rest of the subcontinent.

If the period from 1520 to 1540 was an era of new conquests worldwide, the entire sixteenth century was an era of cultural upheaval in Japan and Europe. Japan, on the verge of becoming a major power in East Asia, chose instead to mostly close itself off from the outside world. European nations continued their aggressive program of overseas trade and exploration but suffered a religious schism that split the continent into violently warring factions.

DAIMYOS AND SAMURAI STRUGGLE FOR POWER IN JAPAN

During the fifteenth and sixteenth centuries, Japan was controlled by daimyos, hereditary landlords who ruled their territories independently. Daimyos maintained private armies as well as cadres of samurai retainers. The samurai, for their part, were an elite warrior class, freed from other obligations through military loyalty to their lords. They had developed an elaborate code of training and behavior based on military skills such as archery and horsemanship in addition to strict codes of honor and loyalty.

Japan was theoretically ruled by a man known as shogun, who stood above the daimyos and supposedly ruled in the name of the semidivine emperors. Yet this entire system was weak and unstable. After 1467, Japan entered a period it calls "the century of the country at war." Factions of daimyos fought one another almost constantly as the shoguns found themselves unable to assert their authority. As the countryside fell into disarray, peasant uprisings became endemic. Finally, certain groups of Buddhist monks grew violent, demanding more land and better terms for their monasteries. Adding to the violence and chaos was the fact that many warriors in all factions took up firearms after they were introduced into the country by Portuguese merchants in the 1540s.

Ironically, Japanese culture and civilization flourished in "the century of the country at war." Commerce expanded as the Japanese, sometimes through outright piracy, expanded their contacts with Korea and China. Agricultural innovations helped to stabilize the food supply and in turn inspire population growth. Zen Buddhists built temples and monasteries and introduced the ritual of the tea ceremony, with its great focus on tranquility and refinement. European merchants transported Japanese luxuries throughout the world, increasing global awareness of this small but highly civilized nation. In these ways Japan truly began to take a place on the global stage.

Meanwhile, Europe entered the era of the Reformation and Counter-Reformation. Religious conflict produced an era of religious wars in Europe that lasted nearly one hundred years. Like the civil wars in Japan, the wars of religion featured not only battles among kingdoms but peasant revolts, activist monks, and massacres.

REFORMATION AND RELIGIOUS WARS IN EUROPE

The Protestant Reformation began in 1517, when a German monk named Martin Luther, according to a widely accepted but probably untrue story, nailed a list of protests, called the Ninety-five Theses, onto a church door in the city of Wittenburg. The theses were questions Luther posed about corrupt church practices such as indulgences, which allowed a sinner to pay a priest for forgiveness of his sins. Luther hoped that the Roman Catholic Church would disavow and would halt such abuse.

Luther was ultimately condemned to death as a heretic by Pope Leo X, although he found protection under German nobles with various financial or territorial conflicts with the papacy. Moreover, Luther's call to end church corruption found sympathetic ears as, thanks to the printing press, his ideas spread widely and quickly to the rest of Europe. Luther was encouraged to develop a newer and more simplifed version of Christianity, which argued that neither priests nor popes nor the entire structure of the Roman Catholic Church were necessary for salvation. This protest, or Protestant, Christianity soon found adherents throughout western Europe who set up congregations without the involvement or approval of Rome.

The rapid spread of Protestantism inspired the Catholic Church to undergo a reformation of its own. At three sessions between 1545 and 1563, church leaders at the Council of Trent decided that certain church practices such as indulgences encouraged corrupt behavior and must be abolished. In addition, the church took a militant stance to stop the spread of the Protestant heresy. Interestingly, and in a true reflection of the nature of European power, the guiding force behind the Catholic Counter-Reformation was not the pope but rather the monarch of Spain, first Charles V and then his successor Philip II.

Meanwhile, Europe had splintered into violent factions, and religious conflict combined with politics to produce nearly a century of religious war. While the kings of France and Spain remained Catholic, the Tudor monarchs of England as well as many of the German kings had adopted Protestantism. The religions of the monarchs, however, were not always the religions of the people, who themselves split along religious lines.

The religious wars were particularly brutal in France. The French royal family sought to maintain peace while Catholic nobles massacred and oppressed Protestant congregations. For their part, French Protestants, or Huguenots, sought to bring the entire nation to Protestantism. After 1560 the dominant force in French politics was Catherine de Medici, mother of King Charles X. Catherine hoped to neutralize Huguenot power; in 1572 she arranged a marriage between her daughter Marguerite and Henry of Navarre, a Huguenot leader.

Thousands of important Huguenots flocked to Paris for the wedding. Among them was Admiral Coligny, the Huguenots' main military strategist but also an adviser and friend to the young Charles X. There Coligny was killed by Catholic nobles, along with thousands of other Huguenots. Ensuing warfare over the next months left thousands more dead, as Protestants not only in France but throughout Europe sought revenge for an event known as the Saint Bartholomew's Day Massacre.

France did not recover from Saint Bartholomew's Day until Henry of Navarre took the French throne in 1589 upon the death of Henry III, Catherine de Medici's last surviving son. Henry IV, as he was titled, was extremely popular among a French populace sick of religious war. Furthermore, deciding that he should practice the same faith as his mostly Catholic people, Henry converted, declaring that "Paris is well worth a mass." But he also proclaimed that Huguenots were free to worship as they chose.

By the time Henry IV took the throne in the 1580s the French, as well as the Dutch and English, had joined the Spanish and Portuguese in global exploration and trade. Ships from these five countries had, in fact, taken command of the world's oceans and constructed a network of exchange that was truly worldwide. Although as before trade was the main aim of European seafarers, the global exchange that began during the Renaissance spread from trade goods to food items, peoples, religious ideas, and of course the diseases that killed so many Native Americans.

A GLOBAL NETWORK OF TRADE AND CULTURAL EXCHANGE

North and South America were incredibly rich in agricultural products. A number of native crops were easy to grow and transport as well as nutritious, and food items from the Americas quickly enriched the cuisines of peoples worldwide, including corn, peppers of various kinds, squash, tomatoes, and potatoes. The cocoa bean provided a mild stimulant in the form of chocolate, which was usually made into a beverage.

The Spanish and Portuguese colonies in the Americas also quickly proved to be fruitful areas for large-scale agriculture, especially once the colonizers determined to make the Americas economically productive for the home kingdoms. Plantations to feed the growing demands of European and global markets appeared in the early 1500s. The first planters grew sugar cane, turning sugar into an important cash crop that changed European tastes forever. Later plantations diversified to include other agricultural products as well as tobacco, the smoking of which Europeans slowly acquired a taste for. By 1604, in fact, tobacco had become so popular in England that King James I tried to legislate against it, claiming that smoking was "a custom loathsome to the eye, hateful to the nose, harmful to the brain, [and] dangerous to the lungs."

The Spanish and Portuguese hoped to use Native Americans as a plantation labor force, but local tribes often resisted subjugation. Moreover, the vast epidemic of European diseases that devasted American populations further reduced the pool of potential workers. The colonists soon turned instead to a labor force of African slaves, who were already being used on sugar cane plantations in North Africa and the Canary Islands.

The African slave trade to the Spanish Caribbean began as early as 1503, importing slaves to work in silver mines; their potential as workers in large-scale agriculture quickly became clear. This marks the beginning of the largest forced migration in human history, and one of the great transformations of the Renaissance. By the time the Atlantic slave trade ended in 1888, slave ships had forcibly transported between 12 and 15 million Africans to the New World.

The slave trade remained small, however, until Atlantic Ocean commerce became mixed up with European political conflict. By the late 1500s Spain's greatest enemy was no longer France but rather England. The reasons were primarily dynastic and religious. In 1533, King Henry VIII of England annulled his marriage to Catherine of Aragon, who was the aunt of Charles V of Spain. In the process of rejecting Catherine in favor of his mistress Anne

Boleyn, Henry also rejected the Roman Catholic Church and brought Protestantism to England.

DYNASTIC STRUGGLE AND THE ATLANTIC SLAVE TRADE

After the death of Henry's only male heir in 1553, Mary, daughter of Henry and Catherine of Aragon, ascended the English throne. Mary was a devout Catholic, and a marriage was quickly arranged between Mary and Philip II, who succeeded Charles V in 1556. Political and religious leaders hoped that Catholicism could be restored to England and peaceful relations could be restored between England and Spain. Mary, however, proved unpopular with both her people and her husband. She died in 1558.

England's new monarch was Elizabeth I, daughter of Henry VIII and Anne Boleyn, the woman for whom Henry had rejected both Catherine of Aragon and the Roman Catholic Church. She was a Protestant, although only a marginally enthusiastic one, and she sought to weaken the influence of Spain in her kingdom. To that end, she adopted the strategy of interference with Spanish shipping in the Atlantic. In 1562, an English mariner named John Hawkins, in defiance of international law, collected a cargo of slaves on the West Coast of Africa and took it across the Atlantic to be sold in Spanish America for a huge profit. Elizabeth, in consequence, grew convinced of the financial and political advantages of adventures such as Hawkins's, and both the slave trade and English attacks on Spanish ships expanded rapidly.

Among the reasons Europeans gave for their growing use of slaves was that doing so brought Africans to Christianity; thus the slave trade was in part a misguided manifestation of the missionary spirit of Reformation Europe. Roman Catholics, particularly, were eager to spread their faith to the rest of the globe, and missionaries quickly followed merchants and explorers to Asia, Africa, and the Americas, where they operated from such cities as Mexico City, Goa in India, and Macao in China. Missionaries not only sought to spread Christianity but also acted as cultural diplomats between Europe and the world.

Among the most active Catholic missionaries in Asia were Francis Xavier and Matteo Ricci. Both were Jesuits, members of a militant order of monks dedicated to the expansion of Counter-Reformation Catholicism. Jesuits used a variety of means in this effort, including education, preaching, good works, and when necessary, intimidation and torture. Xavier devoted his life to bringing Roman Catholicism to Asia, and preached and made conversions in China, Japan, Malaysia, and India. Although he rarely hesitated to punish stray members of his flock and was responsible for bringing the brutal and notorious Inquisition to Asia, he remains revered among the Catholics of Asia.

MISSIONARIES AS CULTURAL AMBASSADORS

Matteo Ricci arrived at the Portuguese enclave of Macao in China in 1582. He quickly endeared himself to Chinese officials and converts alike by becoming an expert in Chinese language and scholarship. In addition he wrote extensively, seeking to explain Chinese culture to Europe while introducing the Chinese to the accomplishments of Europe. Upon a visit to the Ming emperor's Forbidden City in 1601, to which he was the first European ever invited, Ricci demonstrated such devices as navigational tools and musical instruments as well as a modern map of the world and the complicated mathematics of Europe's scientists.

Although he quickly learned that he had to modify Christianity to make it palatable to his Chinese audience, Matteo Ricci hoped to convert all of China to Christianity. He made many converts among the poor and disaffected, but his goals were more ambitious than that. Ricci thought, wrongly, he could convert the Ming emperor Wanli himself, one of the most powerful men on earth.

Wanli reigned from 1572 until 1620. Although during his years on the throne China was increasingly troubled by both Japanese and Korean pirates as well as rebellious nomads, Wanli presided over a China that continued to grow demographically and economically and ranked as the greatest power in East Asia. Thanks to the arrival of American foods such as corn, China's population grew quickly and trade goods flowed through the porous borders and coastal cities. Signs of trouble soon appeared, however, as Wanli increasingly cut himself off from his government and people. Preferring the sanctuary of the Forbidden City, Wanli remained there smoking opium and enjoying other amusements while his court eunuchs took control of the government and exploited their power to enrich themselves.

In Japan, a trio of warlords managed to end the civil wars that had divided the country since 1467. In 1570, a minor daimyo named Oda Nobunaga brought much of central Japan, including the ancient capital of Kyoto, under his control. His successor Hideyoshi continued to unify Japan via conquest and alliances. Moreover, he forbade both peasants and Buddhist monks to carry firearms, declaring that the honor of carrying weapons lay with Japan's military classes, the daimyo and samurai. Probably only his death in an ill-advised military expedition in Korea in

1597 prevented Hideyoshi from fully unifying Japan.

In 1600 the task was completed by Tokugawa Ieyasu, who built on the efforts of his two predecessors and established the Tokugawa Shogunate. Lasting until 1868, the Tokugawa Shogunate brought peace and unity to Japan by putting in place creative measures ranging from restrictions to political centralization. Many daimyos, for instance, were integrated into the government but were also required to keep family members at the Tokugawa court as hostages. Peasants and craftsmen, for their part, were restricted to their professions and lands. Finally, fearing excessive foreign influence, Tokugawa leaders expelled all European merchants and missionaries and forced Japanese who had converted to Christianity to recant. These restrictive measures, however, did not prevent Japan from experiencing a vast economic expansion over the next centuries.

AKBAR THE GREAT ENRICHES MUGHAL INDIA

Another leader of historical significance emerged in Mughal India. Akbar, the grandson of the Mughal conqueror Babur, reigned from 1556 until 1605. Akbar the Great, as he came to be known, transformed the Mughal dynasty from Muslim conquerors into true leaders of the diverse Indian subcontinent. Instead of either dominating or merely tolerating India's majority population, the Hindus, Akbar actively sought to integrate them into the Mughal state. Important Hindu leaders were given prominent offices in the administration and army, and Akbar ended the practice of levying extra taxes on Hindus begun by earlier Muslim leaders. Moreover, Akbar led by example; his four wives included two Hindus, one Muslim, and one Christian.

Akbar presided over the creation of a truly unique Indian culture, a combination of Hindu, Islamic, and Persian elements that would reflect the India he hoped to create. Greatly interested in architecture, Akbar built a new capital at Fatehpur Sikri near Agra that demonstrated this cultural syncretism. Other architectural monuments inspired by Akbar's openmindedness include the huge Red Forts of Delhi and Agra as well as the Taj Mahal, India's best-known symbol, which was built several decades after Akbar's death by his grandson Shah Jahan.

Realizing that the religious diversity of India was a treasure as well as a threat, Akbar displayed great curiosity and openness toward all religions. Although he was illiterate, Akbar liked to surround himself with scholars and experts in Islam and Hinduism, and even with Jesuits from Portugal and Italy. He felt that all religions shared the same goal, and he hoped that in the course of these discussions a new religion, common to all India, could be envisioned. The effort failed, but nonetheless helped provide Akbar the Great's India with a cultural flexibility that later Indian leaders would forget at their peril. Perhaps to commemorate his ideas about both religion and cultural tolerance, Akbar had the following statement inscribed on the Victory Gate in Fatehpur Sikri: "The world is a bridge. Pass over it but do not build upon it. He who hopes for an hour may hope for eternity. The world is but an hour: spend it in devotion. The rest is unseen."

While Akbar tried to create an integrated India, Philip II, king of Spain, tried to preserve an empire that stretched from Europe to the Americas to the Philippines. When Philip took the throne in 1556, Spain was the dominant power in Europe, holding in check threats to Catholic Europe from all sides. In the east, Spanish ships and leadership stopped the expansion of the Ottoman Empire into the Mediterranean at the Battle of Lepanto in 1571. Elsewhere, Spanish missionaries and soldiers sought to halt the spread of Protestantism and convert followers of other religions to their faith. All the while Philip, at least until inflation ruined its value, could enjoy the wealth that poured in from Spain's overseas possessions. Every year a treasure fleet, containing gold and silver from mines in the Americas, crossed the Atlantic to replenish the Spanish treasury, while Spanish coins were valued currency throughout the world.

THE STRUGGLE BETWEEN SPAIN AND ENGLAND FOR MARITIME DOMINATION

However, in the late 1500s the treasure fleets experienced increasing harassment from English pirates who operated with the approval of Queen Elizabeth I, Philip's greatest enemy. Elizabeth, after taking the throne in 1558, had transformed England into a solidly Protestant but reasonably tolerant nation. Her reign, which lasted until 1603, spanned England's evolution from minor kingdom on the fringes of Europe to one of the world's nascent superpowers. Not only did English ships interfere with Philip's treasure fleets, they traversed the globe seeking trading privileges in Africa, India, China, and Russia. Some Elizabethan adventurers had gone so far as to envision English colonies on the Atlantic coast of North America, although the first successful English colony, Jamestown in Virginia, did not appear until 1607.

The vitality and energy of Elizabeth's reign were apparent in philosophy, the sciences, literature, and other endeavors. Francis Bacon, one of Elizabeth's courtiers, played a leading role in Europe's scientific revolution, which was among the great legacies of the Renaissance. In the 1590s, physician William Harvey was the first European to describe the circulation of the blood. Meanwhile, playwrights such as Christopher Marlowe and William Shakespeare produced masterpieces of world literature.

A major turning point not only of the Renaissance but of world history came in 1588. In that year Philip, sick of English interference with his commerce and seeking to replace the "Protestant whore" Elizabeth with a Catholic monarch, preferably his daughter Isabel, organized an invasion of England. His fleet, the Spanish Armada, was the largest ever assembled in European history, containing 130 ships and twenty-five thousand men. But the invasion was a failure as English ships proved quicker and more maneuverable. A fortuitous storm completed the defeat of the Spanish, and one-third of the armada never returned to Spain.

After the defeat of the armada, Philip retreated further into devotions and machinations at his vast palace, the Escorial, near Madrid. The Spanish empire, though it remained wealthy and powerful, never again achieved the heights of power and influence it achieved early in his reign.

Elizabeth could now enjoy her position as the leading Protestant monarch. Moreover, English ships increasingly came to dominate the world's oceans as English merchants, colonists, and adventurers made their presence known throughout the world. In the words of Shakespeare, the greatest Elizabethan writer and one of the greatest products of the Renaissance spirit, "She shall be, to the happiness of England, an aged princess; many days shall see her, and yet no day without a deed to crown it."

New Global Powers: 1450–1520

CHAPTER 1

THE OTTOMAN EMPIRE EXPANDS INTO EUROPE

JASON GOODWIN

During the Renaissance, European powers faced a new challenge from the Middle East. The Ottoman Empire, established by nomadic Turks who had converted to Islam, conquered the city of Constantinople in 1453. Not only did the conquest end the ancient Christian empire of Byzantium, but it also opened the door to further Turkish conquests in southeastern Europe.

In the following selection, Jason Goodwin describes how the Turks consolidated their hold on Constantinople, historically one of the world's great cities. In addition, Goodwin traces the Ottomans' march into southeastern Europe and suggests that military setbacks only temporarily halted the Turkish advance. By 1480, an Ottoman army even reached Italy before being called back upon the death of the sultan, Mehmet II.

Jason Goodwin is an author whose works include *On Foot to the Golden Horn*.

C onstantinople remained the finest city in the world. Christians had torn themselves and the city apart in their efforts to possess it: crusaders, pretenders, ambitious Serb princes, Bulgar khans with long and bitter memories who drank from their enemies' gilded skulls. In a thousand years Constantinople had suffered twenty-nine assaults. It had repulsed twenty-one of them. The King of Naples coveted it still; and as the last of the Byzantine dynasty were dying, Charles II of Anjou bought up their claims and titles and made, in that faded purple, a feint into Italy which disturbed even the Sultan.

It was as if some tilt of geography or politics had always destined this to be the first city of the world. The Byzantines had thought it the navel of the world. The Venetians toyed with the idea of moving Venice there, lock, stock and barrel, after they captured it in 1204; but perhaps their own city on the Veneto was so stuffed with looted treasures from Byzantium that the business of shipping it all back seemed too much trouble. In 1503, fifty years after the Ottoman conquest, Andrea Gritti—who learned his merchanting in Istanbul and later became a doge—wrote that 'its climate, its two seas protecting it on both sides, the beauty of its neighbouring lands, give this city what is thought to be the most beautiful and the most favoured site not only in all of Asia but in all the world', a site, Busbecq noted a century later, 'created by nature to be the capital of the world'. Another Venetian, Benedetto Ramberti, wrung his hands over the beauty of it all. 'The situation of Constantinople is not only beyond description, but it can hardly be grasped in thought because of its loveliness,' he said; and the Roman traveller della Valle, who came in the seventeenth century, described the cascade of buildings with their huge spreading eaves, the big shuttered verandas under the eaves, their shade, the snow-white buildings and green cypresses as a 'sight so beautiful that I do not think there is any city to be found that looks better than this from the outside'. Years later, seeking an image of absolute loveliness to decorate the dome of an Albanian mosque or to brighten the walls of a Greek merchant's house, it was to the eye of empire that people instinctively turned, the kiosks and cypresses of the Golden Horn that people painted, the domes of Istanbul. The poet Nabi wrote: 'Because its beauty is so rare a sight / The sea has clasped it in an embrace.' 'What a city!' wrote [historian] Tursun Bey: 'For an aspre you may be rowed from Asia into Europe.'

CONSTANTINOPLE BECOMES THE TURKISH CAPITAL

Asia came to Europe, the church became a mosque; and Turkish women asked to wear the Byzantine veil in place of the linen hood, with holes for eyes. Mehmet's world-conquering ambitions were crystallised in the new imperial capital. When he rode to Hagia Sophia and the Imam called the faithful there to prayer it was enough, in the rough conquistadorial spirit of the faith, to consecrate the edifice as a mosque. But a hunt was made among the captive Greeks for the fierce old theologian Gennadius the Scholar, the most implacable opponent of the Roman church. They found him in Edirne, in the house of a merchant who had bought him in a job lot, at a knockdown price, at the post-conquest sales, and was now bemusedly according him the courtesy due to his evident dignity and learning. Mehmet invested Gennadius with the robes and honour of the patriarchal office, and he was consecrated by the Archbishop of Heraclea; while thirty-six churches including the Church of the Holy Apostles, whose plan the Venetians had copied at St Mark's, were preserved for his ministers in the city alone. The Chief Rabbi was called to the city from Jerusalem. The Armenian Patriarch was roped in from Bursa. The Sultan's share of captives were released and resettled, and everywhere the Sultan went in the coming years, when laying siege to cities in Greece and the Balkans, he dispatched his share of the captives to populate his capital.

All the while his troops laboured in the summer heat to repair the ravages of centuries of neglect, repairing cisterns and aqueducts, rodding drains, laying paving stones. Motion returned to the fossilised city: ships loading in the roadsteads, lighters bustling about the harbour, processions winding through the streets, the sound of hammers as the streets of the artisans came alive. Greeks sniffed the wind. [Renaissance historian] Kritovolos compared Mehmet to Alexander the Great, and George of Trebizond wrote him a letter: 'No one doubts you are Emperor of the Romans. Whoever holds by right the centre of the Empire is emperor and the centre of the Roman Empire is Constantinople.'

Constantinople was the spot where the long trajectory of the gazi's [Islamic warrior's] fortunes fell to earth. Its conquest blew off the beys [Turkish nobles], just as they had feared; for Mehmet used it to build the edifice of Ottoman power, in which craggy individualists had no place. As the empire began to push against tougher enemies than before, unity was needed if conquest was to proceed at the old rate.

OTTOMAN EXPANSION INTO SOUTHEASTERN EUROPE

Mehmet followed up the conquest of Constantinople with the subjection of the whole Greek-speaking world. From Trebizond to the Peloponnese, he wound up all the Byzantine despots, rivals, and dependants. Kritovolos was a judge on the island of Imbros, the only Byzantine not to run away; he explained the new situation to the papal fleet when it cruised past, was given the governorship of the island, and eventually wrote a convincing history based on Greek and Turkish sources, in which the Sultan was the hero and the Greeks, for all their tragic loss, were urged to reconcile themselves. George Amouritzes negotiated the surrender of Trebizond, by which the Trapuzuntine Emperor David agreed to take his family to exile in Constantinople, and all the men of the city were enslaved. The old Byzantine Emperor's brothers, the Peloponnesian despots Thomas and Demetrius, betrayed their cause by their faithlessness and opportunism, squabbling when Mehmet urged brotherly love, and making war when he urged peace, so that in 1460 he crossed the Gulf of Corinth and finished them off, while the cities of the Peloponnese fell to him one by one. Thomas died in Rome, and his sons never prospered: one married a Roman courtesan and died poor in the city, while the other returned rather hopelessly to Constantinople, dying as a pensioner of the state, and perhaps a Muslim, too. His uncle Demetrius died in Edirne in 1470, last of the Paleologi. Only Thomas's daughter Zoë got away: she married the Russian Grand Duke Ivan III in 1472, taking with her the old Caesaropapist claims, and the double-headed eagle of Byzantium.

In 1456 Mehmet stormed up the Danube with his battle-hardened army of veterans, heroes of Constantinople and Sofia. His objective was an island at the confluence of the Sava and the Danube, the key to all Central Europe, named by the Ottomans Dar-ne-jihad, 'Battlefield of Holy War', and known to us as Belgrade, the White City. At the first news of his approach Janos Hunyadi, the military champion of Hungary, dashed across country to the island citadel with a welcome addition of musketeers, squeaking in just days before the siege commenced. Hunyades cleared the houses round the ramparts for a clear field of fire, and strung up a few Belgrade citizens who had been seen to be friendly with the enemy; but Mehmet's cannon did its work and on 13 August the janissaries advanced through a smoking breach in the walls, trampling over the corpses which lay piled up in the moat.

There was no resistance as they fanned out through the deserted streets and crooked lanes which ran up towards the citadel. Cautiously at first, then more boldly, they pressed through the alleyways, chalking houses for looting later—when a clarion call from the citadel brought the defenders out of their holes. They rose from the ground like the sheeted dead—bounding out of cellars, springing down from rooftops—to fall upon the divided columns of Turkish soldiers. Taken completely by surprise, the janissaries fell back on their fellows streaming through the breach. The defenders chased after them, clearing the trenches with their slashing pikes, and the Turks fled in tumultuous disarray. Not even the exhortations of their Sultan, who must have seen better than they how close to victory his army was, and how easily they could turn the tables on the outnumbered defenders if they would only stand and fight; not even the furious bellow-

ing of the *aga* of the janissaries, or the skirling of the janissary
bands urging attack, could stem the rout. The Sultan cut down
his generals with his own hand, and at his furious reproach the
aga, handling his reins at the Sultan's right, did the decent thing
and plunged into the fray, where he was soon cut down. . . .

Mehmet failed to take Belgrade, and failed to take Rhodes; but
he scoured the Black Sea and the Genoese were booted out of
their colonies there: Kaffa, the Little Constantinople, fell in 1475,
and fifteen hundred young Genoese nobles were enrolled in the
janissary regiments. In the year 1456 he rested his troops; but he
spent the summer reading the classical geographer Ptolemy,
whose concentric vision of the world matched his own. The
Venetians from their rooftops watched the glow of burning villages as the Ottomans swept to the banks of the Piave. In 1480
Mehmet's general Ahmed the Broken-Mouthed, Grand Vizier
and conqueror of the Crimea, landed unopposed on the southern shores of Italy, and seized Otranto, then considered the key
to Italy, with terrifying slaughter, and it was only Mehmet's death
that called him back.

FERDINAND AND ISABELLA TURN SPAIN INTO A MAJOR POWER

JEAN HIPPOLYTE MARIEJOL

For much of the Middle Ages, Spain was a collection of more or less powerful small kingdoms. A number of kingdoms under Arab, or Moorish, control were Muslim rather than Christian, and Spanish history during the Late Middle Ages was characterized by the reconquest of Spain from the Muslims. This "reconquista" was completed by two Spanish monarchs in the second half of the fifteenth century: Ferdinand of Aragon and Isabella of Castile, who went on to unify the country entirely.

Ferdinand and Isabella, who were married in 1469, accomplished much more than the reconquest of Spain, as Jean Hippolyte Mariejol asserts in the following selection. They created a strong, centralized state in which the monarchy held complete authority over both the nobility and the church. Ferdinand and Isabella's Spain was, Mariejol claims, the first of Europe's absolute monarchies, in which opposition to royal authority was suppressed and the will of the monarch was not to be questioned. Perhaps because of the ruthlessness of the "Catholic Sovereigns," Spain went on to become the dominant power in Europe and, thanks to the conquest of America, a global superpower.

Jean Hippolyte Mariejol (1855–1934) was a professor of history at the Universities of Paris and Lyons in the late 1800s and wrote a number of historical works.

Excerpted from *The Spain of Ferdinand and Isabella*, by Jean Hippolyte Mariejol, translated and edited by Benjamin Keen. Copyright © 1961 by Rutgers, The State University. Reprinted by permission of Rutgers University Press.

The reign of Ferdinand and Isabella may be summed up in a few words. These sovereigns wielded very great power, and they used that power for the greatest possible good of the Spanish people. In their hands sovereign authority was an instrument of progress and prosperity. Influence without, peace within, were the first fruits of absolute monarchy.

Absolute monarchy! Theirs is the honor and the responsibility of its creation. When they succeeded Enrique IV, anarchy reigned everywhere, not only in central Spain but in all parts of the country. The crown, weakened by the incapacity of their predecessor, at the mercy of factions, had neither the means nor the servants required for its defense. The provinces, thrown back into their old isolation, were the prey of brigands and the theater of savage struggles. The government retained its feudal character. Great lords sat in the royal council; the affairs of state, all the relations of the sovereign with his subjects and with foreign countries, were subject to the control of this aristocratic body. Dispensations, favors, diplomas, privileges, bore the signatures of the heads of the nobility together with that of the king. Nothing was done without their consent and participation.

These dubious if not hostile collaborators Ferdinand and Isabella replaced with agents drawn from the middle class, men without a past and without attachments, necessarily devoted to their master. In the royal council, or council of justice, which dominated the whole administration, influence and numerical preponderance passed to the legists. The lords and prelates continued to have seats in the body; but the dispatch of business, the work of deliberation and decision, was reserved to the ordinary councilors, that is to say, the men of law. To bar all interference with their actions, the sovereigns took away from the *ricos homes* [nobility] and assigned to a corps of functionaries the confirmation of all diplomas.

The great crown offices were reduced to the status of honorific dignities, used by their owners merely to make a show at court. The Almirante of Castile, who had had command of all naval forces, was reduced by the capitulations of Sante Fe with Columbus, and by royal usurpations, to the status of an unemployed seaman. The Condestable of Castile played no part at all in the Italian Wars. Men of merit chosen by the sovereigns won battles, conquered kingdoms and empires, administered provinces and towns. The ancient dignitaries were surrounded with respect, heaped with honors, invited to all the festivities; they played brilliant parts in the comedy of monarchical prestige, but in the last analysis they had nothing but titles and some satisfactions in the way of vanity or money.

FERDINAND AND ISABELLA DOMINATED BOTH THE NOBILITY AND THE CHURCH

The royal power grew on the ruins of special privilege. The Roman Curia had to yield its supremacy in the disposal of large and small benefices in the Spanish Church. By a mixture of firmness and diplomacy, Ferdinand and Isabella obtained a right of petition which amounted to a right of designation of their candidates (1482). Now they could select the bishops. Isabella displayed such zeal in searching for the worthiest candidates, not in the aristocracy, but in the cloistered orders, that more than once she drew a refusal from these solitary and saintly figures and had to appeal to the Pope for help in overcoming their scruples, as rare as they were admirable. The new clergy was more moral, more learned, more patriotic, and less independent than the old one. The Inquisition placed the civil power at the service of orthodoxy and the fanaticism of the Spanish clergy at the service of Spanish nationality. Church and state worked hand-in-hand on a project that concerned both the future of the nation and the purity of its faith.

The crown sought to assure its preponderance everywhere. The cities and towns were surrounded by vast territories which they administered and over which they exercised undisputed sway. With the pretext of safeguarding order in the towns, the Catholic Sovereigns placed royal officers at their heads and reduced them to a condition of tutelage. The sovereigns even claimed the right to name their magistrates. In certain places the municipal offices became life tenures, and the crown arrogated to itself the right of filling each vacancy. The towns which retained free elections were forbidden to choose their *regidores* [administrators] from among the most powerful lords; thereby the municipalities were detached from the patronage of the grandees as well as deprived of the free initiative and impulses of communal autonomy, so that they were absolutely subject to the action of the central government.

Wherever the crown sensed resistance, it sought means of breaking it. It even took precautions against its own agents. It suppressed venality and inheritability of office, which protected magistrates; it held over the heads of its *corregidores* [councillors] the threat of frequent investigation and accusation by the people.

This concentration of authority, this weakening of provincial and communal life, indicate the tendencies of the new reign. The Catholic Sovereigns advanced toward absolute power; in Castile they achieved their goal. They were as much masters as

Charles V and Philip II. If we are deceived concerning the nature and degree of their power, it is because they governed with intelligence, with moderation, with a constant care for the true interests of the country. Their generosity or genius placed limits on the exercise of their omnipotence. But in the last analysis they were the masters.

MING CHINA BUILT GREAT STRUCTURES BUT FACED INTERNAL WEAKNESS

FRANZ MICHAEL

In the fifteenth century, China was the most populous and perhaps wealthiest region on earth. It was ruled by the Ming dynasty, which had taken power in 1368 following a century of control by Asian invaders, the Mongols. To assert their authority, as Franz Michael points out in the following selection, the Ming emperors built impressive new structures.

One such marvel was the Great Wall of China, an unsuccessful attempt to prevent nomads such as the Mongols from entering China. Although earlier versions of this barrier were erected along China's northern border, the one that stands today is the achievement of the Ming dynasty.

Ming leaders also built, as Michael points out, the Forbidden City, a new capital, in Beijing. While the Forbidden City was an architectural masterpiece, it ultimately reflected the weakness of the Ming emperors. The palace complex isolated them from the Chinese people; moreover, the ongoing conflicts among emperors, Confucian officials (or literati), and court eunuchs were masked by the ritual and pomp of the imperial capital.

Franz Michael was professor of history at George Washington University in Washington, D.C.

Excerpted from *China Through the Ages*, by Franz Michael. Copyright © 1986 by Westview Press, a Member of Perseus Books Group. Reprinted by permission of Westview Press, a member of Perseus Books, L.L.C.

During the fifteenth century, Ming China was immensely powerful. To display their power the Ming emperors became the greatest builders in imperial history. Their chief architectural accomplishments that survived into our time still manifest the dynastic splendor of the imperial era. The Ming palaces, tombs, city walls, and temples, the remaining sections of the Grand Canal, the sinuous lines of the Great Wall as seen today are impressive examples of the scope of architectural enterprises embarked on by Ming emperors and their architects.

THE FORBIDDEN CITY OF THE MING EMPERORS

The city of Peking, a creation of the Ming, was built according to a plan that had been traditionally followed by previous dynasties in the building of their capitals at Ch'ang-an, K'ai-feng, and Hangchow. The overall rectangular shape, the type of city walls, the gates, and the rectangular walled imperial palace within the city, all laid out in a south-north direction appear to have been in one form or another a Chinese tradition also copied by neighboring Asian countries. But the plan of the Ming imperial palace manifests a sense of symmetry and design of such magnificent scope that its grandeur must have awed the audience seeker of the past as much as it affects the casual visitor of the present. Entering through magnificent gates into its spacious courtyards with marble steps, balustrades, and terraces, flanked by official buildings and facing great audience halls, massive colored pillars, elaborate brackets, and sweeping, slightly curved palace roofs covered with brilliant colored glazed tiles, the visitor is struck by an exhilarating impression of symmetry, color, harmony, and grandeur. The northern part of the palace city with its maze of courtyards, alleys, rock gardens, pine trees, and shrubs provided living quarters in which the members of the imperial family had their separate apartments. To the north, across the moat and a modern street, lies the Coal Hill Park, providing a splendid view of the palace and the city.

WEAKNESS CHARACTERIZED MING LEADERSHIP

The splendor of the Ming court cloaked the inherent weakness, both political and cultural, that characterized Ming rule, once its great founder and the second outstanding Ming monarch, Emperor Yung-lo had died. Rule by the emperors through their eunuchs required strong monarchical personalities to stem the corruption and exploitation that in turn would provoke unrest and revolt in the provinces. To satisfy the eunuchs' demands for bribes, provincial and local officials, to retain their positions, exacted heavy payments from the farming population. When a eunuch overplayed his hand too openly, the emperor might act, as in 1510, when the fall of the leading eunuch Liu Chin resulted in the confiscation of all his property, including over a quarter-million taels, jewels, and mansions that in their splendor surpassed the emperor's wealth. But the setback of the eunuchs' power did not last and in the early part of the seventeenth century a deadly, prolonged contest between the eunuchs and a group of scholars and scholar-officials seriously undermined government strength at a time of growing danger of rebellion and outside invasion. Major opposition to the eunuchs' rule came from members of the Tunglin Academy at Wuhsi in Kiangsu province. These scholars had regained political influence at the court under a previous ruler but were severely persecuted under the emperor T'ien-ch'i (1621–1627) when the eunuch Wei Chung-hsien gained control of the administration and the secret police. The eunuch closed the academy, put several hundred of his scholar opponents in prison—where many were executed—while appointing his favorites to official posts and sinecures, instituting a totally corrupt system of appointments. At the death of the emperor, Wei Chung-hsien was assassinated and his clique broken up. For a while the scholar group regained some influence, but the financial and political crisis could not be stemmed and led to the downfall of the dynasty.

Under an autocratic rule, the Ming Dynasty provided no favorable climate for official pursuits in scholarship and the arts. Though the ruling house was Chinese, the scholar-elite remained much of the time in opposition to the court, the eunuchs, and their policies. As under the Mongols, the gap thus widened between the court and the scholar-gentry, and although intermittently some outstanding scholars held high office, for the literati as a whole the tradition of scholarly independence and freedom from government restraint continued, and it became a part of the scholarly creed that independence was morally superior to submission to the discipline of office and authority of the court.

THE SONGHAY EMPIRE EMERGES IN WEST AFRICA

ROLAND OLIVER AND ANTHONY ATMORE

During the thirteenth, fourteenth, and fifteenth centuries, West African empires supplied most of the gold circulated in Europe and Asia. The empire of Mali, with a series of devout Muslim kings, dominated the region into the mid-1400s. Following a series of uprisings the Songhay people, who lived on the Niger River, took control of the gold-producing areas as well as trade cities such as Timbuktu.

In the following selection, historians of Africa Roland Oliver and Anthony Atmore describe how Songhay leaders such as Sonni Ali, who took the throne in 1464, established their authority over much of West Africa. The expansion of Songhay control involved both conquest and missions of plunder, according to the authors. Most importantly however, it required control over trade, including the slave trade. As Oliver and Atmore note, the arrival of Portuguese traders on the West African coast meant little in comparison with the power of Songhay.

Roland Oliver, who teaches at the Cambridge University, and Anthony Atmore, a professor at the University of London, are well-respected scholars of African history.

I t has been estimated that by the end of the fifteenth century the maritime commerce of the Portuguese may have been attracting about a quarter of the total production of West African gold into its net. In addition, by carrying something of the order of 2,000 West African slaves a year to the Cape Verde islands, the Azores and Madeira, as well as to its own homeland, Portugal had established a far-flung sugar industry of great significance for the further development of its world-wide trading system. All this was of revolutionary importance to a small European nation, but it had hardly scratched the surface of life in West Africa. There the first century of Portuguese contact had produced some coastward reorientation in the economic life of peoples living within 100 or 200 kilometres of the ocean, but over most of the region the commercial arteries remained firmly linked to the desert caravans and the Niger waterway. The economic determinant of this pattern, which prevailed until the coming of the railways, was undoubtedly the production and distribution of salt. There was no more economic way of getting this vital mineral into the scattered cooking-pots of the western Sudan than to mine it in mid-Sahara and carry it for a month on camel-back to the banks of the great river of West Africa at the northernmost point of its long course. . . .

SONGHAY WAS A LONG-STANDING POWER

The state which expanded to fill the vacuum left by the break-up of Mali was Songhay. As a kingdom embracing much of the eastern arm of the Niger bend, it already had a long history. It had been the contemporary, and in some respects the counterpart, of ancient Ghana, commanding the caravan routes leading northwards and eastwards from the Niger in much the same way as Ghana controlled those leading to the north and west. With the expansion of Mali in the thirteenth century, Songhay had lost its northern province and its control of the desert routes. For much of the fourteenth century the remainder of the kingdom paid tribute to Mali. Yet the Songhay-speakers were still the predominant population of the river valley far beyond the political boundaries of the state. They were the fishermen, the boat-builders and the river traders right round the great bend of the Niger, forming the main ethnic stratum at Jenne and Timbuktu as well as at Gao and Kukya. Moreover, eastern Songhay, along with the neighbouring country of the Mossi, offered the best conditions for horse-breeding to be found anywhere to the south of the Sahara, and the mounted lancers of Songhay were swift and terrible, whether as slave-raiders on the eastern frontier or as the pillagers of Sahel towns. Thus, the potential existed for a Songhay revival, given only the leadership capable of directing it, and in 1464 this was found with the accession to the throne of Sonni Ali, who in a reign of twenty-eight years placed Songhay in the position formerly occupied by Mali. . . .

The Songhay empire, like that of Mali before it, involved a gigantic effort of state enterprise in production and trade as well as in military operations and civil government. Under Muhammad Ture (1493–1528) its territories were greatly extended, especially towards the west, until it encompassed the whole northern half of the old Mali empire. To the east of Songhay, Muhammad led at least two spectacular military expeditions, the first to Borgu, the second passing through the Hausa states of Zaria and Kano to the city of Agades in Aïr. But these were raids, not wars of conquest. As Muhammad himself explained, they were undertaken to distract the Songhay-speaking element in his armies from meddling in the Mande-speaking western part of his empire, where his own interests were strongest, and where he preferred to rule through slave armies recruited from his own war captives. Not under Muhammad only, but also under the succession of sons and grandsons who followed him as Askiyas [king] until 1591, the real thrust of Songhay was towards the west and the north. It was an impetus based upon Timbuktu, both as the centre of Islamic learning in the western Sudan and as the meeting-point of river and desert communications. It was an impetus, largely successful, to reconstruct as much as possible of the old Mali empire around this northerly base. While it lasted it was certainly more significant in every way than the reconstruction of the coastal fringes of western West Africa under the impact of the European maritime advance.

THE AZTEC AND INCA EMPIRES OF THE NEW WORLD

GEOFFREY W. CONRAD AND ARTHUR A. DEMAREST

In the following selection, anthropologists Geoffrey W. Conrad and Arthur A. Demarest show that the Aztec and Inca Empires established their authority and managed to dominate dozens of other peoples through religious rituals involving human sacrifice and the divinity of rulers.

The Aztec Empire originated with a tribe known as the Mexica, who migrated into southern Mexico, or Mesoamerica, in the thirteenth century. By the late 1400s the Mexica controlled the entire region. Their capital, Tenochtitlán, was one of the largest cities on earth and the Aztec king one of the most powerful monarchs.

The Incas of the Central Andes of South America assembled their empire through both conquest and diplomacy. While they built no large cities, their empire was unified by a vast system of roads and communications as well as an innovative system of social welfare. By the late 1400s, the Inca Empire stretched for two thousand miles along the Pacific coast of South America.

Geoffrey W. Conrad is professor of anthropology at Indiana University. Arthur A. Demarest is professor of anthropology at Vanderbilt University.

A line of men moves slowly up a steep staircase toward the summit of a pyramid. As each man reaches the top, he is seized and pinioned across an altar. A priest approaches, holding a stone-bladed knife with both hands. Raising the knife above his head and concentrating his strength in the blade, the priest intones a prayer, then plunges the knife downward. The man on the altar dies in a shower of his own blood. His heart is torn out and placed in a bowl. His body is carried to the edge of the steps and dropped. As it rolls and bounces toward the bottom, another man is brought forward and stretched across the altar. Hundreds of people have perished since this ceremony started; hundreds more will die before it ends.

Beside the pyramid stands a rack displaying the skulls of tens of thousands of previous victims. Like the broken bodies accumulating at the foot of the staircase, the skulls are those of captives taken in battle. They have been sacrificed to feed the sun. If the sun is not nourished with the vigorous blood of warriors, he will grow too weak for his daily struggle against the forces of darkness, and the universe will be destroyed.

Today the sun is bright and strong, obviously fit for combat. But what of tomorrow? next week? next year? The threat of destruction never passes, and the demand for blood is unrelenting.

An old man sits unmoving in a dimly lighted room. Everything about him attests to his wealth and power. The clothing he wears and the room's furnishings are of the finest quality. Servants come and go, attending to his wishes. Several aides are conferring with him, their voices subdued and postures deferential. One of them asks questions and the others answer; the old man himself does not speak aloud. The interrogation concerns the crops growing on his farmlands and the preparations under way at one of his country estates, where he plans to spend the summer. Everyone can sense that he is deeply pleased, even though he does not smile or shift his gaze as he listens. Instead, he remains aloof and dignified, the perfect image of lordliness.

Indeed, this awesome elder is a king. He claims to be descended from the sun, and his subjects revere him as a god. He has been married several hundred times, but his first and most important wife is his sister. At the moment his happiness stems from the impending visit of his favorite son, the one he has chosen to inherit the throne.

This aged and incestuous ruler, presently conducting a normal day's business, has been dead for thirty-five years. His son, who succeeded him and will dine with him tonight, died three years ago.

Living men die to feed the sun, and dead men live to rule a nation. Surely we have wandered into the realm of nightmares, where everything familiar turns grotesque, and what we hope not to dream about comes to pass.

Quite the contrary. While the events described above are generalized reconstructions, they lie well within the limits of documented fact. Each episode is drawn from a culture that existed less than five hundred years ago. The scene of human sacrifice and skulls mounted on a rack portrays the Mexica Aztecs of Mexico. The vision of a living corpse sitting in his palace depicts the Incas of Peru. As bizarre as these images may seem to twentieth-century Western minds, they were everyday realities for the Mexica and Inca, the two great imperial powers of the Americas on the eve of European discovery.

TWO VAST BUT SHORT-LIVED EMPIRES

For sheer historical drama, few ancient civilizations can match the Mexica and Inca. Both cultures emerged during the thirteenth and fourteenth centuries A.D.—times of turmoil in Mesoamerica and the Central Andes. Throughout this period powerful regional states clashed in contests for political and economic supremacy. In these viciously combative settings the Mexica and Inca appeared as small societies with unsophisticated cultures. Ignored or scorned by their potent and prestigious neighbors, they seemed destined to perish as obscure, almost accidental victims in the struggles of the mighty.

Yet the Mexica and Inca not only survived the bitter conflicts surrounding them, they prevailed. In the early 1400s these two peoples, hitherto so backward and unpromising, suddenly transformed themselves into the most efficient war machines in New World prehistory. Their armies began to march outward in campaigns of conquest. By 1500 they dominated the largest states ever formed in the native Americas—the Aztec and Inca Empires. From the depths of insignificance the Mexica and Inca had vaulted to unrivaled heights of power and affluence.

Still the dramas were unfinished. Only a few decades later, in final acts worthy of Sophocles or Shakespeare, each empire collapsed. In both cases the fall was so swift as to be measured in months. Ostensibly the Aztec and Inca Empires were destroyed by military force, but their defeats had a wildly improbable air. The conquering armies contained only a few *hundred* Spanish adventurers. In lands where soldiers could be mustered by the tens of thousands, the invading forces were so puny that they should have been negligible.

THE AZTEC AND INCA WERE INSECURE EMPIRES OF CONQUEST

DAVID R. RINGROSE

Both the Aztec Empire of Mesoamerica and the Inca Empire of Peru were true empires of conquest, meaning that over many decades the Aztec and Inca tribes established control over numerous other tribes. This control could be achieved in ways ranging from alliance to intermarriage to outright military conquest.

In the following selection historian David R. Ringrose examines the origins and expansion of both empires. He argues that because both were, in effect, multicultural, the Aztec (or Mexica) and Inca rulers had to employ creative means to legitimate their authority, to convince conquered peoples that their rule was justified. Rulers might incorporate conquered tribal leaders into their bureaucracy or require labor service, for example. But, Ringrose points out, both Aztec and Inca leaders relied primarily on religion to justify their authority. Ironically, however, religious machinations helped weaken both empires in the long run.

David R. Ringrose is professor of history at the University of California, San Diego.

R eferred to as the Aztecs in history books, the Mexica entered central Mexico around 1300. After fighting in regional wars with mixed success, around 1350 the Mexica were allowed to settle on a muddy island in the lakes of the central valley of Mexico. In return, they became clients of the Tepanec kingdom, the most aggressive state in the valley, and about 1370 the Tepanec imposed a kinglike military ruler on the tribe. By 1400 the Mexica had become a militarized monarchy, in which a warrior nobility controlled the original kinship groups, and were an important ally of the Tepanec. In the 1420s the Mexica turned on their Tepanec sponsors. They formed an alliance with two small tribes in the valley and in 1428 the Mexica conquered the Tepanecs. This "Triple Alliance," dominated by the Mexica, was the foundation of the Aztec Empire.

The 1420s included a military coup that placed control of the Mexica crown within a single royal family. At the same time, the warrior nobility was strengthened as conquered territory was parcelled out to individual warriors, rather than to the kin groups that were the original basis of Mexica society. The new rulers formalized differences between the priestly, military, and commoner classes. The militarized nobility was allowed distinctive dress and, to expand the supply of noble soldiers, warriors were allowed to have several wives.

THE AZTECS WERE INSECURE CONQUERORS

Between 1428 and 1520 six rulers led the Aztec Triple Alliance in a series of campaigns that brought dozens of kingdoms under Aztec authority and created an empire 700 miles long and 500 miles wide. These successes raise two questions about the Aztec achievement. What gave the Aztec political system its cohesion? What left it so unstable that an empire with several million inhabitants collapsed in the face of a few hundred Spaniards?

Unlike the Turks and the Mongols, the Mexica nomads did not enter agricultural civilization as conquerors. They achieved that goal only after a long period as subordinate mercenaries. This fostered a chronic sense of anxiety about their legitimacy, and the Mexica sought to gain recognition in several ways. Their warriors married women from the elites of the neighboring kingdoms. They also accepted the son of a highly regarded neighboring royal family as founder of their ruling dynasty.

The Mexica also used the religion of central Mexico to reinforce their legitimacy. This manipulation of religion is not easily summarized, but certain elements stand out. To a western observer, the Amerindian religious system has always been hard to comprehend. It apparently viewed the world as driven by a primal force that energized, usually through sun and rain, the actual environment. Worship focused on a collection of what Europeans regarded as gods, although their form and function was confusingly unstable to outside observers. Individual gods were identified with the sun, moon, rain, thunder, and many other phenomena, but their shape and function varied with location and with the religious and seasonal calendar. Thus, at one time and place, a particular god manifested itself with one appearance and power, but at another time of the year its manifestations could be quite different. The nature of these gods also varied from one tribe to another. As a result, the outward forms and powers of Amerindian deities were varied enough to allow the Mexica to reconfigure them to meet specific situations.

A second facet of the religious system is harder to grasp. The Amerindian sense of time and history was cyclical. The past was not a string of events that ran in a continuous line through time. The Amerindians, who were excellent astronomers, had developed an accurate fifty-two year calendric cycle. This cycle was understood as a moment of greatness followed by progressive decline caused by the cyclical waning of cosmic energy. Their view of history, therefore, assumed that distance through time was less important than the place of a past event in the cycle. Events from a particular phase in one historical cycle were readily combined with events from the same phase in other cycles without concern for our idea of chronological sequence. Such combinations simply added insight into the workings of the cyclical pattern, and it was only through understanding that pattern that "history" offered guidance to current events.

SACRIFICES TO THE GODS

Finally, mesoamerican (Mexican and central American) religion fixed on the perception that once a calendric cycle started, it (and human affairs) gradually ran down as the cosmic system used up its store of energy. To counteract that ominous trend, Amerindian societies developed rituals that involved human sacrifice on a scale that is difficult for modern observers to discuss with any kind of objectivity. The practice was to identify sacrificial victims—virgins, children, young men, vigorous warriors—who were full of the energy represented by particular cults. The victims were linked with the god in question and, in theory, were conditioned to think of themselves as joining the divine force. Because this conditioning often involved coercion and narcotics, the degree to which participants really acquiesced in their own death is obviously debatable. Through their ritual death, the personal vital force of these victims replenished the declining power that energized the world, its crops, and its affairs. While mesoamerican religion included many types of human sacrifice, the warriors who entered central Mexico in the 1300s increasingly linked the energy of the sun with the sacrifice of captured warriors and military control of politics. This led to a gruesome increase in the scale of sacrifice of warrior captives during the Aztec–Mexica rise to power.

The leaders of the Mexica coup of 1428 deliberately manipulated this religious system so as to justify their actions. They started with a minor Mexica deity named Huitzilopochtli, who was linked to a Mexica god-hero. They associated Huitzilopochtli with other mesoamerican sun-god cults, each of which reflected a specific time-place-function manifestation of the sun. During the crisis of the 1420s the Mexica apparently destroyed all documents about these deities and replaced them with their own. The new version placed Huitzilopochtli at the top of the pantheon, merging him with other sun-god manifestations. This version of the sun god identified the Aztec emperor as his agent on earth and was "served" by the Mexica warrior class. The warrior class thus had the sacred duty of waging war to provide the sacrifices that replenished the sun's energy.

This arrangement did more than justify war and sacrifice. It reconfigured the entire religious system so that the Aztecs, their warriors, and their emperor became the link between the ordinary world and the energy that drove the heavenly and agricultural cycles that kept human affairs working. This justified the special status of the warrior class. It also justified wars of expansion, because warfare provided the captives whose sacrifice helped keep things running. It also shaped the way in which war was fought, because it put a premium on taking captives, rather than on killing the enemy. This is part of the explanation for some of the Spaniards' dramatic battle victories. Finally, it was a grim way of keeping conquered kingdoms in line. As the empire expanded, it used the threat of force to exact tribute, rather than constructing a bureaucracy and co-opting local elites. Rebellion thus not only was a challenge to religious authority, but also carried the risk that the warriors of a rebel kingdom would become human sacrifices.

If the anthropologists, archaeologists, and historians have it right, this reconstruction of mesoamerican religion played a major role in building the Aztec empire. It turned religion into an ideological support for a militarized empire with a privileged warrior elite. It also made it sacrilegious to challenge Aztec authority and enhanced the risk inherent in challenging that authority.

WEAKNESS AND BAD TIMING

Ironically, this same religious system was undermining Aztec power when the Spaniards arrived. Three things contributed to a sense of impending crisis and to tensions in the society underneath the ruling class. One factor was inherent in the structure of the warrior elite. This noble class was accustomed to increasing its wealth through imperial rewards from new conquests. At the same time, thanks to the practice of polygamy, the number of men in this class grew rapidly. Such trends could be sustained only with new conquests or by extracting higher taxes and tribute from the rest of society.

At the same time, in about 1500, the Aztecs' 52-year cycle of greatness and decline moved into its downward phase. This seemed apparent to religious authorities because of crop failures, revolts, and epidemics, some of which were the initial impact of European disease in a population without immunological resistance. The only solution within the Aztec belief system was to step up the number of warrior sacrifices so as to replenish the energy of the cosmic system. This virtually compelled the later Aztec emperors to launch new wars of conquest.

The third factor that destabilized the empire was its size. By 1515 the Aztec army was stretched to the limit. The many subject kingdoms required constant punitive actions. Meanwhile, the empire had become so big that kingdoms that were candidates for conquest were far from the capital, making military logistics difficult. This reduced the effectiveness of Aztec attacks, meant that victories were not clear-cut, and reduced the numbers of captives just when more were urgently needed. The modest returns from later wars also aggravated internal tensions. Without the rewards of conquest, the oversized military class could not maintain its privileges without raising internal taxes. This alienated subordinate classes and kingdoms and further increased the need for police actions.

By 1519, when Cortez arrived in Mexico, the equilibrium that held the Aztec empire together was very fragile. Left alone, the empire's leadership might have managed a transformation like that of the Ottoman Turks after the invasion by Timurlane. Most observers, however, think it likely that the empire was about to disintegrate into its constituent kingdoms. Either way, Mexico was an ideal world for the Spaniards' tactics of local alliances, participation in local conflicts, and piecemeal conquest, tactics they had learned in Andalusia, Granada, the Canary Islands, and the Caribbean.

THE RISE OF THE INCA EMPIRE

Chronologically, the rise of the Inca Empire is similar to that of the Aztec Empire. Religion played a similar role in shaping the imperial elite and in legitimating imperial authority created by conquest. At the same time, there were differences in the way that this empire evolved and in the crisis that confronted it when the Spaniards landed in Peru. . . .

After about 1100, the Andean interior was divided into several regional kingdoms. The Incas themselves constituted a small tribal state near the city of Cuzco. In the 1200s, and 1300s, several kingdoms contended for power in the Andean valleys and around Lake Titicaca. As a secondary tribe, the Inca participated in the struggle with mixed results. The situation altered in the early 1400s, under the first historically credible Inca ruler, Viracocha Inca (died 1438). After participating in complex diplomatic and military maneuvering around Lake Titicaca, Viracocha Inca and his warriors were nearly defeated by their neighbors in 1438.

After a heroic defense of Cuzco, Viracocha's successor, Pachakuti (ruled 1438–1471), began a remarkable career of internal revitalization and imperial conquest. By 1463 he controlled the Andean valleys from Lake Titicaca to Lake Junin, a strip of territory 600 miles long. Inca armies then moved into the populous and sophisticated Chimu empire, which acknowledged Inca authority by 1465. When Pachakuti died in 1471, the Inca had conquered all of northern Peru and much of highland Ecuador. The next emperor, Topa Inca, turned his attention south. By 1493, when Columbus stumbled upon the Caribbean Islands, Topa Inca had added southern Peru, Bolivia, western Argentina, and Chile as far south as Santiago to the Inca Empire. The last great Inca leader, Huayna Capac (ruled 1493–1525), added the inland valleys of central Peru to the empire and pushed north to the border of modern Colombia. In eighty years these three remarkable rulers created a political empire 3,000 miles (4,300 km) long—the distance from Boston to San Diego.

RELIGION AND POWER

As in the Aztec Empire, this story poses some questions. How did the leaders of an empire of conquest legitimize themselves so as to minimize resistance, and what made their empire collapse when confronted by a few dozen Spaniards? Just as Aztec leaders reconfigured mesoamerican religion to reinforce a military empire, Inca leaders modified Andean religion so as to fit themselves into religious beliefs about the power that controlled the cycles of weather, seasons, and daily life and death. The beginnings of successful expansion in 1438 forced the Inca elite to organize itself into a coherent ruling class and to consolidate royal leadership. Moreover, just as Aztec leadership saw itself confronted by crisis after 1500, the Inca empire confronted an internal crisis in the 1520s. The similarity is deceptive, however, because the policies that integrated the Inca Empire were different from those of the Aztecs, and the crisis that the Spaniards were able to exploit was also different.

Andean religion resembled that of Mexico in basic ways, but had some distinctive traits. Andean culture was conscious of the cyclicality of heavenly events, but was less obsessed by cyclical rise and decline. The conceptual framework was similar in that, while Andean religion had religious figures that Europeans identified as gods, such figures had different features and functions depending on time and location. Leadership in a kin group or kingdom was generally associated with one of these godlike cults, connecting political authority with higher forces through a deity that shared its power with the local leader. Among the manifestations of the power that drove the universe were the sun, the moon, Venus (seen as two entities because it appeared in different places and in different seasons), thunder, and rain. Andean religion included human sacrifice; compared with Mexico, however, it was on a small scale. What emerges is a religion as adaptable as mesoamerican religion, but less pessimistic and bloodthirsty.

To understand how the Inca elite exploited religion, we must understand two other aspects of that religion. One is the concept of the *huaca*. Andean peoples assumed that, although there was a barrier between human affairs and the forces that moved the universe and caused crops and animals to grow, that barrier could be penetrated. The places or objects through which contact between the two spheres took place were called *huacas*. The word could be applied to a magical spring or grotto, to a good-luck amulet, to a tribal god-figure, or to the mummy of a dead ancestor. Priests or rulers who were able to penetrate the barrier and draw upon supernatural forces were respected and powerful people.

The most politically significant practice associated with *huaca* (pl. *huacas*) was a form of ancestor worship. When an individual died (to use a European word), he did not cease to exist or to participate in affairs. Instead, he was thought of as having crossed the barrier between realms. His body was mummified and became a *huaca*, a point at which the barrier between worlds was permeable because the dead individual was assumed able to communicate with the living. Mummified persons were treated with respect and allowed to advise on everyday affairs. They were given lodging, food, and water, and brought out to participate in village festivals and meetings. While they obviously didn't say much, they were treated as members of the spiritual world who sometimes took notice of the material world and signaled good or bad fortune.

Inca leaders reconfigured the Andean religious system after

1438 so as to reinforce their authority. The god-figures associated with the sun and the moon were the most powerful in the Andean pantheon, and the Inca linked together the emperor and the sun god. At the same time, they formalized a hierarchy of god-figures through which cosmic energy descended from the sun and moon to the primal elements of the real world. The sun and moon were identified with emperor and empress, the two Venuses with local kings and queens, and earth and water with man and woman. This placed the sun, and therefore the emperor, above local cults and rulers, and implied that the emperor was the symbolic father of local rulers.

INCORPORATING CONQUERED PEOPLES

This hierarchy was reinforced in other ways. The paternal aspect of rule over subordinate kingdoms was reinforced by "inviting" the children of conquered rulers to the palace in Cuzco. Politically important women became secondary wives of the emperor and the rest entered a form of royal service that prepared food and clothing for ritual use. The men were trained as soldiers and administrators who identified with the imperial government and became officials and army officers. In this way the Inca government recruited a bureaucracy and co-opted regional elites into the imperial ruling class. Simultaneously, Inca rulers transferred the cult images associated with local rulers to Cuzco. This reinforced their subordination to the sun and moon, and toward the imperial government. The recruitment of royal offspring to the court and the transfer of local cults to Cuzco sound suspiciously like hostage taking by Inca conquerors, but, together with the reconfiguring of religious ideology, they suggest a shrewd approach to legitimating imperial rule.

The Incas combined military logistics with a form of paternalist redistribution to strengthen their authority. Conquered peoples were forced to contribute part of their land and labor to construct terraces and irrigation systems. They then had to provide labor to cultivate the terraces in order to produce supplies which were stockpiled in imperial warehouses. These supply depots allowed Inca armies to travel rapidly because they did not have to carry supplies as they marched through the empire. As a result, Inca armies could reach a war zone or a rebel kingdom with remarkable speed. The coercive potential of this arrangement was masked by the fact that emperors released supplies from the royal storehouses when communities were caught short by bad weather and crop failure. In this way the imperial system allowed the emperor to counteract the forces of nature and verify his nearness to the power that drove the universe.

Inca rulers also exploited ancestor worship as a way of enhancing imperial prestige. When an emperor died, his body was mummified. Because he did not die in the European sense, his private property did not pass to his heir. In a form of divided inheritance, the dead emperor was treated as though he had retired from office. The prerogatives of rule passed to his heir, but because he was not really "dead," the late emperor's palaces and property remained "his." The "retired" emperor continued to "live" in his palace and was served by noble families who administered his estates for him, and, of course, supported themselves in the process.

This opulent world of ritual and ceremony enhanced the status of imperial office, but it created a long-term problem for the empire. Each new emperor had to accumulate new wealth and new lands to be personally wealthy. This was one factor that drove successive emperors to make new conquests. As in Mexico, when the empire grew large, conquests became more difficult and the returns were increasingly meager. At the same time, the noble cliques that lived off the estates of the dead emperors constituted a growing aristocracy that was independent of royal favor and thus capable of undermining royal authority.

A SUCCESSION CRISIS AT THE WRONG MOMENT

The potential for internal strife came to a head in the 1520s, just as the Spaniards were preparing to invade. Emperor Huayna Capac died in 1525 of a plague, possibly one that came to America with the Spaniards. This precipitated a succession crisis. Legally, the succession could pass only to a son of the emperor and the empress, who was also the emperor's sister. Brother-sister marriage guaranteed that each new emperor would inherit fully the cosmic power inherent in the identification of the sun with the emperor and the moon with the empress. The emperor also had "secondary" wives from royal families of subordinate kingdoms. The sons of these marriages, being only half divine, were not eligible to rule. At the same time, because they *were* half divine, they became key figures in the army and administration.

When Huayna Capac died, the authorities in Cuzco crowned his legal heir, Huascar, as emperor. Huascar, however, seems to have been an unpleasant, paranoid intriguer who alienated many of his supporters. In his last years, Huayna Capac had favored a half-royal son named Atahualpa, who proved to be a superb general and leader. When the Spaniards arrived in 1532, Atahualpa had just won a series of battles, had captured Huascar, and was on his way to take control of Cuzco, the imperial capital. Thus Francisco Pizarro arrived at a moment when the institutions of empire were challenged both militarily and ideologically. One wonders, however, if things would have been different had the Spaniards arrived a year or two later. Atahualpa might well have used his victory to change the succession and reform the institutions that had created internal dissension. The tenacity with which the Inca sought to recapture Cuzco from the Spaniards in 1536, and the fact that the last Inca government in exile survived until 1572, indicate that the Inca state was not as inherently fragile as the Aztec empire.

A Report on the Aztec Capital

Hernán Cortés

By 1480, the Aztec Empire covered most of southern Mexico and much of Central America. At its center was the capital city of Tenochtitlán, which was built on islands constructed in the center of Lake Texcoco and connected to the mainland by great earthen causeways.

In the following first-person account, taken from official records sent to Charles V, the king of Spain, the Spanish conqueror of Mexico, Hernán Cortés, claims that Tenochtitlán, which he calls Temixtitan, is the equivalent of any Spanish city. Its architecture is striking, and the city is well situated for military defense. The fascinated Cortés also points out the rich array of goods for sale in the markets of Tenochtitlán, indicating that the city is a market center for a vast region.

B efore I begin to describe this great city and the others already mentioned, it may be well for the better understanding of the subject to say something of the configuration of Mexico, in which they are situated, it being the principal seat of Muteczuma's [Montezuma, the king's] power. This Province is in the form of a circle, surrounded on all sides by lofty and rugged mountains; its level surface comprises an area of about seventy leagues in circumference, including two lakes, that overspread nearly the whole valley, being navigated by boats more than fifty leagues round. One of these lakes contains fresh, and the other, which is the larger of the two, salt water. On one side of the lakes, in the middle of the valley, a range of highlands

Reprinted from *The Despatches of Hernando Cortés, the Conqueror of Mexico, Addressed to the Emperor Charles V*, translated by George Folsom (New York: Wiley and Putnam, 1843).

divides them from one another, with the exception of a narrow strait which lies between the highlands and the lofty sierras. This strait is a bow-shot wide, and connects the two lakes; and by this means a trade is carried on between the cities and other settlements on the lakes in canoes without the necessity of travelling by land. As the salt lake rises and falls with its tides like the sea, during the time of high water it pours into the other lake with the rapidity of a powerful stream; and on the other hand, when the tide has ebbed, the water runs from the fresh into the salt lake.

A City as Large as Any in Europe

This great city of Temixtitan [Tenochtitlán] is situated in this salt lake, and from the main land to the denser parts of it, by whichever route one chooses to enter, the distance is two leagues. There are four avenues or entrances to the city, all of which are formed by artificial causeways, two spears' length in width. The city is as large as Seville or Cordova; its streets, I speak of the principal ones, are very wide and straight; some of these, and all the inferior ones, are half land and half water, and are navigated by canoes. All the streets at intervals have openings, through which the water flows, crossing from one street to another; and at these openings, some of which are very wide, there are also very wide bridges, composed of large pieces of timber, of great strength and well put together; on many of these bridges ten horses can go abreast. Foreseeing that if the inhabitants of this city should prove treacherous, they would posses great advantages from the manner in which the city is constructed, since by removing the bridges at the entrances, and abandoning the place, they could leave us to perish by famine without our being able to reach the main land—as soon as I had entered it, I made great haste to build four brigantines, which were soon finished, and were large enough to take ashore three hundred men and the horses, whenever it should become necessary.

Open Squares and Vast Marketplaces

This city has many public squares, in which are situated the markets and other places for buying and selling. There is one square twice as large as that of the city of Salamanca, surrounded by porticoes, where are daily assembled more than sixty thousand souls, engaged in buying and selling; and where are found all kinds of merchandise that the world affords, embracing the necessaries of life, as for instance articles of food, as well as jewels of gold and silver, lead, brass, copper, tin, precious stones, bones, shells, snails, and feathers. There are also exposed for sale wrought and unwrought stone, bricks burnt and unburnt, tim-

ber hewn and unhewn, of different sorts. There is a street for
game, where every variety of birds found in the country are sold,
as fowls, partridges, quails, wild ducks, fly-catchers, widgeons,
turtledoves, pigeons, reedbirds, parrots, sparrows, eagles, hawks,
owls, and kestrels; they sell likewise the skins of some birds of
prey, with their feathers, head, beak, and claws. There are also
sold rabbits, hares, deer, and little dogs, which are raised for eating and castrated. There is also an herb street, where may be obtained all sorts of roots and medicinal herbs that the country affords. There are apothecaries' shops, where prepared medicines,
liquids, ointments, and plasters are sold; barbers' shops, where
they wash and shave the head; and restaurateurs, that furnish
food and drink at a certain price. There is also a class of men like
those called in Castile porters, for carrying burthens. Wood and
coals are seen in abundance, and brasiers of earthenware for
burning coals; mats of various kinds for beds, others of a lighter
sort for seats, and for halls and bedrooms. There are all kinds of
green vegetables, especially onions, leeks, garlic, watercresses,
nasturtium, borage, sorel, artichokes, and golden thistle; fruits
also of numerous descriptions, amongst which are cherries and
plums, similar to those in Spain; honey and wax from bees, and
from the stalks of maize, which are as sweet as the sugar-cane;
honey is also extracted from the plant called maguey, which is
superior to sweet or new wine; from the same plant they extract
sugar and wine, which they also sell. Different kinds of cotton
thread of all colors in skeins are exposed for sale in one quarter
of the market, which has the appearance of the silk-market at
Granada, although the former is supplied more abundantly.
Painters' colors, as numerous as can be found in Spain, and as
fine shades; deerskins dressed and undressed, dyed different colors; earthenware of a large size and excellent quality; large and
small jars, jugs, pots, bricks, and an endless variety of vessels, all
made of fine clay, and all or most of them glazed and painted;
maize, or Indian corn, in the grain and in the form of bread, preferred in the grain for its flavor to that of the other islands and
terra-firma; patés of birds and fish; great quantities of fish, fresh,
salt, cooked and uncooked; the eggs of hens, geese, and of all the
other birds I have mentioned, in great abundance, and cakes
made of eggs; finally, every thing that can be found throughout
the whole country is sold in the markets, comprising articles so
numerous that to avoid prolixity, and because their names are
not retained in my memory, or are unknown to me, I shall not attempt to enumerate them. Every kind of merchandise is sold in
a particular street or quarter assigned to it exclusively, and thus
the best order is preserved. They sell every thing by number or

measure; at least so far we have not observed them to sell any thing by weight. There is a building in the great square that is used as an audience house, where ten or twelve persons, who are magistrates, sit and decide all controversies that arise in the market, and order delinquents to be punished. In the same square there are other persons who go constantly about among the people observing what is sold, and the measures used in selling; and they have been seen to break measures that were not true.

WORLD HISTORY BY ERA

Europe's Cultural Revival

—| CHAPTER 2 |—

THE RENAISSANCE CHANGED EUROPEAN CONCEPTS OF THE WORLD

WILLIAM MANCHESTER

European civilization underwent a major transformation in the fifteenth and sixteenth centuries. During this period, which is known as the Renaissance, European thinkers and artists rediscovered the classical culture of ancient Greece and Rome. Rediscovery preceded the development of a new mentality in Europe, which William Manchester, the author of the following selection, refers to as the "Renaissance spirit." Now, human beings were capable of anything, from creating works of art glorifying God to improving themselves and their societies.

As Manchester points out, the Renaissance spirit was remarkably different from the culture of the medieval period of Europe, from 476 to 1453. During those earlier centuries, little had changed and few people had any reason to expect or work for change. Most people simply expected every year to be the same as the previous one.

Manchester demonstrates that a number of forces were working for change by 1500. The traditional military tactics of the medieval era, characterized by knights on horseback, grew obsolete. Large, centralized kingdoms absorbed hundreds of independent feudal landholdings. And perhaps most importantly, thinkers began increasingly to question the authority of Christianity and the Roman Catholic Church.

Excerpted from *A World Lit Only by Fire*, by William Manchester. Copyright © 1992, 1993 by William Manchester. Reprinted by permission of Little, Brown and Company (Inc.).

William Manchester's works of popular history and biography include *The Glory and the Dream, The Death of a President*, and *The Last Lion: Winston Spencer Churchill.*

I n the medieval mind there was no awareness of time. . . . Inhabitants of the twentieth century are instinctively aware of past, present, and future. At any given moment most can quickly identify where they are on this temporal scale—the year, usually the date or day of the week, and frequently, by glancing at their wrists, the time of day. Medieval men were rarely aware of which century they were living in. There was no reason they should have been. There are great differences between everyday life in 1791 and 1991, but there were very few between 791 and 991. Life then revolved around the passing of the seasons and such cyclical events as religious holidays, harvest time, and local fetes. In all Christendom there was no such thing as a watch, a clock, or, apart from a copy of the Easter tables in the nearest church or monastery, anything resembling a calendar. Generations succeeded one another in a meaningless, timeless blur. In the whole of Europe, which was the world as they knew it, very little happened. Popes, emperors, and kings died and were succeeded by new popes, emperors, and kings; wars were fought, spoils divided; communities suffered, then recovered from, natural disasters. But the impact on the masses was negligible. This lockstep continued for a period of time roughly corresponding in length to the time between the Norman conquest of England, in 1066, and the end of the twentieth century. Inertia reinforced the immobility. Any innovation was inconceivable; to suggest the possibility of one would have invited suspicion, and because the accused were guilty until they had proved themselves innocent by surviving impossible ordeals—by fire, water, or combat—to be suspect was to be doomed. . . .

THE MIDDLE AGES GIVE WAY TO THE RENAISSANCE

And yet, and yet . . .

Rising gusts of wind, disregarded at the time, signaled the coming storm. The first gales affected the laity. Knighthood, a pivotal medieval institution, was dying. At a time when its ceremonies had finally reached their fullest development, chivalry was obsolescent and would soon be obsolete. The knightly way of life was no longer practical. Chain mail had been replaced by plate, which, though more effective, was also much heavier; horses which were capable of carrying that much weight were hard to come by, and their expense, added to that of the costly new mail, was almost prohibitive. Worse still, the mounted knight no longer dominated the battlefield; he could be outmaneuvered and unhorsed by English bowmen, Genoese crossbowmen, and pikemen led by lightly armed men-at-arms, or sergeants. Europe's new armies were composed of highly trained, well-armed professional infantrymen who could remain in the field, ready for battle, through an entire season of campaigning. Since only great nation-states could afford them, the future would belong to powerful absolute monarchs.

By A.D. 1500 most of these sovereign dynasties were in place, represented by England's Henry VII, France's Louis XII, Russia's Ivan III, Scandinavia's John I, Hungary's Ladislas II, Poland's John Albert, and Portugal's Manuel I. Another major player was on the way: in 1492 when the fall of Granada destroyed the last vestiges of Moorish power on the Iberian peninsula, Spaniards completed the long reconquest of their territory. The union of their two chief crowns with the marriage of Ferdinand of Aragon and Isabella of Castile laid the foundations for modern Spain; together they began suppressing their fractious vassals. Germany and Italy, however, were going to be late in joining the new Europe. On both sides of the Alps prolonged disputes over succession delayed the coalescence of central authority. As a result, in the immediate future Italians would continue to live in city-states or papal states and Germans would still be ruled by petty princes. But this fragmentation could not last. A kind of centripetal force, strengthened by emerging feelings of national identity among the masses, was reshaping Europe. And that was a threat to monolithic Christendom.

The papacy was vexed otherwise as the fifteenth century drew to a close. European cities were witnessing the emergence of educated classes inflamed by anticlericalism. Their feelings were understandable, if, in papal eyes, unpardonable. The Lateran reforms of 1215 had been inadequate; reliable reports of misconduct by priests, nuns, and prelates, much of it squalid, were rising. And the harmony achieved by theologians over the last century had been shattered. Bernard of Clairvaux, the anti-intellectual saint, would have found his worst suspicions confirmed by the new philosophy of nominalism. Denying the existence of universals, nominalists declared that the gulf between reason and revelation was unbridgeable—that to believe in virgin birth and the resurrection was completely unreasonable. Men of faith who might have challenged them, such as Thomas à Kempis, seemed lost in a dream of mysticism.

At the same time, a subtle but powerful new spirit was rising in Europe. It was virulently subversive of all medieval society, especially the Church, though no one recognized it as such, partly because its greatest figures were devout Catholics. During the pontificate of Innocent III (1198–1216) the rediscovery of Aristotelian learning—in dialectic, logic, natural science, and metaphysics—had been readily synthesized with traditional Church doctrine. Now, as the full cultural heritage of Greece and Rome began to reappear, the problems of synthesis were escalating, and they defied solution. In Italy the movement was known as the Rinascimento. The French combined the verb *renaître*, "revive," with the feminine noun *naissance*, "birth," to form Renaissance—rebirth.

REPRESENTATIVES OF A NEW SPIRIT

Fixing a date for the beginning of the Renaissance is impossible, but most scholars believe its stirrings had begun by the early 1400s. Although Dante, Petrarch, Boccaccio, Saint Francis of Assisi, and the painter Giotto de Bondone—all of whom seem to have been infused with the new spirit—were dead by then, they are seen as forerunners of the reawakening. In the long reach of history, the most influential Renaissance men were the writers, scholars, philosophers, educators, statesmen, and independent theologians. However, their impact upon events, tremendous as it was, would not be felt until later. The artists began to arrive first, led by the greatest galaxy of painters, sculptors, and architects ever known. They were spectacular, they were most memorably Italian, notably Florentine, and because their works were so dazzling—and so pious—they had the enthusiastic blessing and sponsorship of the papacy. Among their immortal figures were Botticelli, Fra Filippo Lippi, Piero della Francesca, the Bellinis, Giorgione, Della Robbia, Titian, Michelangelo, Raphael, and, elsewhere in Europe, Rubens, the Brueghels, Dürer, and Holbein. The supreme figure was Leonardo da Vinci, but Leonardo was more than an artist trailing clouds of glory.

When we look back across five centuries, the implications of the Renaissance appear to be obvious. It seems astonishing that no one saw where it was leading, anticipating what lay round the next bend in the road and then over the horizon. But they lacked our perspective; they could not hold a mirror up to the future. Like all people at all times, they were confronted each day by the present, which always arrives in a promiscuous rush, with the significant, the trivial, the profound, and the fatuous all tangled together. The popes, emperors, cardinals, kings, prelates, and nobles of the time sorted through the snarl and, being typical men in power, chose to believe what they wanted to believe, accepting whatever justified their policies and convictions and ignoring the rest. Even the wisest of them were at a hopeless disadvantage, for their only guide in sorting it all out—the only guide anyone ever has—was the past, and precedents are worse than useless when facing something entirely new. They suffered another handicap. As medieval men, crippled by ten centuries of immobility, they viewed the world through distorted prisms peculiar to their age.

PRINTING TECHNOLOGY ARRIVES IN EUROPE

S.H. STEINBERG

According to *Life* magazine, the introduction into Europe of printing technology was the most important event of the thousand years from A.D. 1001 to 2000. Printing made knowledge available to anyone by mass-producing books and pamphlets and making them inexpensive. Moreover, earlier hand-copied editions were prone to errors; printing made it possible to standardize information.

Block printing had been invented in China in the eighth century. By the thirteenth century, printed materials from China such as playing cards and paper money had reached Europe. In the mid–fifteenth century, a growing demand among educated Europeans for books stimulated printers to develop effective block-printing technology. The result, in 1455, was a section of the Bible set into print by Johann Gutenberg. In addition to his printing press, Gutenberg invented a durable form of ink. Europe's printing revolution was under way.

In the following selection, S.H. Steinberg describes the spread of printing beyond Gutenberg's shop in Mainz, Germany. Because printing was a profit-making business that required patrons and customers, the early printing centers were also the most important trade centers. Steinberg points out that universities and churches, surprisingly, were slow to accept printing, unable to compete commercially, and opposed to mechanical production on aesthetic grounds.

Excerpted from *Five Hundred Years of Printing*, by S.H. Steinberg, new edition, revised by John Trevitt. Copyright © original text, 1955, 1961, and 1996 B.E. Steinberg; new material © 1996 John Trevitt. Reprinted by permission of the publisher, Oak Knoll Press.

S.H. Steinberg was a teacher and writer whose other works include *A Short History of Germany*, *Steinberg's Dictionary of British History*, and *The Thirty Years War*.

I n view of the fact that printing from movable type was a German invention and first practised in the German city of Mainz, it is not surprising that the first practitioners of the new art in every country of Europe and even in parts of the New World should have been German nationals. It is no exaggeration to describe [Johann] Gutenberg's invention as Germany's most important single contribution to civilization. However, the printers who, from about 1460 onward, went on their travels from Mainz were little concerned with German culture. They were craftsmen and businessmen; they wanted to make a living; and they readily adapted themselves and their art to the conditions of international trade. Until printing had firmly established itself as an everyday commodity—that is to say, until well into the beginning of the sixteenth century—a map showing the places where printers had settled down is virtually identical with a map showing the places where any commercial firm would have set up an agency.

It is quite purposeless to enumerate the dozens of one-horse towns in the Abruzzi or Savoy [in Italy] which can boast of one or perhaps even two early presses or to trace the steps of these wandering printers in their quest for patrons and customers. Fascinating though the study of some of these men and their productions is for the student of incunabula, the history of printing is too much bound up with the history of big business to mention here more than one of these small fry. Except for the high quality of his work, the career of Johann Neumeister of Mainz is typical of that of many of his fellow craftsmen. Perhaps a direct pupil of Gutenberg, Neumeister was invited to Foligno by a humanist scholar and there produced the first edition of Dante's *Divina Commedia* in 1472; he then returned to Mainz, and later set up a press at Albi in Languedoc. In both places he drew on his familiarity with Italian art when he produced Turrecremata's *Meditationes* (1479,1481) with illustrations cut after the mural paintings in S. Maria sopra Minerva in Rome. Finally Neumeister was called by the cardinal d'Amboise to Lyon where he printed the magnificent *Missale secundum usum Lugduni* (1487).

PRINTING WAS FIRST AND FOREMOST A BUSINESS

Individual patrons, however, were not enough to guarantee the printer a livelihood and to secure the sale of his books. Right

Johann Gutenberg pulls a freshly printed sheet from a bed of type.
Gutenberg revolutionized the printing process with his invention of
moveable type.

from the beginning, the printer (who, be it remembered, was his
own publisher and retailer) was faced by the alternative, unchanged ever since, of basing his business on the support of organized institutions or of relying on the fairly stable market of a
literate, book-loving and book-buying clientele of sizable di-
mensions. Official backing was (and is) provided mainly by governments, churches and schools; private patronage, by the educated middle class.

The aristocracy, which in the following centuries was to build
up those magnificent libraries, most of which have eventually
found their last refuge in public libraries, greeted the new invention with little enthusiasm if they did not condemn it outright. The attitude of the Duke Federigo of Urbino as reported by
Vespasiano da Bisticci was at the time, about 1490, shared by
most connoisseurs. In his splendid library 'all books were su-
perlatively good and written with the pen; had there been one
printed book, it would have been ashamed in such company'. It
is in keeping with this contempt of the mechanically produced
book that Cardinal Giuliano della Rovere (later Pope Julius II)
had [ancient Roman writer] Appian's *Civil Wars* copied by a superb scribe in 1479 from the text printed by Wendelin of Speier
in 1472. The calligrapher even adopted the printer's colophon;

he only changed 'impressit Vindelinus' to 'scripsit Franciscus Tianus'. As late as the second half of the eighteenth century a voluptuary aesthete, Cardinal Rohan, used only handwritten service books when he celebrated mass.

It was, then, people of moderate means, who could not afford to be squeamish about the outward appearance of the tools of their profession, to whom the early printers had to look for custom. It was the binders rather than the printers who overcame the reluctance of highbrow connoisseurs in admitting printed books to their stately shelves; and down to the present the sumptuousness of choice bindings frequently contrasts oddly with the shoddiness of printing and the worthlessness of contents thus bound.

PRINTING SPREAD RAPIDLY AND WIDELY

It is quite in keeping with the well-organized and world-wide net of international trade at the end of the Middle Ages that printing by no means spread in ever-widening circles from Mainz over southern Germany, central Europe, and to the fringes of the then known world. On the contrary, the ease of firmly established communications all over the Continent permitted the printers to reach out at once to those places which offered the brightest prospects, that is to say the flourishing centres of international trade. So it came about that printing presses were established in quick succession in Cologne (1464), Basel (1466), Rome (1467), Venice (1469), Paris, Nürnberg, Utrecht (1470), Milan, Naples, Florence (1471), Augsburg (1472), Lyon, Valencia, Budapest (1473), Cracow, Bruges (1474), Lübeck, Breslau (1475), Westminster, Rostock (1476), Geneva, Palermo, Messina (1478), London (1480), Antwerp, Leipzig (1481), Odense (1482), Stockholm (1483). University towns as such had no attraction for printers: learning and diligence is no substitute for ready cash. Cologne, Basel, Paris, Valencia, Seville and Naples acted as magnets because they were thriving centres of trading, banking and shipping, and seats of secular and ecclesiastical courts.

The only university town which seems to be an exception was Wittenberg; but there it was one professor only who made printing a success, and before and after Martin Luther's connection with Wittenberg University the place does not occur in the annals of printing. In fact, Wittenberg can be said to owe its fame partly to the one blunder the shrewd Nürnberg printer, Anton Koberger, ever committed when he turned down Luther's invitation to become his publisher.

The church, and especially the monastic orders and congregations with their far-flung connections, too, provided easy ways of transmitting the art regardless of political frontiers. When in

1463 the two printers, Conrad Sweynheym and Arnold Pannartz, went to the Benedictine abbey of Subiaco near Rome to set up the first press outside Germany, they most probably travelled via Augsburg. Both abbeys excelled in the zeal and quality of their scriptoria, and it was in SS. Ulric and Afra that a few years later the first Augsburg press was established. As the Subiaco abbey was under the supervision of the great Spanish cardinal, Torquemada, it was a natural step for the two printers to move to Rome very soon, after they had printed four books. Later their literary adviser, Giovanni Andrea dei Bussi, was rewarded with a bishopric in Corsica; and Sweynheym received a canonry at St Victor's in Mainz (1474).

However, the shelter of a monastery and the patronage of a prince of the church were not sufficient to maintain a steady output and sale. Intellectual impetus and economic power had long since become the property of the laity. It was the big towns and the world of industry and commerce which became the mainstay of book production.

In northern Europe the net of international trade which the Hanse towns had spun from Russia to England and from Norway to Flanders now provided easy openings for the printer's craft. The trade routes which the south German merchants had established to Milan and Venice, Lyon and Paris, Budapest and Cracow were now trodden by printers and booksellers. The very first printer next to Gutenberg, Johann Fust, died in 1466 in Paris where he had gone on business. The 'Great Trading Company' of Revensburg, which had a virtual monopoly in the trade with Spain, was instrumental in establishing presses in Valencia, Seville, Barcelona, Burgos and elsewhere; and one of their emissaries, Juan Cromberger of Seville, introduced printing in the New World, when in 1539 he dispatched a printer and a press to the capital of the then Spanish colony of Mexico.

THE WELL-ROUNDED RENAISSANCE MAN

JACOB BURCKHARDT

Renaissance scholarship fostered a new form of education in Europe based on the ancient Greek ideal of humanism. A humanistic education involved a thorough study of philosophy, history, languages, and the arts. It also might include training in etiquette and athletics and, many argued, should liberate the mind and spirit from the restrictions of society or religion.

In the following selection, nineteenth-century Swiss historian Jacob Burckhardt describes the sort of person produced by an education in the "humanities" or "liberal arts." These men were capable of greatness in many fields ranging from painting to architecture to literature. Moreover, they cut an impressive figure not only in philosophical discussions but also on horseback or the duelling ground.

The most obvious Renaissance men were artists and thinkers, and Burckhardt uses as his example Leon Battista Alberti, who is best known as a painter. But Burckhardt points out that even politicians and merchants had wide humanistic educations.

Jacob Burckhardt's *The Civilization of the Renaissance in Italy* was the first major historical work on the subject. Published in the mid-1800s, it set the standard for Renaissance studies for decades.

A n acute and practised eye might be able to trace, step by step, the increase in the number of complete men during the fifteenth century. Whether they had before them as a conscious object the harmonious development of their spiritual and material existence is hard to say; but several of them attained it, so far as is consistent with the imperfection of all that is earthly.

Excerpted from *The Civilization of the Renaissance in Italy*, vol. 1, by Jacob Burckhardt, translated by S.G.C. Middlemore (New York: Harper & Row, 1929).

It may be better to renounce the attempt at an estimate of the share which fortune, character, and talent had in the life of [Florentine despot and art patron] Lorenzo the Magnificent. But look at a personality like that of [comic writer] Ariosto, especially as shown in his satires. In what harmony are there expressed the pride of the man and the poet, the irony with which he treats his own enjoyments, the most delicate satire, and the deepest goodwill!

When this impulse to the highest individual development was combined with a powerful and varied nature, which had mastered all the elements of the culture of the age, then arose the "all-sided man"—*l'uomo universale*—who belonged to Italy alone. Men there were of encyclopaedic knowledge in many countries during the Middle Ages, for this knowledge was confined within narrow limits; and even in the twelfth century there were universal artists, but the problems of architecture were comparatively simple and uniform, and in sculpture and painting the matter was of more importance than the form. But in Italy at the time of the Renaissance we find artists who in every branch created new and perfect works, and who also made the greatest impression as men. Others, outside the arts they practised, were masters of a vast circle of spiritual interests. . . .

THE RENAISSANCE MAN WAS SKILLED IN MANY FIELDS

The fifteenth century is, above all, that of the many-sided men. There is no biography which does not, besides the chief work of its hero, speak of other pursuits all passing beyond the limits of dilettantism. The Florentine merchant and statesman was often learned in both the classical languages; the most famous humanists read the ethics and politics of Aristotle to him and his sons; even the daughters of the house were highly educated. It is in these circles that private education was first treated seriously. The humanist, on his side, was compelled to the most varied attainments, since his philological learning was not limited, as it now is, to the theoretical knowledge of classical antiquity, but had to serve the practical needs of daily life. While studying Pliny, he made collections of natural history; the geography of the ancients was his guide in treating of modern geography, their history was his pattern in writing contemporary chronicles, even when composed in Italian; he not only translated the comedies of Plautus, but acted as manager when they were put on the stage; every effective form of ancient literature down to the dialogues of Lucian he did his best to imitate; and besides all this he acted as magistrate, secretary, and diplomatist—not always to his own advantage.

But among these many-sided men some who may truly be called 'all-sided' tower above the rest. Before analysing the general phases of life and culture of this period we may here, on the threshold of the fifteenth century, consider for a moment the figure of one of these giants—Leon Battista Alberti. His biography, which is only a fragment, speaks of him but little as an artist, and makes no mention at all of his great significance in the history of architecture. We shall now see what he was apart from these special claims to distinction.

In all by which praise is won Leon Battista from his childhood excelled. Of his various gymnastic feats and exercises we read with astonishment how, with his feet together, he could spring over a man's head; how in the cathedral he threw a coin in the air till it was heard to ring against the distant roof; how the wildest horses trembled under him. In three things he desired to appear faultless to others, in walking, in riding, and in speaking. He learned music without a master, and yet his compositions were admired by professional judges. Under the pressure of poverty he studied both civil and canonical law for many years, till exhaustion brought on a severe illness. In his twenty-fourth year, finding his memory for words weakened, but his sense of facts unimpaired, he set to work at physics and mathematics. And all the while he acquired every sort of accomplishment and dexterity, cross-examining artists, scholars, and artisans of all descriptions, down to the cobblers, about the secrets and peculiarities of their craft. Painting and modelling he practised by the way, and especially excelled in admirable likenesses from memory. Great admiration was excited by his mysterious *camera obscura*, in which he showed at one time the stars and the moon rising over rocky hills, at another wide landscapes with mountains and gulfs receding into dim perspective, and with fleets advancing on the waters in shade or sunshine. And that which others created he welcomed joyfully, and held every human achievement which followed the laws of beauty for something almost divine. To all this must be added his literary works, first of all those on art, which are landmarks and authorities of the first order for the Renaissance of Form, especially in architecture; then his Latin prose writings—novels and other works—of which some have been taken for productions of antiquity; his elegies, eclogues, and humorous dinner-speeches. He also wrote an Italian treatise on domestic life in four books; various moral, philosophical, and historical works; and many speeches and poems, including a funeral oration on his dog. Notwithstanding his admiration for the Latin language, he wrote in Italian, and encouraged others to do the same; himself a disciple of Greek science, he maintained the doctrine that without Christianity the world would wander in a labyrinth of error. His serious and witty sayings were thought worth collecting, and specimens of them, many columns long, are quoted in his biography. And all that he had and knew he imparted, as rich natures always do, without the least reserve, giving away his chief discoveries for nothing. But the deepest spring of his nature has yet to be spoken of—the sympathetic intensity with which he entered into the whole life around him. At the sight of noble trees and waving cornfields he shed tears; handsome and dignified old men he honoured as a "delight of nature," and could never look at them enough. Perfectly formed animals won his goodwill as being specially favoured by nature; and more than once, when he was ill, the sight of a beautiful landscape cured him. No wonder that those who saw him in this close and mysterious communion with the world ascribed to him the gift of prophecy. He was said to have foretold a bloody catastrophe in the family of Este, the fate of Florence, and the death of the Popes years before they happened, and to be able to read into the countenances and the hearts of men. It need not be added that an iron will pervaded and sustained his whole personality; like all the great men of the Renaissance, he said, "Men can do all things if they will."

And Leonardo da Vinci was to Alberti as the finisher to the beginner, as the master to the *dilettante*. Would only that [historian Georgio] Vasari's work were here supplemented by a description like that of Alberti! The colossal outlines of Leonardo's nature can never be more than dimly and distantly conceived.

THREE GREAT ARTISTS OF RENAISSANCE FLORENCE

VINCENZO LABELLA

The Renaissance began in Italy, which at that time was a collection of independent city-states rather than a unified nation. Some cities, Venice and Genoa in particular, were major trade centers. Rome remained the seat of the papacy. Florence, however, became the great cultural and artistic center of Renaissance Italy.

Located in central Italy's Tuscany region, Florence rose to major power status under the leadership of the Medici family in the mid-1400s. The Medici had risen from shopkeepers to become Europe's richest bankers, and later members of the family became popes and queens. Under the leadership of Cosimo de Medici and his grandson Lorenzo in the 1400s, the Medici added artistic and cultural patronage to their many accomplishments. Painters, sculptors, architects, and humanistic philosophers all enjoyed the support of the Medici.

Among the artists who enjoyed the patronage of the Medici and the vibrant cultural atmosphere of Florence were Leonardo da Vinci, Michelangelo, and Raphael, whom Vincenzo Labella describes in the following selection. Leonardo's father brought his family from his native village of Vinci to seek employment as a Medici civil servant, while many of Leonardo's first paintings were completed under the patronage of Lorenzo. Michelangelo, for his part, began work as a sculptor for Lorenzo while still in his teens and later studied in the Philosophic Academy begun by Cosimo. Raphael came to Florence in the early 1500s to study the works of Leonardo, Michelangelo, and other masters. Vincenzo

Labella is a film and television producer whose works include *Jesus of Nazareth* and *A Season of Giants*.

<hr>

T here happened a time in the history of humankind when the ravages of wars, plagues and social conflicts were overshadowed by artistic achievements of such excellence and power as to find but rare parallel.

This was the season that saw the sudden blossoming of painters, sculptors, architects, poets, scientists and musicians, in a manner and quantity so amazing that it was reasonably considered the rebirth or "renaissance" of the human creative energy.

This flowering of genius found its natural humus in the central part of Italy formed by four regions: Tuscany, Umbria, the Marches and Lazio. Florence was its ideal center, a city-state governed by the Medici, a genial dynasty of merchants and art patrons who had risen from their druggist shops to become the first and most successful bankers in Europe. They were represented in every major city, and even as far as Turkey.

Just when the Genovese Christopher Columbus was about to land in the New World, soon to be followed by the Florentine Amerigo Vespucci, whose name would be given to the discovered continent, Florence was under the gentle rule of His Magnificence Lorenzo de Medici, who had gathered at his court some of the highest intellects of his time. He hosted a school for young sculptors, painters and architects, including his young "adopted son" Michelangelo Buonarroti, who stood out as the harbinger of the glory that Lorenzo's champions would garner for Florence.

The "city of the flower," as Florence was known because of the red lily (or iris) that shone in its blazon, earned the title of "new Athens." The *fiorino,* or florin, its gold currency, held financial credit all over Europe.

In the efflorescence of this season, three names rose above all others: Leonardo, Michelangelo, Raphael. For a brief, magical span in the course of time, they worked side by side in Florence, divided by rivalry, yet united by the common denomination of genius. And humankind is still being uplifted by them.

They were not supermen; to the contrary, even as they climbed to the highest peaks of excellence and fame, they retained their natural vulnerability. Far from being unassailable, they were hurt, and in turn, hurt others by envy, jealousy and pride. They were arrogant in the self-assurance of their talent, humble in the knowledge that beyond any finishing line there was another, and yet another, to be crossed. The threads of their lives were spun from different origins, yet were interwoven, and often entangled, in that unique loom of the Renaissance tapestry that was Florence.

They were all attracted to this city by the same magnet of love and common spirit, like desert farers looking for the oasis to quench their thirst. One thing they had in common was the premature death of their mothers while they were still infants. Each of them bore the mark of this loss in his conscience, and each drew from it a cathartic inspiration that was translated into his works.

*Completed in 1516, Michelangelo's **Moses** has been hailed as one of the most extraordinary statues of its time.*

THE THREE GENIUSES WERE VERY DIFFERENT FROM ONE ANOTHER

Otherwise, they differed greatly. Leonardo was the prober of all that was human, or pertained to the condition of humankind on planet Earth, and the mysteries beyond. In the opening words of his Madrid Codex, he proclaimed, "Come, men, to see the wonders which may be discovered in nature by my studies." His multifarious interests so stimulated his intelligence that he found it hard to complete all that he commenced. His continual search for innovation and invention led him to extraordinary accomplishment, and to dismal failure. He was handsome and possessed a natural elegance that won him the esteem of lords and artisans, of masters and apprentices alike. He was the champion of a nobility derived from his constant celebration of aesthetic values and the harmony of nature and its wonders.

Whether designing an equestrian monument or experimenting with a new painting technique in his fresco *The Last Supper,* Leonardo never ceased to surprise and amaze. He was called to paint a simple portrait, and he turned it into an invitation to enter a world of magic and mystery. The *Mona Lisa,* exhibited at the Louvre in Paris, was a window he left open for generations to pass from mere portraiture to a dimension of wider horizons. The property of genius is just this: to stimulate, to provoke *intelligence,* the quality of *intus legere* (to read inside), to decipher what life proposes in all its aspects.

"I have never had one day that I could call my own," wrote Michelangelo from the stronghold of his solitude, where very few friends were admitted, and where he defended his will to concentrate on the driving force of his vocation. Impervious as the stony mountains that he loved, he did not impress by his stocky and ungraceful appearance. Misunderstood by his family, opposed by a father who disapproved of what he considered the demeaning craft of stonecutting, Michelangelo found solace only in his work. When he lost his great patron, the man that all of Florence hailed as the Magnificent Lorenzo de Medici, and his beloved city was shaken by the stormy drama of Friar Girolamo Savonarola, he was left alone to defend his visions, and battle frequent humiliations such as a commission to shape a statue in snow, an exercise as vain as it was painful. But on his path to glory he unearthed giants who proclaimed his greatness: the *Pietà,* the *David,* the *Moses.*

He rose in fame so as to stand face to face with another giant, Pope Julius II, daring to challenge him. From the excruciating adventure of the Sistine Chapel he emerged victorious, and his triumph, unlike those of the Caesars, was for all seasons, as proved by the recent stunning restorations of his work.

Raphael, the youngest in this triad of geniuses, was not a Florentine. He came from a town in the Marches region where another enlightened ruler held a court that shored up the energy of the Renaissance. Raphael, the son of an honest painter, was soon introduced into the practice of the art, and was so precocious that, at age seventeen in an official contract, he was called "master."

Enamored of life and almost prescient of the brief span it would allow him, he produced a wealth of images that partake of humanity while tending to a superior sphere in which the spirit moves freely and powerfully. His Madonnas are portraits of real women, captured tales of motherly love, transfigured by the artist and steeped in the inimitable ambient light that flooded his work.

Raphael, too, had an appointment with destiny in the *Stanze*—the rooms that Pope Julius II commissioned him to decorate in order to endow the Vatican palace with art treasures worthy of the new era he had inaugurated. In his *School of Athens*, the triad of champions of the Renaissance found consecration, as Raphael portrayed himself and his great traveling companions, Leonardo and Michelangelo.

PAINTING IS SUPERIOR TO THE OTHER ARTS

LEONARDO DA VINCI

Among the most accomplished men of the Renaissance was the illegitimate son of a public notary from the small Tuscan town of Vinci. Born in 1452, his name was Leonardo. Interested from a very young age in the workings of nature, Leonardo was able to gain practical knowledge in painting when his father moved to Florence to seek employment under the Medici.

Leonardo, whose works include the *Mona Lisa, The Last Supper,* and other works of deep emotional subtlety and richness, was indeed a great painter. But his accomplishments spread far beyond painting into science, engineering, and even human psychology. He drew sketches of, among other devices, helicopters and machine guns centuries before they were actually invented.

In the following selection from his *Notebooks,* Leonardo argues that painting is superior to other arts such as poetry and sculpture because it depicts the richness and vitality of nature most truly.

How painting surpasses all human works by reason of the subtle possibilities which it contains:

The eye, which is called the window of the soul, is the chief means whereby the understanding may most fully and abundantly appreciate the infinite works of nature; and the ear is the second, inasmuch as it acquires its importance from the fact that it hears the things which the eye has seen. If you historians, or poets, or mathematicians had never seen things with your eyes you would be ill able to describe them in your writings. And if you, O poet, represent a story by depicting it with your pen,

Excerpted from *The Notebooks of Leonardo da Vinci,* arranged and rendered into English, with introductions, by Edward MacCurdy (New York: Scribner's, 1906).

the painter with his brush will so render it as to be more easily satisfying and less tedious to understand. If you call painting 'dumb poetry', then the painter may say of the poet that his art is 'blind painting'. Consider then which is the more grievous affliction, to be blind or to be dumb! Although the poet has as wide a choice of subjects as the painter, his creations fail to afford as much satisfaction to mankind as do paintings, for while poetry attempts to represent forms, actions and scenes with words, the painter employs the exact images of these forms in order to reproduce them. Consider, then, which is more fundamental to man, the name of man or his image? The name changes with change of country; the form is unchanged except by death.

And if the poet serves the understanding by way of the ear, the painter does so by the eye, which is the nobler sense.

I will only cite as an instance of this how if a good painter represents the fury of a battle and a poet also describes one, and the two descriptions are shown together to the public, you will soon see which will draw most of the spectators, and where there will be most discussion, to which most praise will be given and which will satisfy the more. There is no doubt that the painting, which is by far the more useful and beautiful, will give the greater pleasure. Inscribe in any place the name of God and set opposite to it His image, you will see which will be held in greater reverence!

THE VISUAL SENSE SURPASSES MERE WORDS

Since painting embraces within itself all the forms of nature, you have omitted nothing except the names, and these are not universal like the forms. If you have the results of her processes we have the processes of her results.

Take the case of a poet describing the beauties of a lady to her lover and that of a painter who makes a portrait of her; you will see whither nature will the more incline the enamoured judge. Surely the proof of the matter ought to rest upon the verdict of experience!

You have set painting among the mechanical arts! Truly were painters as ready equipped as you are to praise their own works in writing, I doubt whether it would endure the reproach of so vile a name. If you call it mechanical because it is by manual work that the hands represent what the imagination creates, your writers are setting down with the pen by manual work what originates in the mind. If you call it mechanical because it is done for money, who fall into this error—if indeed it can be called an error—more than you yourselves? If you lecture for the Schools do you not go to whoever pays you the most? Do you do any work without some reward?

The emotional subtlety and richness of Leonardo da Vinci's work is demonstrated in one of his most famous paintings, the **Mona Lisa.**

And yet I do not say this in order to censure such opinions, for every labour looks for its reward. And if the poet should say, 'I will create a fiction which shall express great things', so likewise will the painter also, for even so Apelles [ancient Roman painter] made the Calumny [moralistic painting]. If you should say that poetry is the more enduring,—to this I would reply that the works of a coppersmith are more enduring still, since time preserves them longer than either your works or ours; nevertheless they show but little imagination; and painting, if it be done upon copper in enamel colours, can be made far more enduring.

In Art we may be said to be grandsons unto God. If poetry

treats of moral philosophy, painting has to do with natural philosophy; if the one describes the workings of the mind, the other considers what the mind effects by movements of the body; if the one dismays folk by hellish fictions, the other does the like by showing the same things in action. Suppose the poet sets himself to represent some image of beauty or terror, something vile and foul, or some monstrous thing, in contest with the painter, and suppose in his own way he makes a change of forms at his pleasure, will not the painter still satisfy the more? Have we not seen pictures which bear so close a resemblance to the actual thing that they have deceived both men and beasts?

If you know how to describe and write down the appearance of the forms, the painter can make them so that they appear enlivened with lights and shadows which create the very expression of the faces; herein you cannot attain with the pen where he attains with the brush. . . .

How he who despises painting has no love for the philosophy in nature:

If you despise painting, which is the sole imitator of all the visible works of nature, it is certain that you will be despising a subtle invention which with philosophical and ingenious speculation takes as its theme all the various kinds of forms, airs and scenes, plants, animals, grasses and flowers, which are surrounded by light and shade. And this truly is a science and the true-born daughter of nature, since painting is the offspring of nature. But in order to speak more correctly we may call it the grandchild of nature; for all visible things derive their existence from nature, and from these same things is born painting. So therefore we may justly speak of it as the grandchild of nature and as related to God himself.

A New Elite: The Renaissance Prince and Courtier

E.R. Chamberlin

During the Renaissance, centralized political authority in the form of monarchies grew stronger throughout Europe. Even the powerful monarchs of Spain, France, and England, however, increasingly imitated the merchant-princes who ruled the Italian city-states. The greatest of these were the Medici of Florence, who, scholar E.R. Chamberlin claims in the following passage, not only dominated their city for centuries but influenced politics and cultural development throughout Europe.

Moreover, since the Renaissance was an era of scholarship and instruction, humanist scholars wrote guidebooks describing proper forms of rule and diplomatic conduct. Among the most famous of these, Chamberlin notes, are *The Prince* by Niccolò Machiavelli and *The Courtier* by Baldassare Castiglione. According to Machiavelli, a prince should be guided by the necessities of power and not concern himself with moral questions. Castiglione, on the other hand, described the qualities necessary for success and influence within a prince's court. Both books were widely read, finding favor not only in Italy but in the faraway courts in Madrid, Paris, and London.

A t the peak of Renaissance society stood the prince, the single, powerful man who, by a combination of political skill and hereditary authority, virtually ruled absolute over his state. It seems a curious contradiction that this period, which stressed, above all, the freedom of the individual, should have accepted the concept of the single ruler. There was good reason for it. In Italy, where the prince achieved his most brilliant and characteristic form, he was born of the fierce and endless tumults between factions in the cities. Despairing of ever finding peace except under the rule of one man, cities deserted the republican ideal, placing power freely in the hands of a leading citizen. Theoretically, that power was merely lent, not given, but once having enjoyed it few men intended to yield it back. Elsewhere in Europe, similar causes were at work in every country which did not possess a strong, central monarchy. . . .

Theoretically, the term 'prince' could be applied to all who held power, whether over thousands or millions, and it is in this sense that Machiavelli and other political writers used the term. Those princes who contributed most to the new society, however, tended to be smaller rather than larger rulers, exerting a social influence out of proportion to their power until their courts were edged off the European stage by the development of the huge, modern nations. Federigo da Montefeltro, whose court at Urbino set a standard in civilised behaviour for 300 years, ruled perhaps 150,000 souls; those over whom the Medici exercised direct control probably did not exceed a quarter of a million. Even the powerful dukes of Burgundy maintained their independence only through the disordered condition of France. In earlier centuries, much of the energies of these princes would have been expended in war, for military victory meant both glory and survival; the Renaissance prince needed less the virtues of courage and military genius than to be versed in the subtle skills of finance and politics, for war now was in the hands of the professionals. His fame depended less upon battle honours than upon the culture of his court, the extent to which he patronised the arts and showed himself capable of conversing with the learned.

The most brilliant of the Renaissance princes were those early members of the house of Medici which dominated Florence for nearly three hundred years. Rarely can a single family have so influenced an entire continent. It was largely through their munificence and taste that there was gathered in the small city of Florence, during the late fifteenth and early sixteenth centuries the band of men who created the Renaissance. The Medici rule in Florence was tempestuous: three times they were thrown out of the city; three times they returned, creating an ever-closer grip upon the constitution. They took much—but they gave more. The ancient republican history of the city came to an end under them but, under them too, the city became the engine-house of the Renaissance. They poured their enormous wealth into the patronage of the arts and sciences. They spent the better part of four million pounds in less than half a century, not merely in adorning their palaces with works of art but also in endowing seats of learning. Cosimo de' Medici, called 'Pater patriae' [father of his country] by a grateful city, displayed the fantastic generosity of the family to the full in 1439 when the Council of Florence met in the city. He made himself the personal host of the scores of dignitaries attending it, among them the Pope, the Emperor of the East and the Patriarch of Constantinople. The conference was an attempt to achieve a working unity between the Church of Rome and the Eastern Church. It failed, but during the five months that it was in Florence it contributed something possibly even greater to Europe. Some of the most learned people of the world were gathered within the confines of the city between March and July of 1439, and outside the deliberations of the Council they found a ready audience in the Florentines, ever hungry for new ideas. Predominant among these scholars were the Greeks whose language provided the key to the sciences which had so long been lost to Europe. Through their influence Cosimo founded the Platonic Academy which his successors cherished.

In 1444 Cosimo began the construction of the first of the Medici palaces. His fellow-citizens protested, thinking it both unfitting and ominous that a so-called private citizen should build upon such a scale. They tried to unseat him but he weathered that particular storm although others were to follow. Later, when the Medici became overlords in law as they were in fact, and took the title of Duke, they built an enormous palace on the far side of the Arno—a sprawling, arrogant building which proclaimed the superior status of the family. But Cosimo's palace, where the Renaissance can be said to have been born, appears more as a private house in its exterior for it fits into the line of the street. It was the first of the Renaissance palaces, providing the model for scores to come. Medici rule was still far from absolute and the palace still had to discharge the function of a castle where the family could shelter from the rage of their fellows. The ground storey therefore appears solid, almost forbidding, but the upper stories are elegant. The great street door gave on to a little court, graceful and airy, and here were placed the statues of *David* and *Judith* which Donatello had been commissioned to produce while the palace was being constructed. The *David* was a work of a kind which had not been seen in Europe for over a thousand years, for it was executed in the round and, like the palace in which it stood, created a precedent for others to follow. . . .

In 1469 Lorenzo de' Medici became head of the family and of the State. He was only twenty years old at the time and, although bred to responsibility, was vividly aware of the burden he had to bear. 'The second day after my father's death, the principal men of the city and of the State came to our house to condole with us on our loss, and to encourage me to take on the care of the city and of the State as my father and grandfather had done. This proposal being against the instincts of my immature age, and considering that the burden and danger were great, I consented to it unwillingly.' His reason for acceptance was the sound, practical reason of finance which the Medici never quite abandoned. 'I did so in order to protect our friends and property for it fares ill in Florence with any who possesses wealth without any share in the government.' The Florentines thereby gained a leader who combined in his person all the qualities of the rich and diverse period. Financier and poet, statesman and scholar, economist and strategist—it seemed that there was no activity in which he could not excel if he so desired. The consummate political and military skill with which he steered Florence through the dangerous shoals of Italian politics ultimately left no trace, for Florence, with all Italy, became subject to foreigners. It was the manner in which he cherished and directed the new-born arts and learning which left its mark upon Europe. His patronage made heavy inroads even

Lorenzo de Medici

upon the great Medici fortune, but he looked upon himself as a custodian, rather than an owner, of wealth. 'Some would perhaps think it more desirable to have a part of it in their purse but I conceive it to have been spent to the great advantage of the public and am therefore perfectly satisfied.' The vast library which he amassed became the first true public library in Europe for it was freely available to all. Agents were engaged not only in Europe but in the East with the express purpose of discovering ancient manuscripts. One scholar brought back 200 Greek works, eighty of which had never before been known in Europe. The names of the innumerable artists he encouraged would be a catalogue of the creators of the Renaissance. Botticelli, five years his senior, had shared his childhood home and later worked for him; Leonardo da Vinci owed his appointment to the Milanese court to him; he gave the 15-year-old Michelangelo a home in his palace with a monthly allowance; Verrocchio, Ghirlandajo, Filippino Lippi—so the list could be extended until it included

every talented man working in Florence during the brief years of
Lorenzo's life. He died at the age of forty-three, but, though no
other Medici could equal the versatility of 'Il Magnifico', yet they
continued his work. One of them became pope as Leo X and infused into the most powerful court in Europe some of the ideals
which Lorenzo had cherished.

   Renaissance society, having perforce accepted the single ruler,
did not thereby accept him as a natural phenomenon to be en-
dured or adored. His office was analysed, as it had never been
before, in an attempt to explain its growth and function, to pre-
pare a blue-print of a piece of political machinery which was to
drive Europe for nearly three hundred years. The machinery was
'political' in the fullest sense, for it governed in some degree
every aspect of the lives of men gathered together in communities, decreeing how they should be judged, how they should earn
their bread, refresh their minds and bodies, protect themselves
from enemies within and without the State. Two books appeared
in the early years of the sixteenth century which placed the
prince and his court under the microscope, *The Prince* by Niccolo
Machiavelli and *The Courtier* by Baldassare Castiglione. They appeared within four years of each other, in 1528 and 1532, respec-
tively, but both had been written, quite independently, many
years before—testimony to the fact that the phenomenon of the
prince was beginning to engage European attention. Machiavelli's intention was to dissect the mechanics of statecraft in
terms of its effectiveness. Morality was irrelevant: if a strategy
worked, it was good; if it failed, it was bad. There have been few
writers so grossly misjudged as this Florentine republican who
produced the classic textbook for the practice of tyranny. It is as
though a doctor, having diagnosed a disease, were to be accused
of inventing it. Machiavelli was well aware of the construction
likely to be placed upon his work and went out of his way to
stress that this was the picture of things as they were—that, given
that the prince was necessary in civil life, then it was best that he
should learn how to conduct himself in the most perilous craft in
the world. He should indeed be a wise and virtuous man, but
'the manner in which men now live is so different from the manner in which they should live that he who deviates from the common course of practice and endeavours to act as duty dictates,
necessarily ensures his own destruction'. Every man has a price,
every seemingly disinterested action can be shown to be rooted
in self-interest. A prince should keep his word—but few successful men actually do so. Is it better for a prince to be loved or
feared? It depends, Machiavelli replies; circumstances alter cases
but, on the whole, it is safer to be feared, for most men are fickle

and timid and will abandon in the hour of need those who have favoured them and have no other call upon them than the claims of gratitude. A prince as a commander of troops should always be feared, never worrying about a reputation for cruelty, for this was the only possible way to keep cruel men in order. It was a jaundiced view of the world; none knew better than Machiavelli that men could, and did, die for no other price than love of their country. But such love presupposed freedom; where there was no longer freedom the only incentives were self-interest or fear.

Machiavelli's prince was the first among men but was still a man; the Latin mind declined to invest him with that tinge of divinity which, in the north, came to infuse the idea. In Burgundy, the concept of the duke as being the personification of the State, and therefore as being something greater than a common man, was erected into a principle and a ritual. All the trappings of adoration, more commonly reserved for the worship of God, were his. Religious texts which spoke of the Trinity were freely applied to his comings and goings. After certain festivities in Arras, le Clerc wrote: 'If God were to descend from heaven I doubt if they could do him greater honour than was made to the duke.' Another remarked of the enthusiasm shown in the streets, 'It seemed as though they had God himself by the feet'. The most precious metals were considered only just good enough to touch his sacred flesh, be viewed by his holy eyes. The attendance at table upon him echoed the ritual of the Holy Mass; his very cup-bearer was seen as the priest who, in another church, elevated the chalice. Even as at the altar, the napkin with which the duke dried his hands was kissed as it was passed from courtier to courtier. The torches which lit his way to table were kissed, as were the handles of the knives placed before him. Such adulation would have astonished the Italians. Lorenzo de' Medici, popular and competent though he was, came under heavy and sustained criticisms for his pretensions: 'He did not want to be equalled or imitated even in verses or games or exercises and turned angrily on any one who did so.' No one would have dared even attempt to be the equal of a duke of Burgundy. The excess was to bring its reaction: a king of England lost his head through too much devotion to the Divine Right and the monarchy of France ultimately collapsed in bloody ruin.

Machiavelli's *Prince* was a cold exercise in logic; Castiglione's *Courtier* was a warm, living portrait of the ideal man. 'I do not wonder that you were able to depict the perfect courtier', a friend wrote to him, 'for you had only to hold a mirror before you and set down what you saw there.' The graceful compliment was essentially true for Castiglione possessed most of the qualities he praised: piety, loyalty, courage, an easy learning and wit. Indeed, his life was almost a demonstration of Machiavelli's opinion that a virtuous man was at a disadvantage. As envoy between Pope Clement VII and the Emperor Charles V during the perilous days which culminated in the Sack of Rome in 1527, he was deluded by both, failed in his mission and died a discredited man. The Emperor, who so sorely tried him, said sadly, 'I tell you, one of the finest gentlemen in the world is dead'. Castiglione would have been proud of the epitaph and history, too, remembers him, not as diplomat but as gentleman.

The Courtier was the outcome of four brief years spent at the little court of Urbino. Afterwards, Castiglione was to mix with the truly great and powerful. As representative of the duke at the Papal Court, he came into intimate contact with Raphael, Michelangelo, Bembo; later he was Apostolic Nuncio to the Emperor's court. But always he looked back with nostalgia to the little court set among the hills of the northern Marches. He left Urbino in 1508, but for twenty years thereafter he lovingly polished and repolished his account of a civilised society, creating a monument to his own Golden Age. The duchy of Urbino owed its foundation to Federigo da Montefeltro, a professional soldier who yet managed to create a court in which the new humanist values were dazzlingly embodied. Piero della Francesca's portrait of him shows a man in whom strength is combined with tolerance, who would be surprised by nothing, expected nothing and was well able to defend his own rights. . . . He was a man who made a fortune from soldiering, played off his enemies one against the other and so kept inviolate the 400-odd hill villages and towns which acknowledged him as prince. But he was also a man who, in childhood, had been schooled by Vittorino da Feltre, the greatest humanist teacher in Europe, who infused in his pupils the new view of man. The great library at Urbino was Federigo's work. 'He alone had a mind to do what had not been done for a thousand years and more; that is, to create the finest library since ancient times.' Not for him was the common product of the new printing press; he employed thirty or forty scribes so that all his books should be 'written with the pen, not one printed, that it might not be disgraced thereby'.

In 1450 he began the construction of the palace which Castiglione knew and which attracted travellers on the Grand Tour long after the brief life of the duchy had passed. 'It seemed not a palace but a city in the form of a palace', Castiglione affirmed, 'and [he] furnished it not only with what is customary such as silver vases, wall hangings of the richest cloth of gold, silk and other like things but for ornament he added countless ancient statues of marble and bronze, rare paintings . . .' In this twofold role, admirer of ancient art and patron of modern painters, Federigo was essentially of the Renaissance. He died in 1482 and the dukedom passed to his son, Guidobaldo, who maintained the intellectual atmosphere of the court although he proved himself unable to hold back the militant world outside. It was his court which Castiglione described in the process of building up the portrait of the courtier. It is the picture of a group of brilliant minds, familiar with each other and therefore at ease, who have turned aside briefly from the cares of state and seek refreshment in conversation. There are feasts and entertainments of wide variety; during the day the members go about their business but each evening they meet again, under the presidency of the duchess (for the duke is grievously afflicted by gout and retires early). They talk into the small hours, pursuing each topic informally but with sobriety and order—and merriment too—fashioning between themselves the perfect man. So vividly did the memory stay with Castiglione that he could describe the end of one of these sessions with the poignancy of a paradise lost. . . .

After Castiglione's day, the image of the courtier suffered a decline, becoming either the image of a fop or an intriguing social climber; even the Italian feminine of the word—'la cortegiana' or courtesan—became a synonym for a high-class harlot. But for Castiglione, the courtier was the cream of civilised society. He did not have to be nobly born; admittedly, he usually was, for only those born into the upper classes had the leisure or the opportunities to practice the arts, but this recognition that 'courtesy' was a quality of mind, and not of class, went far to explain the wide influence of the book. The courtier must be able to acquit himself in all manly exercises—wrestling, running, riding, but should be equally at home with literature, able to speak several languages, play musical instruments, write elegant verse. But everything should be done with a casual air so that his conversation, though sensible, was sprightly; he was even enjoined to study the form and nature of jokes. In love, he was to be discreet and honourable; in war, courageous but magnanimous. Above all, he was to be a man of his word, loyal to his prince, generous to his servants. He was altogether far removed from that other ideal man, the knight, with his fantastic code of personal honour. In modern language, Castiglione's courtier would be described as a well-educated, 'decent' man, with a strong code of personal morals but tolerant of the weakness of others. It was an ideal by which most men probably measured their lapses, for the standard demanded was high. But that the book filled a void is well shown by the speed with which it entered other languages and how long it maintained its influence. It was translated into French in 1537, into Spanish in 1540, into English in 1561, and, 200 years after Urbino ceased to exist as a state, Samuel Johnson gave his benediction to the book which enshrined its memory. 'The best book that ever was written upon good breeding, Il Cortegiano, by Castiglione, grew up at the little court of Urbino and you should read it.'

THE LIVES OF WOMEN DURING THE RENAISSANCE

KATE SIMON

According to Kate Simon, the author of the following selection, it is difficult to generalize about the lives of women in Italy during the Renaissance. Some women, indeed, enjoyed political and cultural influence. Others were immortalized by artists such as Leonardo da Vinci. The vast majority of women, however, lived undocumented lives, and an unfortunate few fell into slavery.

Simon notes that few careers were open to women, and that, for most, marriage was the best option. Marriage itself could be a difficult and complex affair. Upper-class women married young, were expected to provide dowries, and hoped to produce sons for their philandering husbands. Poorer women, Simon claims, bore a variety of burdens, although they might have more influence on their husbands. The women who enjoyed the greatest individual freedom were concubines and entertainers.

Kate Simon is the author of many books of travel and history, including *Italy: The Places in Between*, *Rome: Places and Pleasures*, and *England's Green and Pleasant Land*.

The stage on which the Renaissance woman lived is often bathed in the luminous nostalgic glow of a "Golden Age." It was a Golden Age for a few women, very few, and the light was less a broad glow than a spotlight, strengthened by energetic display and the scribblings of ambitious chroniclers and court sycophants. As we know, the Renaissance recorded itself in

Excerpted from *A Renaissance Tapestry*, by Kate Simon (New York: Harper & Row, 1988). Copyright © 1988 by Kate Simon. Reprinted by permission of International Creative Management, Inc.

minute detail, and when there was concentration on one or two figures it was intense and large, pointing up every singularity, every distinction. The ladies who protected courts and fortresses, foiled enemies and placated popes, and who were mythologized in their time and after, though stubbornly strong and bold were not always as effective as some reports would have them. The usually keen Isabella d'Este-Gonzaga, for example, a prototype of the Renaissance Athena, made several serious political mistakes, using a good deal of her energy and cleverness to smooth or explain them away.

WOMEN IN POLITICS

The warrior-politician-lady usually came to high responsibility when her husband became a victim of the politics or wars he himself often helped design. In the handsome Renaissance library of the Accademia Lincei in Rome, there is a folio of letters that defined the mature life of Lucrezia Gonzaga of the collateral line of Gazzuolo, a vulnerable territory claimed by various Gonzaga cousins at various times. They are angry letters, servile letters, letters that plead, that grovel, that praise, that beg. Her husband was the prisoner of the duke of Ferrara and his allies. She apologizes for the actions of the spouse, "who was, I think, born a twin of unhappiness," and begs pardon for his grave error. Won't the duke please have him released? His sin was stupidity and nothing more. How can such a flea menace an eagle! What force has a puppy against a lion? There was no response to this flattery; nor did reference to the fact that they were connected by blood and shared honored relatives make an impression on the Este. She also writes for help from the duke of Parma, to the powers of Genoa, Verona, Padua, and to relatives in Mantua. To her sister she writes of the dreadful wariness one has to maintain as a mentor of a court, as a politician, and of the danger and exhaustion inherent in the position. To Pope Paul II and to Julius III she writes letters trembling with piety and humility, and then to her sister she speaks of the unkindness of popes, bishops, archbishops, abbots, as cold as kings and emperors. Nor can she stop the letter-writing in widowhood; it gives her purpose and dimension. We find her groveling gracefully at the feet of Solimano, the emperor of Constantinople, and sending flattering notes to the king of Bohemia.

There were luckier women almost constantly in view. We frequently hear Isabella d'Este dictating to her scribes on a world of matters, and hear her sister Beatrice describing the gold brocade of her vest and the rubies laced into her hair for festivities to celebrate the birth of her first son. The shine of Lucrezia Borgia's

golden hair, washed, dried in the sun, and touched with an al-
chemist's bleach during a day of rest on her progress toward Ferrara to marry Alfonso d'Este, is still refulgent across the centuries.
The poetry and letters of devout, learned Vittoria Colonna to
Pietro Bembo, to Castiglione, and most famously the sonnets and
letters she exchanged with Michelangelo, who wrote a moving
poem on her death, still sound for us from yellowed pages. We
know of Cecilia Gonzaga's learning, of the cultivated and wise
spirit of Elisabetta Gonzaga, of Caterina Sforza's outrageous
scheming and courage, and her experiments in magic and medicine that might produce a "celestial water," a panacea for most
ills. The intellectual career of Renée of France, who married into
the court of Ferrara, where she gathered an "academy" of learned
scholars and which she embarrassed profoundly—to the point
of being removed to a nunnery by her husband—through her
friendship with Calvin and other leaders of the Reformation, is
richly documented. The Treaty of Cambria, involving pan-
European affairs and often referred to as the "Peace of the
Ladies," is praised as a step in the advancement of women. The
"ladies," however, were Louise, the mother of the king of France,
and Margaret, aunt of the emperor, women in conspicuous positions who may simply have been window dressing in matters actually handled by ambassadors and papal envoys at least as
clever and seasoned as they.

Were it not for Leonardo [da Vinci], we might have lost the
beauty and the poised, sly charm of such court mistresses as Cecilia Gallerini and Lucretia Crivelli, painted for Ludovico il Moro
of Milan. Were it not for court chroniclers, we might have lost the
translations from the classics, the poetry, and the disquisitions on
philosophy written by other court mistresses. Nor did marriage
always diminish the gifts of talented and privileged women. Ip-
polita Gonzaga, the daughter of Isabella's brother Ferrante, continued to study music and astronomy, to write poetry and remain
for years "one of the most beautiful and accomplished women of
her day." We know of a few polymaths, a few writers, and a few
artists, but there must have been many gifted girls lost in
anonymity. Large, busy ateliers like those of Squarcione and the
Bellini in Padua quite possibly put their daughters to work with
the boy apprentices. Who knows what telling passages in which
paintings may have been theirs? Who knows what a prospering
merchant gleaned from the hints and suggestions of his observant
wife (in spite of the fact that, having followed Alberti's injunc-
tions, he kept his papers hidden from her)? Who knows about the
management of properties controlled by the wives of Italian
bankers who made long, frequent voyages to their branches in

Antwerp and London? There are, of course, extant diaries and records, but they touch on comparatively few female lives.

WOMEN PREPARE FOR THEIR FEW CAREERS

Careers open to women were the three perennials: housewifery and childbearing, the religious life, and whoredom. The little girls of princely houses were, with a few notable exceptions, taught mainly the feminine arts of embroidering, singing, dancing, playing a musical instrument or two, and being able to handle a few Latin phrases. The daughter of a merchant or a well-paid artisan acquired household skills and a knowledge of numbers, while she ate sturdily to achieve the buxom figure that promised fecundity. She was betrothed at about thirteen or earlier, but was not considered of interest until she was ready for childbearing, when her career actually began. The marriage celebration which she had anticipated for years was the fulfillment of a dream with nightmare components. The feasting and dancing were lovely, but how was a fifteen- or sixteen-year-old to react, no matter how sophisticated or well prepared by her female relatives, to heavy practical jokes of attempted rape or being bedded with a proxy, who might go as far as touching her nude leg with his, hardly the *amore* she had heard so much about in stories and carnival songs. Titillating jokes made around the marriage bed, and the display of her bed sheets to prove her virginity and her husband's capability, were familiar customs of her time, yet must have been confusing, even appalling, to a girl who might have been brought up on a blend of piety and romances about gentle knights.

Dowries frequently created problems, particularly in the courts that had inlaid boxes prepared with ingenious mechanisms to safeguard dowries of accumulated pearls and emeralds. Their ambassadors and secretaries rushed back and forth between courts, lawyers argued fine points, scribes scribbled, parents weighed and disputed, grew indignant, melted into acquiescence—acts and scenes that often absorbed protracted lengths of time. Where there was no money or too little, girls were sent to nunneries to weave and embroider, their chastity guarded by nuns who might or might not themselves be chaste and even if chaste, subject to rape—nuns and little girls alike—by gangs of adventuresome young men, who might be severely punished *if* they were caught. When nunneries were overwhelmed with little girls pushed into their doors, they asked for admission fees, spoken of as "dowries." Or a community might gather a dowry fund to distribute to poor girls or design regulations to hold down the size of dowries, always a failure. No one could discourage this prime symbol of upward mobility, particularly flexible among a growing class of prosperous merchants who felt they had the right to buy their way into the ranks of the elite, who often needed the dowry gold.

DOWRIES AND MARRIAGE GIFTS

Among the many pieces of advice and instructions given a girl by her mother was the important matter of being patient and forbearing, of not, by either "learning or magics," attempting to match her husband's accomplishments. Some of the exquisitely painted *cassoni*, wedding chests that held a bride's new finery, presented Mamma's lessons graphically. Although many featured the popular subjects of Hercules' labors and Horatio's defense of his bridge, considerable attention was given the patient Griselda, the heroic Queen Esther, Ulysses' faithful Penelope, and Lucrezia, who stabbed herself rather than live with dishonor after she had been raped.

The rare artifacts that portrayed "woman triumphant" were the birth trays which carried food to women in labor, the most elaborate of them kept and displayed as commemorative pieces. In tempera on wood, a master painter of *cassoni* and trays, taking his theme from Plutarch's *Triumph of Love*, paints a triumphal chariot driven by Cupid. In the foreground, Aristotle acts as beast of burden for his Phyllis; nearby, Delilah cuts Samson's hair. The white-bearded philosopher is made stupid by the bit in his teeth, while Phyllis, young, ravishing, and splendidly dressed, holds the reins that direct and pull the old man. Another variation on the theme has Socrates playing the docile donkey for an exultant Xanthippe.

One tray, luxuriant with gold leaf, Medici symbols, horses, dogs, and armored knights, which compose a bravura display of the miniaturist's art, centers on a winged Fame, holding in one hand a sword, in the other a minute Cupid, bow at the ready. Probably designed by Domenico Veneziano after a passage in Boccaccio, the tray celebrates the birth of Lorenzo de' Medici. One side depicts a birthing-room scene, complete with attendants, visitors, and a lady harpist playing to the swaddled baby. The obverse displays a baby boy with a disconcertingly muscular body, sitting on a rock. He wears a coral amulet and urinates a streamlet of gold and silver, a symbol of the wealth to which he was born and the additional wealth he will achieve.

The same little stream of silver and gold appears in at least one other extant birth tray, decorated with the legend: "May God give health to all women who give birth and to the fathers. May there be no exhaustion or danger. I am an infant on a rock [a symbol of strength and endurance?] and I piss silver and gold." Such prayers, plus the magical amulets, plus the no-nonsense symbol of golden piss, were often accompanied by a weight of religious medals, which the mother of a princeling attached to his swaddling clothes and his cradle. She might also see to it that measures against the power of the evil eye be carefully maintained. (One was a prohibition against cutting the infant's nails for a proscribed time.) When she was no longer fed off the beautiful, flattering trays, when the baby left her care entirely—turned over to a wet nurse or put in the care of members of the court—she returned to being a lesser human being, an enfeebled version of noble man. Frequent literary references point up woman's perfidy and ridicule the barbaric practices to achieve false beauty: filling her wrinkles with unsightly paste, pulling her hair out by the roots to make her forehead taller, wearing wigs made of the hair of corpses.

THE HARDSHIPS OF MARRIAGE

The daughter of a moneyed family had no hope of inheriting more than a pittance of the family fortune; her dowry was considered her inheritance, and that was secure only if she behaved herself—good behavior frequently meaning her acceptance of her husband's dalliance anywhere, with anyone. If she made her husband a cuckold, a favorite form of fool, or if he merely suspected her and for obscure reasons chose not to have her beheaded or poisoned or shut up forever in a dungeon, he claimed her dowry, never again hers. She was, literally, a chattel of her husband, subject to what one historian called "moral lynching." Should she be maltreated—and many were, and hideously—her family might sympathize, invite her for long cosseting visits, but not rescue her. So notorious was the maltreatment of these golden lambs that [the respectable essayist Baldassare] Castiglione, an affectionate husband, actually condoned adultery in women and advocated divorce. Occasionally a girl would suffer the humiliation of being repeatedly offered and rejected, like a piece of faulty merchandise. Francesco Sforza of Milan, old enough to have fathered two dozen children, was betrothed to Bianca Maria Visconti when she was seven. The accompanying festivities were attended by nobles, knights, and relations, but not the little fiancée. As time passed, the contract was dissolved and the girl sent to Leonello d'Este for his approval. When he returned her, she was readied for a Gonzaga marriage, which also fell through. Eighteen years after the first marital foray, her long road rounded back to Milan, where she became Francesco Sforza's not too happy duchess.

Annulments were rare, affordable only by those who could

make large gifts to the Church and unattainable altogether, as in the case of Henry VIII, by those who scorned papal authority. Leprosy, impotence, and absences of many years were grounds for annulment. Even when armed with such reasons, women were frequently reluctant to avail themselves of annulments; second marriages for women were frowned on by the Church and society, and in any case, chances of improvement might be slim: better the devil one knew.

A woman was eager to produce sons to protect the family and its interests, and happily proud to help arrange consequent jubilation, but her own birth and that of her daughters was rarely cause for celebration. Isabella d'Este owned a magnificent cradle, prepared for the birth of her firstborn, who, however, turned out to be a girl, Leonora, followed by another and yet another girl child. The cradle was kept under wraps for ten years, until Federico, the future marquis and first duke of Mantua, was born. It was then refurbished and shown in its full splendor, appropriate to a son. ("May all your children be sons" is still a common form of "Best wishes" in Italy.)

Should her husband bring home an illegitimate child, as Leonardo da Vinci's father brought him to his stepmother's household, she took care of him no matter how she might feel, among his half-siblings. The humanist tenet that a man's beginnings were of little importance and what a man made of himself, of his own free will, was all that mattered essentially, created a casual acceptance of the illegitimate child. (Illegitimacy rarely caused much inconvenience, except where property and power might be involved, and these matters were carefully settled, frequently by allotting portions of an inheritance to promising bastards. Illegitimate heirs were sometimes needed to continue a dwindling line; at least one pope repeopled his family tree with the help of a number of women. To answer particular problems, formal legitimacy was arranged with the Church, as when the Borgia pope, Alexander VI, established the legitimacy of his son Cesare before he declared him a cardinal.)

FEW RECORDS SPEAK OF WOMEN FROM POOR BACKGROUNDS

Of the poor, unchronicled woman we know little, her life as unmarked as the vanished hovels in which she and her family lived with their animals and feed. She might not escape the plague by fleeing to a country villa, as her duchess did, but puerperal fever was more democratic, and her children might last longer than princelings did, since the poor woman was likely to nurse them herself rather than have them nursed by hired, not always sound, women. If he survived death in infancy, the peasant child might die of diseases related to malnutrition; drought, famine, and invasions left him weeds, acorns, and grasses for nourishment. When a sharecropper husband was tagged for military service to protect or expand his overlord's holdings, his wife could not apply to an agrarian guild for help. She might ask for help from church confraternities or petition the nuns and monks to take one or two of her young to teach them reading and writing or a useful craft. When taxes, always higher in rural areas, and church tithing became overwhelmingly burdensome, when she realized that surpluses of wheat, oats, millet, barley, and rice were amassed in the city, leaving farmlands scarce of these essentials, she might induce her husband to join the mass that was searching the cities for employment. A son might become an apprentice weaver, a daughter might learn to spin. A boy who could draw or carve might be taken into one of the art ateliers and be fed while he studied and ground colors. A winsome little girl might be taken on as a servant; a dramatically deformed child might become a court toy or a beggar; a blind child might earn a bit more as a street singer. Life in the city offered greater opportunities and, what with frequent guild holidays and theatricals, church and court festivities, considerably more diversion.

A rung below the peasant woman, though not immutably, was the slave. Slavery was a solid institution, waxing and waning with mortality figures and degrees of general prosperity. The busiest slave markets, the concentration mainly on girls, were the ports—Genoa and Venice the most active—where the captives arrived in large numbers from the east, from the Carpathians, from the Black Sea and beyond. These exotics with broad cheekbones and honeyed skin were used as domestics and wet nurses in well-to-do households. A letter dated 1474 written by Barbara of Brandenburg, the wife of Ludovico II, mentions the purchase of a slave arranged for her by Catherine, Queen of Bosnia, a country that supplied slave girls in considerable numbers. The need to ask a highly placed friend to find a slave may indicate a diminished supply that resulted from the fall of Constantinople in 1453 and the consequent collapse of eastern trade. The near disappearance of slaves comforted a few humanists but not householders or the Church, which had found with iterations of dogma—as in the American South centuries later—rationalizations for supporting slavery.

THE FREEST WOMEN

Vain and courageous girls, and as often the most hapless, found their way to brothels, and with luck, to the "paradise of whores,"

Venice; two of her ripe, bored, elaborately golden-haired *puellae lupanaris* [prostitutes] were forever and wondrously set at rest on their terrace by the Venetian painter Carpaccio. From the ranks of these middle range prostitutes came the apogee of the Renaissance courtesan, who, like a present-day rock star, had male groupies follow her through the streets as she tottered on her exceedingly tall pattens, supported at each side by a servant. Golden hair, perilous shoes, attentive servants, and adoring admirers frequently enlivened services in churches favored by the aristocracy. Near the crest of the courtesan hierarchy were women like the magnificently dressed beauty painted by Palma Vecchio, who gave her no other name than "La Bella." At the very crest were La Boschetta, to whom Federico Gonzaga was attached most of his life; Vanozza Cataneo, the mother of Lucrezia, Cesare, and several other children of the Borgia pope; the gifted mistresses of Ludovico Sforza; and an impressive additional list of talented Aspasias, who were the companions and ornaments of cardinals and popes, and frequently the mothers of their numerous "nephews." The ruthless Bianca Capello, who rose from the stews of Venice to become the mistress of Francesco de' Medici, reached the summit of her eventful career by marrying him, to rule and misrule, as the Grand Duchess, in Tuscany and wherever else she could put her troublesome hand.

Among the freest women were the singers and actresses of traveling companies, the most capable groups attached for long periods to one court or another, as in Mantua and Ferrara. England would not have women on the stage, although its throne was held by a woman: actresses were bawds, said the English, and so did Spain, and the Papacy protested their presence as well. The sophisticated Italians countered by pointing out the moral danger of having boys, too many already inclined and encouraged to feminine airs, actually playing pretty nymphs and foul-mouthed old whores. The Church especially loathed the freedom of the commedia dell'arte companies acting lascivious matter, irresistible to the young who sat in audiences among prostitutes male and female. Some of the actresses, encouraged by their husbands, found "protectors" at court, who supported the husband and often the whole company. But there were a few dedicated professionals who scorned favors and ran their own companies, with distinction while they also translated classics, studied the learned sciences and the arts of painting and music. Fighting the characterization of "loose women," a universal accusation often justified, they strove to make acting one of the respected arts. One phenomenon still remembered in theater history was Isabella Andreini, a poet, the author of several plays, a member of a learned academy, a musician, a fine actress, the mother of seven, and revered enough to have her head cast—like royalty—in several medals. It was her son's wife, Virginia, who mastered in six days—and sang exquisitely, it was reported—the *Arianna* of Monteverdi and (almost as distinguished an act) never became the sexual property of Duke Vincenzo, preferring to remain the faithful wife of a footloose husband.

Europe's Age of Exploration Begins

—|— CHAPTER 3 |—

EXPLORATION BEGINS WITH THE PORTUGUESE

J.H. PARRY

Global exploration was one of the clearest expressions of Europe's aggression and dynamism during the Renaissance. Between 1420 and 1610, European ships connected almost the entire world in a single network of trade, a feat that had never been accomplished before.

While Christopher Columbus is the most famous explorer, he was in fact a relative latecomer to the enterprise. European exploration began in the early 1400s when Portugal, a small kingdom on the southwestern fringe of Europe, began sending merchant ships south along the west coast of Africa. Credit for beginning the movement is often given to Prince Henry of Portugal (1393–1464), who enthusiastically sought to both expand Christendom and find new sources of gold.

In the following selection, J.H. Parry examines how Portuguese explorers proceeded south along Africa's coast until, in 1489, Bartolomeu Dias traveled around the Cape of Good Hope into the Indian Ocean. Parry goes on to mention how Vasco da Gama, in hopes of preceding Columbus to India, sailed farther in 1497, ultimately establishing trade connections with East African cities and the great spice markets of India itself.

J.H. Parry is the author of several books on European exploration, including *Trade and Dominion* and *The Spanish Seaborne Empire*.

Prince Henry used his monopoly generously, and financed foreign as well as Portuguese traders and explorers. The Venetian Cadamosto, for example, made voyages under

Prince Henry's licence to the Atlantic islands and West Africa as far as the Gambia, in 1455 and 1456. Cadamosto wrote journals which contain vivid descriptions of the places he visited, observations on trade and navigation, and a wealth of entertaining details such as the most convincing early description of a hippopotamus and some useful hints on how to cook ostrich eggs. This garrulity on Cadamosto's part is a welcome change from the silence of his Portuguese contemporaries. The official Portuguese policy was one of secrecy concerning discoveries, and this secrecy grew closer and stricter after Prince Henry's death. . . .

PORTUGUESE SHIPS MOVE DOWN THE AFRICAN COAST

Although African exploration began as Prince Henry's private hobby, it had the sympathy and probably the support of at least one of his brothers, the regent Prince Pedro, and during the lifetime of the two princes it became for a time a matter of considerable national interest. After Pedro's death in 1449, however, the pace of exploration slackened; and when Prince Henry himself died and his monopoly passed to the Crown, a pause ensued of over ten years without any major discovery. The next important date was 1471, when Fernando Po discovered the island which bears his name near the mouth of the Niger, and discovered also the sharp southerly trend of the African coast just north of the equator. This must have been a severe disappointment to men who had hoped that India was just round the corner; and four years later, in 1475, a still more serious interruption occurred, in the shape of war with Spain, arising out of a Portuguese claim to the Castillian throne. In this war, which was bitter and destructive, Portugal was defeated and Isabella was confirmed as Queen of Castille; but as often happened, the Portuguese, having lost the war, won the treaty, at least from the colonial point of view. Among its many clauses, the treaty of Alcaçovas in 1479 confirmed to Portugal the monopoly of the trade, settlement and exploration of the West African coast and the possession of all the known Atlantic islands except the Canaries, which remained to Spain. The first of the long series of European treaties regulating colonial spheres of influence was thus a diplomatic triumph for the Portuguese.

Two years later Affonso V died, to be succeeded by John II, one of the ablest and least scrupulous princes of his century, a competent geographer and an enthusiast for discovery. One of his first acts was a decree which laid down that all foreign ships visiting the Guinea coast might be sunk or captured without inquiry. If captured, their officers and men were to be thrown to the sharks, notoriously plentiful in those waters. Partly in order to enforce this legislation, partly to facilitate trade and to defend the traders against native attack, John II embarked in 1482 on the building of a second fortress and warehouse on the African coast, on a more ambitious scale than the old one at Arguim. The site chosen was at Elmina on the Bight of Benin. The stone used in the construction of the keep was all shipped out from Portugal, with a small army of workmen. Elmina soon became the naval and commercial capital of the African discoveries and the centre of a thriving trade in slaves, ivory, gold-dust and Malaguette pepper—the coarse pungent pepper of the Guinea coast. Part of the profit of this trade was applied to financing a hydrographical office and a school of navigation.

With the financial resources of the Crown at his disposal, and with none of Prince Henry's patience with unprofitable servants, John II secured rapid results in African exploration. The most distinguished of the captains whom he employed were Diogo Cão and Bartholomeu Dias. In 1483, Cão reached the mouth of the Congo and explored some way up the river. In 1486, in a second voyage, he sailed as far as Cape Cross. In the following year Bartholomeu Dias left Lisbon on the famous voyage which was to solve the problem of the southern extremity of Africa.

DIAS SAILS AROUND AFRICA

Very little is known about Dias. There is no portrait of him in existence and no detailed and reliable account of his voyage. He was probably a man of quite humble origin, like most professional seamen of his day, but he must have been a very capable navigator, for Vasco da Gama ten years later was able to follow his directions with accuracy and success. We know that his experience was employed in designing and fitting out the ships of Vasco da Gama's fleet.

Dias's achievement was more than a mere continuation of southerly sailing. The Cape of Good Hope is not the southerly extremity of Africa. The southernmost point is Cape Agulhas, considerably farther east. Between them lie False Bay and a difficult stretch of coast with a current setting from east to west. But Dias was a fortunate as well as a capable seaman. He was in the latitude of Walfisch Bay, or thereabouts, when his ships were caught by a northerly gale which blew them south under reduced canvas for thirteen days out of sight of land. When the wind moderated Dias squared away on the port tack in order to regain the West African coast; but he had already passed the Cape without knowing it, and eventually made his landfall at Mossel Bay on the Indian Ocean. Dias himself would have liked to explore far-

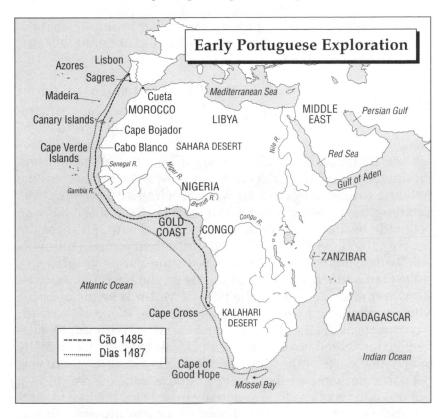

Early Portuguese Exploration

Azores
Lisbon
Sagres
Madeira
Canary Islands
Cueta
MOROCCO
Mediterranean Sea
Cape Bojador
Cabo Blanco   SAHARA DESERT
Cape Verde Islands
Senegal R.
Niger R.
Gambia R.
NIGERIA
Benue R.
GOLD COAST   CONGO
Congo R.
Atlantic Ocean
Cape Cross
KALAHARI DESERT
LIBYA
MIDDLE EAST
Persian Gulf
Nile R.
Red Sea
Gulf of Aden
ZANZIBAR
MADAGASCAR
Indian Ocean
Cape of Good Hope
Mossel Bay

------ Cão 1485
·········· Dias 1487

ther; but his men were tired and frightened and inclined to be mutinous and his two caravels were small and ill-provided for sailing farther into the unknown. He had left his storeship at Walfisch Bay; and so he agreed to return there to rejoin it. It was on the homeward passage, therefore, that Dias first sighted the great cape which he had been seeking. According to the chronicler Barros, he first called it the Cape of Storms; it was the king who, upon Dias's return, renamed it the Cape of Good Hope.

It was to be for some years the cape of hope deferred. The way to India seemed to lie open; but voyages to India were not to be undertaken by small European kingdoms without due thought. The king's attention was taken by political troubles and succession disputes; and to confuse the situation, in March, 1493, Columbus's *Niña* put into the Tagus, having returned—so her company said—across the Atlantic from easternmost Asia. If Columbus were right, the best part of a century of Portuguese exploration would be wasted; the prize which seemed within the Portuguese grasp would fall undeserved into the hands of Spain; inevitably there would be trouble. In fact, Columbus's assertions did not deceive the Portuguese for long; but they led to long and intricate negotiations, designed by the Portuguese to prevent or to limit further Spanish exploring. It was not until 1495 that the decision was taken to send a fleet to India; and not until 1497 that the fleet actually sailed.

Vasco da Gama Is the First to India

Vasco da Gama's fleet consisted of four sail: three ships, square-rigged with lateen mizens, and a lateen caravel; he was to trade, therefore, and not only to explore. Apart from its results, the voyage was memorable in itself as a magnificent feat of seamanship. Profiting by Dias's experience, da Gama stood far out across the Atlantic until the trade belts were reached and passed; thus avoiding the Doldrums and making by far the longest passage yet made by a European ship out of sight of land. This was the course which generations of later Indiamen were to follow; a bold course then, when celestial navigation was in its infancy.

Da Gama touched at several places on the East African coast for water and fuel, and at the port of Malindi he picked up a Muslim pilot, Ibn Majid, as luck would have it one of the leading experts of his day in celestial navigation. With Ibn Majid's help he navigated across the Indian Ocean to Calicut, one of the main spice ports of the Malabar coast. His reception there was not particularly promising. The Portuguese trade goods—mostly trinkets and woollen cloth—were unsuitable for the Indian market; the local Hindu ruler at Calicut was naturally unwilling to give up his profitable Arab connections, and the resident Arab merchants put every pressure upon him to refuse facilities to the Portuguese. Nevertheless da Gama, with great difficulty and great persistence, collected a quantity of pepper and cinnamon. With this cargo he cleared for home; and the long story of European intrigue with the native princes of India was begun. During his voyage, which lasted over two years in all, da Gama had spent more than three hundred days at sea, and had lost over a third of his company, probably as the result of scurvy.

Columbus Sought the Gold and Spices of the Indies

Samuel Eliot Morison

Europeans began their global explorations for both religious and economic reasons. Among the important religious reasons were the hope of finding legendary communities of lost Christians and the desire to continue the Crusades of the Middle Ages. Of the economic motivations, two predominated. First, explorers hoped to find new sources of gold and silver. Second, they hoped to enter into the rich spice trade of a region they knew of as only the Indies. The expansion of the Turkish empire in the Middle East, along with Turkish control of traditional overland trade routes, gave further urgency to the exploration movement.

According to Samuel Eliot Morison, the author of the following selection, Europeans knew little about the globe in the 1400s. They knew simply that it was round and that there were rich lands to the east, in Asia. They had no concept of the distances involved or of the existence of two vast continents, the Americas, that lay between Europe and the Indies along the western route that Columbus hoped to pursue.

Renowned historian and naval authority Samuel Eliot Morison taught history at Harvard and Oxford Universities. His biography of Christopher Columbus, *Admiral of the Ocean Sea*, won the Pulitzer Prize in 1942.

Excerpted from *Christopher Columbus, Mariner*, by Samuel Eliot Morison. Copyright © 1942, 1955 by Samuel Eliot Morison; copyright © renewed 1983 by Emily Morison Beck. Reprinted by permission of Little, Brown and Company (Inc.).

The Indies, meaning most of Eastern Asia—India, Burma, China, Japan, the Moluccas and Indonesia—cast a spell over European imagination in the fifteenth century. These were lands of vast wealth in gold, silver and precious stones, in silk and fine cotton, in spices, drugs and perfumes, which in small quantities were taken by caravans across Asia to Constantinople or to Levantine ports, thence distributed through Europe by ship, wagon and pack train. The cost of handling by so many middlemen and over such long and complicated routes made the prices of Oriental goods to the European consumer exorbitant; yet the increase of wealth and luxury in European cities kept the demand far ahead of the supply. That is why the kings of Portugal made repeated attempts to get around Africa to India, where Oriental products could be purchased cheap. Columbus decided that the African route was the hard way to the Indies; he proposed to find a bold but easy way, due west by sea.

Christopher Columbus

And there were other reasons for seeking a new and easy contact with the Far East, which appealed to so religious a man as Columbus, and still more to the churchmen who held many of the highest posts in European governments. It was a matter of intense mortification to them that the Crusades had failed, that Christians had been forced to evacuate the Holy Land, and that the Holy Sepulchre at Jerusalem, and the birthplace of Our Lord, were now controlled by infidel Turks. Somewhere in the Orient, it was believed, existed a powerful Christian state ruled by a monarch known as Prester John. The substance behind this legend was the Kingdom of Ethiopia, over which Haile Selassie's [a twentieth-century Ethiopian king] ancestors then ruled. If only contact could be made and an alliance concluded with Prester John, who was rumored to have enormous wealth and a big army, the Christian hosts might recover the Holy Land and send the Turks reeling back to Central Asia.

ASIA WAS A MYSTERY, AMERICA UNKNOWN

European knowledge of China at that time was slight and inaccurate. The Spanish Sovereigns, as their letter of introduction furnished to Columbus indicates, thought that the Mongol dynasty of Kubla Khan still reigned in the Celestial Empire, although the Ming dynasty had supplanted it as far back as 1368. Most of the information (and misinformation) that Europe had about China came from *The Book of Ser Marco Polo,* the Venetian who spent about three years in China around the turn of the fourteenth century. This account of his experiences was circulated in countless manuscript copies and was one of the earliest books to be printed. Marco Polo not only confirmed the rumors that Chinese emperors were rolling in wealth, but he wrote a highly embellished account of an even wealthier island kingdom named Cipangu (Japan) which, he said, lay 1500 miles off the coast of China.

We must constantly keep in mind that nobody in Europe had any conception or suspicion of the existence of the continent that we call America. The voyages of the Northmen in the eleventh century to a part of the east coast of the future Canada or New England, which they called Vinland, were either unknown or forgotten in Southern Europe; and if Columbus had heard about them on his voyage to Iceland, they were of no interest to him, since he was not interested in wild grapes, pine trees and codfish, but in gold and spices. Everyone regarded the Ocean Sea as one and indivisible, flowing around Europe, Asia and Africa, which formed, as it were, one big island in one big ocean. The great questions before Columbus, and before the various monarchs and officials who must decide whether or not to support him, were, "How far west *is* the Far East? How many miles lie between Spain and China or Japan? How long would the voyage take? And is such a voyage practicable?"

COLUMBUS'S SHIPS REACH THE NEW WORLD

CHRISTOPHER COLUMBUS

After nearly a decade of petitions for sponsorship among the courts of Portugal, Spain, and France, Christopher Columbus finally persuaded Queen Isabella, one of Spain's dual monarchs, to supply him with ships and crews in 1492. Columbus, the son of a weaver from Genoa, Italy, had devised a plan to sail directly west across the Atlantic Ocean from Europe. He calculated that the rich lands of the Indies, particularly China and Japan, lay only three thousand miles away along that route.

In the following selection from Columbus's official journal of the voyage, part of which was rewritten by Bartolome de las Casas, a cleric who accompanied the expedition, the "Admiral of the Ocean Seas," as he was deemed by Isabella, describes how sailors from his ships finally sighted land on October 11, 1492. The Spaniards made landfall on an island in what is today the Bahamas, where, as Columbus reports, they found a people known as the Guanahani. Columbus claimed the islands for the Crown of Spain and the Roman Catholic Church, little suspecting that what he had located was not a minor group of islands off the coast of Japan, but a new hemisphere.

Wednesday, Oct. 10th. Steered W.S.W. [west southwest] and sailed at times ten miles an hour, at others twelve, and at others, seven; day and night made fifty-nine leagues' progress; reckoned to the crew but forty-four. Here the

Excerpted from *Journal of First Voyage to America*, by Christopher Columbus, with an introduction by Van Wyck Brooks (New York: Albert and Charles Boni, 1924).

men lost all patience, and complained of the length of the voyage, but the Admiral encouraged them in the best manner he could, representing the profits they were about to acquire, and adding that it was to no purpose to complain, having come so far, they had nothing to do but continue on to the Indies, till with the help of our Lord, they should arrive there.

Thursday, Oct. 11th. Steered W.S.W.; and encountered a heavier sea than they had met with before in the whole voyage. Saw *pardelas* [a tropical bird] and a green rush near the vessel. The crew of the *Pinta* saw a cane and a log; they also picked up a stick which appeared to have been carved with an iron tool, a piece of cane, a plant which grows on land, and a board. The crew of the *Nina* saw other signs of land, and a stalk loaded with roseberries. These signs encouraged them, and they all grew cheerful. Sailed this day till sunset, twenty-seven leagues.

THE *PINTA* SIGHTS LAND

After sunset steered their original course W. and sailed twelve miles an hour till two hours after midnight, going ninety miles, which are twenty-two leagues and a half; and as the *Pinta* was the swiftest sailer, and kept ahead of the Admiral, she discovered land and made the signals which had been ordered. The land was first seen by a sailor called Rodrigo de Triana, although the Admiral at ten o'clock that evening standing on the quarter-deck saw a light, but so small a body that he could not affirm it to be land; calling to Pero Gutierrez, groom of the King's wardrobe, he told him he saw a light, and bid him look that way, which he did and saw it; he did the same to Rodrigo Sanchez of Segovia, whom the King and Queen had sent with the squadron as comptroller, but he was unable to see it from his situation. The Admiral again perceived it once or twice, appearing like the light of a wax candle moving up and down, which some thought an indication of land. But the Admiral held it for certain that land was near; for which reason, after they had said the *Salve* [a prayer] which the seamen are accustomed to repeat and chant after their fashion, the Admiral directed them to keep a strict watch upon the forecastle and look out diligently for land, and to him who should first discover it he promised a silken jacket, besides the reward which the King and Queen had offered, which was an annuity of ten thousand maravedis. At two o'clock in the morning the land was discovered, at two leagues' distance; they took in sail and remained under the square-sail lying to till day, which was Friday, when they found themselves near a small island, one of the Lucayos, called in the Indian language Guanahani.

Presently they described people, naked, and the Admiral

After sailing for more than a month, Columbus lands on the island of San Salvador in the Bahamas on October 11, 1492.

landed in the boat, which was armed, along with Martin Alonzo Pinzon, and Vincent Yanez his brother, captain of the *Nina*. The Admiral bore the royal standard, and the two captains each a banner of the Green Cross, which all the ships had carried; this contained the initials of the names of the King and Queen each side of the cross, and a crown over each letter. Arrived on shore, they saw trees very green, many streams of water, and diverse sorts of fruits. The Admiral called upon the two Captains, and the rest of the crew who landed, as also to Rodrigo de Escovedo, notary of the fleet, and Rodrigo Sanchez, of Segovia, to bear witness that he before all others took possession (as in fact he did) of that island for the King and Queen his sovereigns; making the requisite declarations, which are more at large set down here in writing. Numbers of the people of the island straightway collected together.

COLUMBUS DESCRIBES THE PEOPLE

Here follow the precise words of the Admiral: "As I saw that they were very friendly to us, and perceived that they could be much more easily converted to our holy faith by gentle means than by force, I presented them with some red caps, and strings of beads to wear upon the neck, and many other trifles of small value, wherewith they were much delighted, and became wonderfully attached to us. Afterwards they came swimming to the boats, bringing parrots, balls of cotton thread, javelins and many other things which they exchanged for articles we gave them, such as glass beads, and hawk's bells; which trade was carried on with the utmost good will. But they seemed on the whole to me, to be a very poor people. They all go completely naked, even the women, though I saw but one girl. All whom I saw were young, not above thirty years of age, well made, with fine shapes and faces; their hair short, and coarse like that of a horse's tail, combed toward the forehead, except a small portion which they suffer to hang down behind, and never cut. Some paint themselves with black, which makes them appear like those of the Canaries, neither black nor white; others with white, others with red, and others with such colours as they can find. Some paint the face, and some the whole body; others only the eyes, and others the nose. Weapons they have none, nor are acquainted with them, for I showed them swords which they grasped by the blades, and cut themselves through ignorance. They have no iron, their javelins being without it, and nothing more than sticks, though some have fish-bones or other things at the ends. They are all of a good size and stature, and handsomely formed. I saw some with scars of wounds upon their bodies, and demanded by signs the cause of them; they answered me in the same way, that there came people from the other islands in the neighbourhood who endeavoured to make prisoners of them, and they defended themselves. I thought then, and still believe, that these were from the continent. It appears to me, that the people are ingenuous, and would be good servants; and I am of opinion that they would very readily become Christians, as they appear to have no religion. They very quickly learn such words as are spoken to them. If it please our Lord, I intend at my return to carry home six of them to your Highnesses, that they may learn our language. I saw no beasts in the island, nor any sort of animals except parrots." These are the words of the Admiral.

Magellan's Fleet Circumnavigates the Globe

Simon Winchester

In the following selection, Simon Winchester notes that Ferdinand Magellan, a Portuguese explorer who sailed for Spain, is commemorated in many parts of the world as the first sailor to successfully travel completely around the globe. Magellan had no idea, Winchester asserts, of the distances he would have to travel or the dangers he would face.

Magellan set sail in 1519. By then, Spanish conquistadors had claimed much of the Western Hemisphere as their own while Portuguese merchants had established a strong presence in the trade of the Indian Ocean. Both countries wanted to be the first to circumnavigate the globe and assert their territorial claims. The greatest challenge was crossing the Pacific Ocean, as no one had any idea how vast it was.

Magellan and his men were the first Europeans to cross the Pacific, finally reaching the Philippines in 1521 after losing two of their five ships and many men. Magellan himself did not complete the voyage, as he was killed in a political uprising on the island of Cebu in the Philippines. The circumnavigation was completed under the command of Juan Sebastian d'Elcano, who returned to Spain with one of the five original ships and 17 of the original 277 men.

Simon Winchester is a journalist and film producer who specializes is Asian and Pacific Ocean subjects. He is also the author of *The Sun Never Sets* and *Korea*.

Excerpted from *Pacific Rising: The Emergence of a New World Culture,* by Simon Winchester. Copyright © 1988 by Simon Winchester. Reprinted by permission of Sterling Lord Literistic, Inc.

There is a statue to Ferdinand Magellan in the main square of Punta Arenas, at the southernmost tip of Chile. He sits by a globe with his back to the police station, looking south towards the Cabo de Hornos Hotel, towards the low hills of Tierra del Fuego and the unseen coast of the distant Antarctic. Another monument to him is in the main square of the city of Cebu in the central Philippines, a canopy with the kind of gaudy murals one expects in this flamboyant tropic city. The paintings illustrate the notable moments of his forty years of life, including that most singular to the Filipinos, the bringing of Christianity to their islands. Nearby, on a small, marshy, mosquito-ridden island called Mactan—the site of Cebu airport, and some of the region's hundreds of guitar factories—there is a simple memorial (looked after by a caretaker with the improbably contradictory name of Jesus Baring). Doubtless there are other statues to Magellan—near Sabrosa in Portugal's Trás-os-Montes, where he was born; in Sanlucar de Barrameda, from where he set sail. But the life that will be always remembered stems from a journey which will never be forgotten—that commemorated by the space of sea between the statues in Chile and Cebu, a distance of some 12,000 miles. Edward Gaylord Bourne, in his masterly series *Spain in America,* written at the beginning of the twentieth century, offers a view with which few would take issue:

Ferdinand Magellan

> The first navigation of the Straits of Magellan was a far more difficult problem of seamanship than crossing the Atlantic. . . . Columbus's voyage was over in thirty-five days; but Magellan's had been gone a year and weathered a subAntarctic winter before the real task began— the voyage over a trackless waste of waters exactly three times as long as the first crossing of the Atlantic. . . . Magellan is to be ranked as the first navigator of ancient or modern times, and his voyage is the greatest single human achievement on the sea.

Yet when he set off on 20 September 1519, with a royal mandate to search for a passage through to the *Mar del Sur* [Southern

Ocean], and thus to determine for certain that the Spice Islands
were within the Spanish domains, he had not the foggiest notion
how far he might have to travel. Not only was there great per-
plexity about the existence of a Strait—for all the men in their five
little ships knew, Balboa's Panama and the Columbia that
Columbus had sighted in 1499 might be the equatorial portions
of a continent that extended without a break to the Antarctic
pole, and the Southern Sea would be quite unreachable from the
west. And even if a break were to be found, the five *naos* [ships]
and the 277 men would have to sail—how far? [German geogra-
pher] Schoener's globe of the world then known shows Japan a
few hundred miles off Mexico; the historian López de Gómara
says that in his negotiations with the Emperor Magellan always
insisted that the Moluccas [in modern Indonesia] were "no great
distance from Panama, and the Gulf of San Miguel which Vasco
Núñez de Balboa discovered". He would rapidly discover precisely what "no great distance" meant.

FINDING A NEW ATLANTIS

FRANCIS BACON

By 1600 Europeans had grown accustomed to stories of adventurous seafarers and exotic discoveries in foreign lands. Explorers, often with the support of their kings and queens, had circumnavigated the globe and were still actively seeking new sea routes. Meanwhile, merchants and pirates returned to their homelands laden with goods as well as stories of their exploits. Indeed, overseas exploration had become an accepted part of life, and seemed to suggest to Renaissance Europeans the many opportunities that lay open to them to both enrich themselves and improve their world.

The following selection is by Francis Bacon, a philosopher and courtier in Elizabethan England (1557–1602). Taken from a text entitled *New Atlantis and the Great Instauration*, not published until 1627, Bacon's story is of a group of Europeans discovering in a faraway ocean a fictional civilization called Bensalem. In this passage, the sailors experience an unexpected welcome and find themselves in a place surprisingly as Christian and at least as "civilized" as their homeland.

We sailed from Peru, (where we had continued by the space of one whole year,) for China and Japan, by the South Sea; taking with us victuals for twelve months; and had good winds from the east, though soft and weak, for five months' space and more. But then the wind came about, and settled in the west for many days, so as we could make little or no way, and were sometimes in purpose to turn back. But then again there arose strong and great winds from the south, with a point

Excerpted from *New Atlantis and the Great Instauration*, by Francis Bacon, rev. ed., edited by Jerry Weinberger. Copyright © 1989 by Harlan Davidson, Inc. Reproduced by permission.

east; which carried us up (for all that we could do) towards the north: by which time our victuals failed us, though we had made good spare of them. So that finding ourselves in the midst of the greatest wilderness of waters in the world, without victuals, we gave ourselves for lost men, and prepared for death. Yet we did lift up our hearts and voices to God above, who *showeth his wonder in the deep;* beseeching him of his mercy, that as in the beginning he discovered the face of the deep, and brought forth dry land, so he would now discover land to us, that we might not perish. And it came to pass that the next day about evening, we saw within a kenning before us, towards the north, as it were thick clouds, which did put us in some hope of land; knowing how that part of the South Sea was utterly unknown; and might have islands or continents, that hitherto were not come to light. Wherefore we bent our course thither, where we saw the appearance of land, all that night; and in the dawning of the next day, we might plainly discern that it was a land; flat to our sight and full of boscage; which made it shew the more dark.

AN UNDISCOVERED LAND AND HESITANT WELCOME

And after an hour and a half's sailing, we entered into a good haven, being the port of a fair city; not great indeed, but well built, and that gave a pleasant view from the sea: and we thinking every minute long till we were on land, came close to the shore, and offered to land. But straightways we saw divers of the people, with bastons in their hands, as it were forbidding us to land; yet without any cries or fierceness, but only as warning us off by signs that they made. Whereupon being not a little discomforted, we were advising with ourselves what we should do. During which time there made forth to us a small boat, with about eight persons in it; whereof one of them had in his hand a tipstaff of a yellow cane, tipped at both ends with blue, who came aboard our ship, without any show of distrust at all. And when he saw one of our number present himself somewhat afore the rest, he drew forth a little scroll of parchment (somewhat yellower than our parchment, and shining like the leaves of writing tables, but otherwise soft and flexible,) and delivered it to our foremost man. In which scroll were written in ancient Hebrew, and in ancient Greek, and in good Latin of the School, and in Spanish, these words; "Land ye not, none of you; and provide to be gone from this coast within sixteen days, except you have further time given you. Meanwhile, if you want fresh water, or victual, or help for your sick or that your ship needeth repair, write down your wants, and you shall have that which belongeth to mercy." This scroll was signed with a stamp of cherubins' wings, not spread but hanging downwards, and by them a cross. This being delivered, the officer returned, and left only a servant with us to receive our answer. Consulting hereupon amongst ourselves, we were much perplexed. The denial of landing and hasty warning us away troubled us much; on the other side, to find that the people had languages and were so full of humanity, did comfort us not a little. And above all, the sign of the cross to that instrument was to us a great rejoicing, and as it were a certain presage of good. Our answer was in the Spanish tongue; "That for our ship, it was well; for we had rather met with calms and contrary winds than any tempests. For our sick, they were many, and in very ill case; so that if they were not permitted to land, they ran danger of their lives." Our other wants we set down in particular; adding, "that we had some little store of merchandise, which if it pleased them to deal for, it might supply our wants without being chargeable unto them." We offered some reward in pistolets unto the servants and a piece of crimson velvet to be presented to the officer; but the servant took them not, nor would scarce look upon them; and so left us, and went back in another little boat which was sent for him.

A LOST COMMUNITY OF CHRISTIANS

About three hours after we had dispatched our answer, there came towards us a person (as it seemed) of place. He had on him a gown with wide sleeves, of a kind of water chamolet, of an excellent azure colour, far more glossy than ours; his under apparel was green; and so was his hat, being in the form of a turban, daintily made, and not so huge as the Turkish turbans; and the locks of his hair came down below the brims of it. A reverend man was he to behold. He came in a boat, gilt in some part of it, with four persons more only in that boat; and was followed by another boat, wherein were some twenty. When he was come within a flight-shot of our ship, signs were made to us that we should send forth some to meet him upon the water; which we presently did in our ship-boat, sending the principal man amongst us save one, and four of our number with him. When we were come within six yards of their boat, they called to us to stay, and not to approach farther; which we did. And thereupon the man whom I before described stood up, and with a loud voice in Spanish, asked, "Are ye Christians?" We answered "We were;" fearing the less, because of the cross we had seen in the subscription. At which answer the said person lifted up his right hand towards heaven and drew it softly to his mouth (which is the gesture they use when they thank God,) and then said: "If ye will swear (all of you) by the merits of the Saviour that ye are no pirates, nor have shed blood lawfully nor unlawfully within forty days past, you may have licence to come on land." We said, "We were all ready to take that oath." Whereupon one of those that were with him, being (as it seemed) a notary, made an entry of this act. Which done, another of the attendants of the great person, which was with him in the same boat, after his lord had spoken a little to him, said aloud; "My lord would have you know, that it is not of pride or greatness that he cometh not aboard your ship; but for that in your answer you declare that you have many sick amongst you, he was warned by the Conservator of Health of the city that he should keep a distance." We bowed ourselves towards him, and answered, "We were his humble servants; and accounted for great honour and singular humanity towards us that which was already done; but hoped well that the nature of the sickness of our men was not infectious." So he returned; and a while after came the notary to us aboard our ship; holding in his hand a fruit of that country, like an orange, but of color between orange-tawney and scarlet, which cast a most excellent odour. He used it (as it seemeth) for a preservative against infection. He gave us our oath; "By the name of Jesus and his merits:" and after told us that the next day by six of the clock in the morning we should be sent to, and brought to the Strangers' House, (so he called it,) where we should be accomodated of things both for our whole and for our sick. So he left us; and when we offered him some pistolets, he smiling said, "He must not be twice paid for one labour:" meaning (as I take it) that he had salary sufficient of the state for his service. For (as I after learned) they call an officer that taketh rewards, *twice paid*.

THE STRANGERS ARE WELCOMED ASHORE

The next morning early, there came to us the same officer that came to us at first with his cane, and told us, "He came to conduct us to the Strangers' House; and that he had prevented the hour, because we might have the whole day before us for our business." "For," said he, "if you will follow my advice, there shall first go with me some few of you, and see the place, and how it may be made convenient for you and then you may send for your sick, and the rest of your number which ye will bring on land." We thanked him, and said, "That this care which he took of desolate strangers God would reward." And so six of us went on land with him: and when we were on land, he went before us, and turned to us, and said, "He was but our servant, and our guide." He led us through three fair streets; and all the way we went there were gathered some people on both sides standing in a row; but in so civil a fashion, as if it had been not to wonder at us but to welcome us; and divers of them, as we passed by them, put their arms a little abroad; which is their gesture when they bid any welcome. The Strangers' House is a fair and spacious house, built of brick, of somewhat a bluer colour than our brick; and with handsome windows, some of glass, some of a kind of cambric oiled. He brought us first into a fair parlour above stairs, and then asked us, "What number of persons we were? And how many sick?" We answered, "We were in all (sick and whole) one and fifty persons, whereof our sick were seventeen." He desired us to have patience a little, and to stay till he came back to us; which was about an hour after; and then he led us to see the chambers which were provided for us, being in number nineteen: they having cast it (as it seemeth) that four of those chambers, which were better than the rest, might receive four of the principal men of our company, and lodge them alone by themselves; and the other fifteen chambers were to lodge us two and two together. The chambers were handsome and cheerful chambers, and furnished civilly. Then he led us to a long gallery, like a dorture, where he showed us all along the one side (for the other side was but wall and window) seventeen cells, very neat ones, having partitions of cedar wood. Which gallery and cells, being in all forty, (many more than we needed,) were instituted as an infirmary for sick persons. And he told us withal, that as any of our sick waxed well, he might be removed from his cell to a chamber; for which purpose there were set forth ten spare chambers, besides the number we spake of before. This done, he brought us back to the parlour, and lifting up his cane a little, (as they do when they give any charge or command,) said to us, "Ye are to know that the custom of the land requireth, that after this day and to-morrow, (which we give you for removing of your people from your ship,) you are to keep within doors for three days. But let it not trouble you, nor do not think yourselves restrained, but rather left to your rest and ease. You shall want nothing, and there are six of our people appointed to attend you, for any business you may have abroad." We gave him thanks with all affection and respect and said, "God surely is manifested in this land." We offered him also twenty pistolets; but he smiled, and only said; "What? twice paid!" And so he left us.

GENEROUS TREATMENT

Soon after our dinner was served in; which was right good viands, both for bread and meat: better than any collegiate diet that I have known in Europe. We had also drink of three sorts, all wholesome and good; wine of the grape; a drink of grain, such as is with us our ale, but more clear; and a kind of cider made of a fruit of that country; a wonderful pleasing and refreshing drink. Besides, there were brought in to us great store of those scarlet oranges for our sick; which (they said) were an assured remedy for sickness taken at sea. There was given us also a box of small grey or whitish pills, which they wished our sick should take, one of the pills every night before sleep; which (they said) would hasten their recovery. The next day, after that our trouble of carriage and removing of our men and goods out of our ship was somewhat settled and quiet, I thought good to call our company together; and when they were assembled said unto them; "My dear friends, let us know ourselves, and how it standeth with us. We are men cast on land, as Jonas was out of the whale's belly, when we were as buried in the deep: and now we are on land, we are but between death and life; for we are beyond both the old world and the new; and whether ever we shall see Europe, God only knoweth. It is a kind of miracle hath brought us hither: and it must be little less that shall bring us hence. Therefore in regard of our deliverance past, and our danger present and to come, let us look up to God, and every man reform his own ways. Besides we are come here amongst a Christian people, full of piety and humanity: let us not bring that confusion of face upon ourselves, as to show our vices or unworthiness before them. Yet there is more. For they have by commandment (though in form of courtesy) cloistered us within these walls for three days: who knoweth whether it be not to take some taste of our manners and conditions? and if they find them bad, to banish us straightways; if good, to give us further time. For these men that they have given us for attendance may withal have an eye upon us. Therefore for God's love, and as we love the weal of our souls and bodies, let us so behave ourselves as we may be at peace with God, and may find grace in the eyes of this people." Our company with one voice thanked me for my good admonition, and promised me to live soberly and civilly, and without giving any the least occasion of offence. So we spent our three days joyfully and without care, in expectation what would be done with us when they were expired. During which time, we had every hour joy of the amendment of our sick; who thought themselves cast into some divine pool of healing, they mended so kindly and so fast.

The morrow after our three days were past, there came to us a new man that we had not seen before, clothed in blue as the former was, save that his turban was white, with a small red cross on the top. He had also a tippet of fine linen. At his coming in, he did bend to us a little, and put his arms abroad. We of our parts saluted him in a very lowly and submissive manner; as looking that from him we should receive sentence of life or death. He desired to speak with some few of us: whereupon six of us only stayed, and the rest avoided the room. He said, "I am by office governor of this House of Strangers, and by vocation I am a Christian priest; and therefore am come to you to offer you my service, both as strangers and chiefly as Christians. Some things I may tell you, which I think you will not be unwilling to hear. The state hath given you licence to stay on land for the space of six weeks: and let it not trouble you if your occasions ask further time, for the law in this point is not precise; and I do not doubt but myself shall be able to obtain for you such further time as may be convenient. Ye shall also understand that the Strangers' House is at this time rich, and much aforehand; for it hath laid up revenue these thirty-seven years; for so long it is since any stranger arrived in this part: and therefore take ye no care; the state will defray you all the time you stay; neither shall you stay one day the less for that. As for any merchandise ye have brought, ye shall be well used, and have your return either in merchandise or in gold and silver: for to us it is all one. And if you have any other request to make, hide it not. For ye shall find we will not make your countenance to fall by the answer ye shall receive.

WORLD HISTORY BY ERA

An Era of Global Conquest: 1520–1540

CHAPTER 4

THE OTTOMAN EMPIRE THRIVED ON CONQUEST

ANDREW WHEATCROFT

The Turkish Ottoman Empire expanded rapidly during the Renaissance. The conquest of Constantinople in 1453 gave the Ottomans control of one of the world's great cities as well as command of trade routes connecting Europe with Asia. Meanwhile, the Ottoman army developed into perhaps the most cohesive fighting force on earth. At the heart of the army was the janissary corps, elite soldiers recruited from among the empire's Christian population.

In the following selection, Andrew Wheatcroft examines how the military successes of the Ottoman conquerors took them to the walls of Vienna, the gateway to western Europe, by 1528. The way lay open after the victory over the Hungarians at Mohács, which gave the Turks control of Budapest, only one hundred miles from Vienna. Moreover, Wheatcroft demonstrates, the Ottomans established control over their Islamic challengers in the Middle East and North Africa as well as the Christian kingdoms of southeastern Europe. The Ottomans failed to capture Vienna, but the sultan who made the attempt, Suleiman the Magnificent, the grandson of the conqueror of Constantinople, could enjoy the wealth and power gained by many other victories.

Andrew Wheatcroft, the author of three popular histories, teaches at the University of Stirling in the United Kingdom.

If the Turks lost a battle, they generally returned to win the war. For war was not a single campaign but a state of being until the whole of the Domain of War was embraced within the Domain of Peace. [The Ottomans divided the world between the Domain of Peace (Muslims) and the Domain of War (non-Muslims).] War was a season of the year, like winter or summer. So, while Mehmed [the conqueror of Constantinople in 1453] failed to capture Belgrade, his great-grandson, Suleiman, succeeded sixty-five years later. The island of Rhodes resisted Mehmed, but succumbed to Suleiman in 1522. For fifteen years the Ottomans suffered raids into Anatolia by Iranians and Mamelukes from Egypt. Then, in 1515, Selim, Mehmed's grandson, moved to the offensive, turning the Ottoman armies south. In two years, he checked the advance of the Iranian empire at the battle of Chaldiran (1515) and smashed the Mamelukes [of Egypt] at Merj-Dabik, just to the north of Aleppo in Syria. Within six months Selim's army had marched across the Sinai desert at Gaza, and on 25 January 1517 it captured Cairo. In the Egyptian capital, Selim hanged the Mameluke leader, Tuman Bey, from the city gates, and resistance quickly subsided. The sultan received the submission of local rulers, among them the chiefs of the Bedouin tribes of Arabia and the sherif of Mecca, guardian of the holy places of Islam.

As a direct consequence of this conquest, Selim and his successors gained immense prestige as the 'Servant and Protector of the Holy Places'. Attempts were even made to buttress his rights of conquest by constructing a pedigree which 'proved' that the sultan—a born Turk—was a lineal descendent of the Prophet. He received the keys to the Holy Kaaba in Mecca and the sacred relics of the Prophet and his family: the robe, the sword of Omar, the sacred banner—which were dispatched immediately to the palace in Constantinople. With the title and the emblems of Islam, the Ottoman sultans assumed the unquestioned leadership of the Islamic world. Legitimacy was ultimately less important than the capacity to defend and then advance the boundaries of the Domain of Peace.

SETTING OFF FROM CONSTANTINOPLE

War was thus the *raison d'être* [reason for being] of the Ottoman state. The Ottomans planned systematically for each campaign. They garrisoned all the key strategic towns with detachments of janissaries and special fortress troops, partly to control the countryside, but principally to provide the staging-posts for the advancing host. Year after year the army marched the same route, going north-west from the capital to Adrianople, through the

Balkan mountains to Sofia, and onward into Serbia. After Suleiman captured Belgrade in 1521, that city became the last Ottoman stronghold, before the army set out along the line of the Danube into the Domain of War, through the debatable lands of Hungary, towards Vienna and the west. If the sultan had decided to wage his campaign in the east, the process was reversed. The host would then gather at the heights above Üsküdar, on the opposite shore of the Bosporus to the Yeni Saray. The long procession which wound through the city towards the Cyrpyci Meadow for the war against Christendom was transformed into a string of caiques [galleys] and barges heading from the Golden Horn to the opposing shore. After pausing to pray at the shrine by the shore, the sultan would appear before his army and launch them on their march eastwards. Thereafter, the host would head towards Erzerum, Van and Diyabakir, which were the traditional departure points for the campaign against Iran; or the army might meet the fleet (and its supplies) at Aleppo or concentrate its forces farther south at Mosul. But, either in the north or the east, there was a limit to the extent and duration of any campaign. The Ottomans did not spend winter in the field—that would be almost impossible in the harsh wastes of Anatolia, and difficult in the extreme in the eastern recesses of Europe. The Army of the Divine Light that left the Cyrpyci Meadow or Üsküdar in the spring returned in late autumn. Leave it too late, ran a Turkish proverb, and all the horses would die. . . .

THE WAY TO VIENNA IS OPENED

Mohács was a disaster for Hungary's Magyar nobility—the 'tomb of the nation', as one historian described it. Throughout Europe the battle was portrayed as the destruction of a tiny band of Christian paladins by the overwhelming hosts of Islam. The truth was very different. The effective strengths of the two armies were very similar, since most of the conscripts and the *akincis* and *delis* [irregulars and tribesman] who made up the bulk of the Ottoman army were of little value. The Ottomans were also weary, after eighty days on the march before they joined battle at Mohács, while the Hungarians had been fresh and eager for a fight. In fact to the Turks, on the day after the battle, it appeared something of a pyrrhic victory, since the piles of dead on both sides were roughly equal. Most Ottoman battles were like that, showing little evidence of tactical or strategic skill but an astonishing power of endurance.

After the battle the Ottomans took the capital, Buda, and then slowly retreated, pillaging. By November 1526 Suleiman was back in Constantinople, displaying the two vast Turkish cannon

which the Hungarians had carried off in triumph from Hunyadi's victory over the Ottomans, and, more privately, enjoying
the remarkable library assembled by the scholar-monarch
Matthias Corvinus in the castle at Buda. Behind him, Suleiman
left chaos along the Danube following the virtual elimination of
the Hungarian élite. The vacuum was slowly filled by the triumph of the Habsburg candidate, Ferdinand of Austria, for the
vacant thrones of Hungary and Bohemia.

Austria, Hungary and Bohemia, united, threatened the Turkish position, and by the early autumn of 1528 the sultan was
planning a new expedition to the north—this time aimed beyond
Buda, at the city of Vienna itself.

BABUR, THE FIRST MUGHAL EMPEROR, CONQUERS INDIA

PERCIVAL SPEAR

Indian civilization reached a high point during the era of the Mughal emperors, who governed from 1529 until 1757. During this era India's richness in both culture and trade goods attracted people from all over the world, while the Mughals sponsored an artistic and intellectual flowering that produced such masterpieces as the Taj Mahal.

The Mughal emperors, however, were foreign to India. Their ancestors were Turkish-speaking nomads from Central Asia who had settled in Afghanistan, where they converted to Islam and adopted Persian as their language of administration. Claiming they were descended from Genghis Khan and Tamerlane (or Taimur), two earlier nomadic conquerors, the Mughals believed fully in their right to govern.

In the following selection, Percival Spear describes the first Mughal, Babur the Tiger, whose armies conquered a disunified north India between 1517 and 1529. Spear claims that Babur never felt at home in India, finding the country disorganized and the people uncultured.

Percival Spear taught history at both St. Stephen's College in Delhi, India, and Cambridge University in England.

Given that India at this time was in a state of confusion and conflict, and that it was also bubbling with life and energy, we may ask whether there were any great forces moving the minds of men beneath the surface of events. Such forces I find difficult to see at this time. On the Muslim side the *élan* [energy] of Muslim proselytism had died away; the tendency was now, apart from moments of passion or fanaticism, to live and let live. The Turkish enthusiasm for conquest and empire-building had wilted under the hammer blows of Taimur [Tamerlane]. What was left was a general spirit of adventure. There were numbers of young men ready, in the unsettled conditions of north-west India and the Iranian plateau, to seek their fortunes in foreign parts. They would attach themselves to some great man in a distant kingdom and hope to achieve promotion and fame by their ability. Such a career was eminently open to talent, as the career of many dynasty founders shows. Everyone was in need of able young followers, and promotion, like disgrace, could be dazzling in its speed. This social fact meant that India contained many enterprising and relatively unattached men ready to take advantage of any twist of fortune and to rally to any outstanding leader. On the Hindu side we find no such tendency. The Hindu magnates were too busy trying to preserve what they still retained or to win back something that they had lost for their people to have time for adventuring. Within Hinduism there was intellectual and social activity but in both spheres the dominant interest was adjustment to the fact of Islam in their midst, with its strange and repugnant ideas, values, and practices. Hindu society was on the defensive and not ready for any large new constructive venture.

THE FIRST MUGHAL: BABUR THE TIGER

It was on this scene that the Mughal or Turkish chief Babur appeared in the year 1517. He himself was an adventurer, though not one of those who seek to gain fortune from nothing. Babur was trying to recover in one direction what he had lost in others. Babur's dynasty is entitled Mughal or Mongol but it should in fact be thought of as Turkish, which language they spoke. Turk and Mongol have been much intermixed in the ebb and flow of Central Asian intertribal warfare, and though some Mughals had decidedly Mongoloid features they were physically more Turkish than Mongolian. Babur was fifth in descent from the great Taimur. As a younger branch, however, his father's kingdom was reduced to the small principality of Farghana in Badakshan. Babur succeeded as a boy of eleven in 1494 but soon found himself threatened by the Uzbeg chief Shaibani Khan. He was soon a fugitive and spent the years between 1494 and 1513 trying to maintain himself in Farghana and recover Samarkand. As a descendant of Taimur, Babur considered he had a right to all Taimur's possessions. He was thus a king by profession and an adventurer by force of circumstances. . . .

Babur is one of the most attractive characters in Indian or any other history. He was not only a soldier-statesman of a familiar type, but a poet and man of letters, of sensibility and taste and humour as well. Wherever he went he laid out Persian gardens and his memoirs are dotted with references to natural beauties. It was the absence of the hills and streams of his homeland that he felt so keenly in India. His memoirs, written in Turki and translated thence into Persian and English, are a masterpiece in their genre. He had a zest for life which carried him cheerfully through the hardships of his early life when he was often a hunted man, and a sense of humour which could make even treachery look ridiculous. His love of sport was infectious and spontaneous and he treated life as one long game of polo. He lacked the vindictiveness common at that time of fanaticism and intense power struggle and had a personal magnetism which could galvanize his followers as in those hot dusty days in Agra and in the camp before Rana Sanga's Rajputs [the greatest Hindu power]. Any good soldier at that time could collect followers. Babur had the rarer gifts of retaining their loyalty, of inspiring them to further efforts, and of reconciling enemies as well as defeating them.

BABUR CONQUERED A POOR, DISORGANIZED INDIA

The state which Babur took over was an aristocratic confederation and had little bureaucratic machinery. Babur had therefore no ready-made apparatus of government, but he did have a free hand to shape new institutions. His genius was for personal government and he died before he had the chance or need to organize. The general state of north India at this time is much more difficult to determine because of lack of evidence. Such clues as we have suggest that the prosperity of the fourteenth century had not returned by the early sixteenth century. The agricultural Hindu mass remained at a subsistence level, punctuated by famines and floods. The upper classes, though better off than in 1400, were still relatively impoverished by constant wars and the reduced trade with a disturbed north-west. If the building of mosques, colleges, and tombs, acts of both piety and prestige, can be taken as a guide, it would appear that prosperity increased as one went south-eastwards, becoming pronounced in eastern Uttar Pradesh, where the Sharqi dynasty adorned Jaunpur. Babur himself took a poor view of the Delhi-

Agra tract and its inhabitants. [The following is] an extract from his own description of Hindustan:

> Hindustan is a country that has few pleasures to recommend it. The people are not handsome. They have no idea of the charms of friendly society, of frankly mixing together, or of familiar intercourse. They have no genius, no comprehension of mind, no politeness of manner, no kindness or fellow-feeling, no ingenuity or mechanical invention in planning or executing their handicraft works, no skill or knowledge in design or architecture; they have no horses, no good flesh, no grapes or musk melons, no good fruits, no ice or cold water, no good food or bread in their bazaars, no baths or colleges, no candles, no torches, not a candlestick.

CORTÉS COMPLETES THE CONQUEST OF MEXICO

BERNAL DIAZ DEL CASTILLO

The Spanish concluded their conquest of the Aztec Empire of Mexico after the Aztec emperor, Moctezuma II (Montezuma), died in battle and by blockading and starving the capital, Tenochtitlán. In the following selection, Bernal Diaz del Castillo describes how the Spanish were able to persuade Moctezuma's successor, Cuahtemoc (Guatimotzin in this translation), to surrender the city. Diaz, who was an officer under Hernán Cortés, the leader of the conquest, wrote his account of the story in his old age, forty-seven years after the conquest.

Diaz describes the meeting between Cuahtemoc and Cortés as one between honorable leaders. He even notes how Cortés promised Cuahtemoc that he might remain the leader of his people under Spanish authority. However, Diaz also mentions the frightful scene in Tenochtitlán, where thousands lay dead or dying of starvation as a result of the conflict.

Cortes gave orders to Sandoval [the chief lieutenant] to go with the flotilla against that part or nook of the city whither Guatimotzin [Cuahtemoc] had retired, cautioning him at the same time not to kill or injure any Mexican, unless he was attacked, nor even then to do more than was absolutely necessary for his own defence; but to level all the houses, and the many advanced works which the enemy had made in the lake. Cortes ascended then into the great temple, with several of his of-

Excerpted from *The True History of the Conquest of Mexico,* by Bernal Diaz del Castillo, translated by Maurice Keatinge (New York: McBride, 1927).

ficers and soldiers, to observe the movements of his fleet. When Sandoval approached the quarters of Guatimotzin, that prince, who had great apprehensions of being made prisoner, availed himself of the preparations which he had made for his escape, and embarking himself, his family, his courtiers, and officers, with their most valuable effects, on board fifty large piraguas [canoes], the whole body set off for the main land, as did all his nobility and chiefs in various directions.

THE SPANISH CAPTURE THE AZTEC PRINCE

Sandoval who was at this time occupied in making his way by tearing down the houses, received immediate notice of the flight of Guatimotzin. He instantly set out in the pursuit, giving strict orders that no injury or insult should be offered, but that each should keep a steady eye upon the royal vessel, and do his utmost to get possession of it. He particularly directed however Garci Holguin, his intimate friend, and captain of the quickest sailer of the fleet, to make for that part of the shore whither Guatimotzin was most likely to go. Accordingly this officer followed his instructions, and falling in with the vessels, from certain particulars in its appearance, structure, and awning, he ascertained that which the king was on board of. He made signs to the people in it to bring to, but without effect; he then ordered his crossbow-men and musqueteers to present, upon which Guatimotzin called out to them not to shoot, and approaching the vessel, acknowledged himself for what he was, declaring his readiness to submit, and go with them to their general, but requesting that his queen, his children, and attendants should be suffered to remain unmolested. Holguin received him with the greatest respect, together with his queen, and twenty of his nobility. He seated them on the poop of his ship, and provided refreshments for them, commanding, that the piraguas which carried the king's effects, should follow untouched.

Sandoval at this moment made a signal for the flotilla to close up to him, and perceived that Guatimotzin was prisoner to Holguin, who was taking him to Cortes . . . then on the summit of the great temple in the Taltelulco, . . . Cortes instantly dispatched Captain Luis Marin and Francisco de Lugo, to bring the whole party together to his quarters, and thus to stop all litigation; but he enjoined them not to omit treating Guatimotzin and his queen with the greatest respect. During the interval, he employed himself in arranging a state, as well as he could, with cloths and mantles. He also prepared a table with refreshments, to receive his prisoners. As soon as they appeared, he went forward to meet them, and embracing Guatimotzin, treated him and all his attendants with every mark of respect. The unfortunate monarch, with tears in his

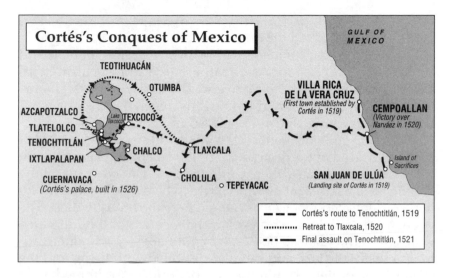

eyes, and sinking under affliction, then addressed him in the following words. "Malintzin! I have done that which was my duty in the defence of my kingdom and people; my efforts have failed, and being now brought by force a prisoner in your hands, draw that poinard from your side, and stab me to the heart." Cortes embraced, and used every expression to comfort him, by assurances that he held him in high estimation for the valour and firmness he had shewn, and that he had required a submission from him and the people at the time that they could no longer reasonably hope for success, in order to prevent further destruction; but that was all past, and no more to be thought of; he should continue to reign over the people, as he had done before.

CORTES TAKES CONTROL OF MEXICO

Cortes then enquired after his queen, to which Guatimotzin replied, that in consequence of the compliance of Sandoval with his request, she and her women remained in the piraguas until Cortes should decide as to their fate. The general then caused them to be sent for, and treated them in the best manner his situation afforded. The evening was drawing on, and it appeared likely to rain; he therefore sent the whole royal family to Cuyoacan, under the care of Sandoval. The rest of the troops then returned to their former quarters; we to ours of Tacuba, and Cortes, proceeding to Cuyoacan, took the command there, sending Sandoval to resume his station at Tepeaquilla. Thus was the siege of Mexico brought to a conclusion by the capture of Guatimotzin and his chiefs, on the thirteenth of August, at the hour of vespers, being the day of St. Hyppolitus, in the year of our Lord one thousand five hundred and twenty one. Glorified be our Lord Jesus

Christ, and our lady the Holy Virgin Mary and his blessed
mother, amen! . . .

Guatimotzin was of a noble appearance both in person and
countenance; his features were rather large, and chearful, with
lively eyes. His age was about twenty three or four years, and his
complexion very fair for an Indian. His queen the niece of Montezuma, was young, and very handsome. . . .

What I am going to mention is truth, and I swear and say amen
to it. I have read of the destruction of Jerusalem, but I cannot conceive that the mortality there exceeded this of Mexico; for all the
people from the distant provinces which belonged to this empire
had concentrated themselves here, where they mostly died. The
streets, the squares, the houses, and the courts of the Taltelulco
were covered with dead bodies; we could not step without tread-
ing on them; the lake and canals were filled with them, and the
stench was intolerable. For this reason, our troops immediately
after the capture of the royal family retired to their former quarters. Cortes himself was for some time ill from the effect of it.

SPANISH CONQUISTADORS HELD MANY ADVANTAGES OVER THE AZTECS AND INCAS

DAN O'SULLIVAN

Columbus's voyage to the New World was followed in the early 1500s by waves of settlers and explorers from Spain who sought gold and glory—the conquistadors. In 1519 Hernán Cortés led the first expedition onto the Mexican mainland. By 1521, through a combination of luck, treachery, and greater firepower, Cortés had conquered the vast Aztec empire. In 1531, Francisco Pizarro led another small force into the South American Andes, where he found the rich Inca empire. It, too, fell to the Spanish. After the victories over the Aztecs and Incas, the Americas lay completely open to Spanish settlement and economic exploitation.

In the following selection, Dan O'Sullivan discusses the various advantages that allowed small groups of conquistadors to control huge and powerful empires. He goes on to describe how Spanish authorities replaced the rapacious conquerors with more seasoned administrators to ensure that the New World would be of lasting economic benefit.

A historian of early modern Europe, Dan O'Sullivan is the author, with Roger Lockyer, of *Tudor England*.

Excerpted from *The Age of Discovery, 1400–1550,* by Dan O'Sullivan. Copyright © Longman Group Limited 1984. Reprinted by permission of Pearson Education Limited.

Why did these empires fall so easily to the Spaniards? Both the Aztecs and the Incas were familiar with organised war and had large numbers of men trained and under arms. Their weapons were by no means negligible; the Aztec axe, with its obsidian blade, could cut off a horse's head; the Incas possessed bronze spears and shields. Partly, it was due to a characteristic they shared. Their considerable degree of cultural, artistic and political development was combined with technological weakness when compared with Europe. They had no written alphabet, no iron, no wheeled vehicles, no ships except the most rudimentary, few domestic beasts of burden, and not even the plough. Another characteristic they shared was a high level of social conformity and docility. Without the subservience of the individual to the state such impressive empires could hardly have arisen, given their primitive technology. Inca irrigation, in particular, needed large-scale collective labour. Their system of rule, centred on semi-divine emperors and small elites of nobles, tended to produce passive obedience rather than active loyalty. These political systems were especially vulnerable to an enemy with technical superiority and mobility, who could reach and seize the centres of power.

THE CONQUISTADORS HAD GREATER WEAPONS AND CONFIDENCE

The conquistadors had such superiority. As well as cannon and musket—neither of which played a vital part in the conquests, though they were no doubt terrifying and contributed to the Spaniards' god-like image—they had the great advantage of steel over bronze or stone. The Indians had no answer to razor-sharp Toledo steel blades, handled by experienced swordsmen. The Spaniards also possessed horses, although not many—Cortés had only 16 when he landed in Mexico. Even more important were factors of motivation and temperament. The conquistadors were tough individualists from the harsh uplands of Castile. The narrative of the conquest brings out the three strands in their psychology: a wolfish greed for gold; a passionate longing to strike down the heathen and win souls for Christ; a chivalric love of great deeds for their own sake.

Other factors were that, in the case of both Mexico and Peru, the Spaniards were able to exploit the legends and superstitions of the enemy so as to weaken opposition, at least temporarily. Again, the Aztec preoccupation with taking prisoners for sacrifice rather than killing them put them at a disadvantage in battle. More important was the disunity of which the Spaniards took full advantage: in Mexico between the Aztecs and their subservient peoples, especially the Tlaxcalans; in Peru between the followers of Atahualpa and Huáscar. Finally, the fatalism of both Aztec and Inca religions could not stand up to the truculent confidence of Renaissance Christianity. In the Old World this had been less of an advantage because the enemy was usually Moslem, an equally optimistic faith, with similar attitudes towards war and death. But, as J.H. Parry puts it, 'Amerindian religion . . . was profoundly pessimistic, the sad, acquiescent faith of the last great Stone Age culture. The Indian believed that his religion required him to fight, and if need be, to die bravely. The Spaniard believed that his religion enabled him to win'.

The rule of the conquistadors was quarrelsome and brief. By 1550 they had been largely supplanted by a bureaucracy of officials, lawyers and priests sent out from Spain to govern the new lands. The process took longer in Peru than in Mexico, where Cortés enjoyed a unique prestige so that there was no other conquistador faction to challenge him. But even Cortés was not fully trusted, precisely because he had such prestige.

In 1528 he returned to Spain and met Charles V who greeted him warmly and confirmed the vast *encomienda* [an award of Indian labor and service] he had granted to himself, of over 23,000 Indian families. Nevertheless, Charles sent out a viceroy and an *audiencia*, or committee of lawyers, to govern Mexico. In 1539 Cortés finally retired to Spain, a disillusioned man. During the last years of his life his house in Madrid became the centre for a circle of humanist intellectuals including John Dantiscus, the Polish ambassador to the Imperial Court and a friend of Copernicus. These humanists did much, after Cortés's death in 1539, to perpetuate his fame and his ideas.

In Peru bureaucratic rule was held up by civil wars between factions of the victorious conquistadors. The first of these, the war of Las Salinas, ended with the defeat of Almagro by the Pizarro brothers in 1538. Three years later, Francisco Pizarro was murdered by supporters of the late Almagro, and a second struggle, the war of Chupas, broke out. In 1546 there was more violence—a rising of the settlers led by Gonzalo Pizarro, the last of the five brothers, against an incompetent viceroy from Spain who tried to enforce the New Laws. Not until 1548 was the fighting finally concluded.

SPAIN ORGANIZES AND EXPLOITS AMERICA

By mid-century both Mexico and Peru were relatively peaceful and starting to prosper. Cities had sprung up, either newly sited as at Lima, which the Spaniards built as a more suitable capital for Peru than the mountainous Cuzco—or on old Indian sites.

Mexico City was the largest settlement in the New World. By 1550 it may have had nearly 100,000 inhabitants, larger than Santo Domingo and far out-distancing any city in Spain. New World cities were independently run by self-perpetuating but civic-conscious *cabíldos,* or councils, and were often well planned, with elegant churches and public buildings. Charles V tended to favour municipal self-government, and there was some chance during his reign that the *cabíldos* would increase in influence. There was talk of setting up a colonial Cortés (Parliament) like that of Castile. However, centralising tendencies eventually took over, and the power of the cities declined relative to that of the bureaucracy. . . .

In 1545 the rich silver mines at Potosí in Peru (modern Bolivia) were opened up. The discovery of this mountain of silver has been called one of the turning points in the history of the western world. The ensuing silver rush turned Potosí into a vast shanty town, even though the mines lay at 18,000 metres, a dangerous altitude for heavy manual labour. Silver was mined in Mexico as well as Peru, and gold also, though in much smaller quantities; by now the gold-bearing rivers of Hispaniola had been exhausted. The main export to Europe next to silver was cochineal, the tiny red beetle parasitic on cactus, which when crushed yielded a valuable dye.

By this time, too, the New World was producing its own food, including wheat, grapes and olives, and the import of bulk food-stuffs from Spain was becoming uneconomic. The rearing of cattle and sheep, both introduced from Spain, was a highly successful activity, especially in Mexico, where beef became so cheap that carcasses were often left to rot once the hide and the fat, for tallow, had been removed. In spite of this self-sufficiency, trade between Seville and the New World had steadily increased, and in exchange for silver came books, textiles, weapons, and other products of Old World civilization, as well as fresh supplies of manpower. In 1550, 133 ships crossed the Atlantic west-bound, and 82 east-bound.

RENAISSANCE ITALY FALLS TO CHARLES V

HARRY HEARDER

The independent city-states of Renaissance Italy stood little chance of military success against the aggressive national monarchies of the early sixteenth century. In the following selection, Harry Hearder describes how France and Spain turned Italy into a battleground. Ironically employing the strategies of the Italian writer Machiavelli, who claimed that power justified virtually any means, Francis I of France and Charles V of Spain sought to dominate the rich cities of Italy.

Charles V, the grandson of Ferdinand and Isabella, became king of Spain as Charles I in 1517. But, as Hearder notes, he held other titles as head of the Hapsburg family, Europe's greatest. Charles was king of Austria and the Netherlands; in addition, he was elected Holy Roman Emperor, giving him control of Germany. Finally, Spanish conquistadors added much of North and South America as well as the Philippines to Charles's holdings. Shortly after an army of troops from the Holy Roman Empire sacked Rome in 1527, Charles V could indeed claim to be ruler of half the world.

Harry Hearder is emeritus professor of history at the University of Wales.

A n Italian writer who anticipated the Europe of self-sufficient embryonic nation states—the 'New Monarchies' of France, Spain and England—was Niccolo Machiavelli (1469–1527). His knowledge came from two sources: the ancient Roman world, and his own contemporary Italian world, where secular principalities and republics acquired a sense of identity as independent units recognizing no higher authority, whether it be of pope or emperor. Fifteenth-century Italy was a microcosm of sixteenth-century Europe, where powerful monarchs nationalized their churches, and acquired a form of independence which was total in practice, and which would have been difficult for the medieval mind to conceive.

Machiavelli's most influential work was the short handbook for rulers which he called *The Prince*. He had held public office under the republic, and when the Medici dismissed him in 1513 he wrote his cynical, yet perceptive, commentary on the necessary skills for securing and retaining power. His argument took the secular spirit of the Renaissance to its most extreme point. In his eyes *raison d'état* [political necessity] required the ignoring of all moral values; in his eighteenth chapter, he wrote:

> A prince, and especially, a new prince, cannot observe all those things for which men are held to be good, it being often necessary, to maintain the State, to operate against integrity, against charity, against humanity, against religion.

. . . Machiavelli's hope for a native [Italian] prince to drive out the foreigners was a vain one. After [King of France] Charles VIII's invasion of Italy in 1494, the Italian states tried to play off the great powers against each other, but without success. If the fox showed occasional subtlety, he was not subtle enough to persuade the lion to depart. After each successive invasion, however, when the French, German or Spanish armies returned to their homelands, they took with them a knowledge and some of the new skills of the Italian Renaissance. If, in the first half of the sixteenth century, Italy was conquered militarily and politically, the end result was to be an Italian cultural conquest of Western and Central Europe.

INVASIONS FROM FRANCE AND SPAIN

But the foreign invasions divided, rather than united, the Italians. And it divided them not only between states, but within cities. Since the Medici in Florence opposed Charles VIII's march southwards to Rome and Naples, the republican anti-Medici party acquired the support of the French, and the domestic politics of Florence came to rely on the struggle between the great powers. Initially it was a struggle between France and the Empire, but it was to become in practice one between France and Spain. When the Spanish army entered Florence in 1512 it meant that the Medici were restored.

Charles VIII had entered Naples in February of 1495, but his rapid successes led to the formation of a strong league against him. Milan, Venice and Pope Alexander VI secured the help of the Emperor Maximilian and Ferdinand of Aragon. Charles withdrew from Italy, and died in 1498. Other barbarian invasions followed. The new king of France, Louis XII, laid claims to Milan, and secured an alliance with the Venetian Republic. In a strictly defensive spirit, fearful of the ambitions of Ludovico Sforza, the Venetians seized the opportunity to extend their land empire to its farthest extent, by the acquisition of Cremona, only some fifty miles from Milan. But their success was counter-productive. The League of Cambrai of 1508, formed to drive back the Venetians, included not only neighbouring Italian cities (Mantua and Ferrara), but also Pope Julius II, France and Spain. For a brief interlude the two great powers were aligned in Italy. Although the Venetians were defeated in the battle of Agnadello in May of 1509, most of their mainland conquests were retained. Venetian rule was efficient and enlightened, and Italian cities evidently accepted it with some gratitude.

THE SACK OF ROME

A yet grimmer and more significant phase of the Italian wars of the fifteenth century started with the succession of Francis I to the French throne in 1515. He immediately invaded Italy and occupied Milan. He was a firm believer in the Machiavellian doctrine that a ruler must have no moral scruples in his pursuit and retention of power. Later in his reign Francis was to send many Calvinists to the stake, not because he had any religious convictions, but because he regarded Protestantism as subversive. But on the international field he was to be faced with a formidable opponent. The grandson of Isabella of Castile and Ferdinand of Aragon became King Charles I of Spain in 1517, and was elected Emperor Charles V in 1519. With his possession of the Netherlands, the Spanish settlements in the New World and his Aragonese inheritance of Naples, he could claim sovereignty over a considerable portion of the known world. . . .

Spanish successes led to the sack of Rome in 1527, the last of the many barbarian sackings of the city since its foundation. Rome herself had not been sacked for several centuries, but the appalling event of 1527 was only one of the many similar atrocities committed on a smaller scale on other cities since the invasions had started in 1494. An imperial army under the command of the Duke of Bourbon marched on Rome and in May of 1527 about 20,000 troops, some German and some Spanish, mostly mercenaries, broke into the city. Of the Germans some were Protestants, who were not likely to respect the sanctity of Rome, but the whole force was out of control, especially after the Duke of Bourbon had been killed in the fighting outside the walls. The pope found refuge in the Castel Sant'Angelo, the formidable fortress which had been built from the remains of the tomb of the Emperor Hadrian. A horrific massacre and unrestrained devastation ensued. Normal life came to a halt for almost a year. No one can tell how many art masterpieces were destroyed. If a date had to be fixed for the ending of the Renaissance, 1527 would have the strongest claim.

MACHIAVELLI DESCRIBES HOW A PRINCE GAINS PRESTIGE

NICCOLÒ MACHIAVELLI

Machiavelli's *The Prince* is the most famous and most notorious work of Renaissance political thought. The author, a humanist scholar well versed in the literature of ancient Greece and Rome as well as a Florentine civil servant, was distressed by the weakness of Florence in comparison with monarchies such as France or Spain. He hoped that a prince might emerge to unify the Italians in the face of such political threats. *The Prince*, published in 1513, is his guidebook for such a leader to acquire and maintain power, emphasizing strong and decisive action. From the date of its publication the book has remained controversial, since Machiavelli appears to claim that power is more important than religion or morality and that the maintenance of power justifies any action.

In the following selection, Machiavelli examines the importance of successful wars, which allow a prince to expand his power abroad while inspiring support and enthusiasm at home. He uses as his example King Ferdinand of Spain, who not only fought successfully, but also used religion to justify his actions.

Nothing brings a prince more prestige than great campaigns and striking demonstrations of his personal abilities. In our own time we have Ferdinand of Aragon, the present king of Spain. He can be regarded as a new prince, because from being a weak king he has risen to being, for fame and glory, the first king of Christendom. If you study his achievements, you will find that they were all magnificent and some of them unparalleled. At the start of his reign he attacked Granada; and this campaign laid the foundation of his power. First, he embarked on it undistracted, and without fear of interference; he used it to engage the energies of the barons of Castile who, as they were giving their minds to the war, had no mind for causing trouble at home. In this way, without their realizing what was happening, he increased his standing and his control over them. He was able to sustain his armies with money from the Church and the people, and, by

Niccolò Machiavelli

means of that long war, to lay a good foundation for his standing army, which has subsequently won him renown. In addition, in order to be able to undertake even greater campaigns, still making use of religion, he turned his hand to a pious work of cruelty when he chased out the Moriscos [Muslims] and rid his kingdom of them: there could not have been a more pitiful or striking enterprise. Under the same cloak of religion he assaulted Africa; he started his campaign in Italy; he has recently attacked France. Thus he has always planned and completed great projects, which

have always kept his subjects in a state of suspense and wonder, and intent on their outcome. And his moves have followed closely upon one another in such a way that he has never allowed time and opportunity in between times for people to plot quietly against them.

It is also very profitable for a prince to give striking demonstrations of his capabilities in regard to government at home, similar to those which are attributed to messer Bernabò of Milan; in the event that someone accomplishes something exceptional, for good or evil, in civil life, he should be rewarded or punished in a way that sets everyone talking. Above all, in all his doings a prince must endeavour to win the reputation of being a great man of outstanding ability.

A prince also wins prestige for being a true friend or a true enemy, that is, for revealing himself without any reservation in favour of one side against another. This policy is always more advantageous than neutrality. For instance, if the powers neighbouring on you come to blows, either they are such that, if one of them conquers, you will be in danger, or they are not. In either case it will always be to your advantage to declare yourself and to wage a vigorous war; because, in the first case, if you do not declare yourself you will always be at the mercy of the conqueror, much to the pleasure and satisfaction of the one who has been beaten, and you will have no justification nor any way to obtain protection or refuge. The conqueror does not want doubtful friends who do not help him when he is in difficulties; the loser repudiates you because you were unwilling to go, arms in hand, and throw in your lot with him.

Political Chaos and Cultural Change in Europe and Japan

—| CHAPTER 5 |—

THE MOVEMENT TO REFORM THE ROMAN CATHOLIC CHURCH

J.M. ROBERTS

According to British historian J.M. Roberts, the author of the following selection, the Protestant Reformation was a pivotal event in Renaissance Europe, dividing the continent along religious lines, causing decades of warfare, and inspiring the Roman Catholic Church to reform itself. As Roberts claims, the criticism of the church that resulted in the Reformation began during the Middle Ages, but became more widespread as the Renaissance church grew worldly, taking an ever greater part in financial, political, and cultural affairs. When Martin Luther, a passionate German monk, protested the worldliness of the church in 1517, his arguments were printed and spread rapidly to the rest of Europe.

Roberts notes that the movement to reform the church could neither be separated from politics nor contained, as new reformers such as John Calvin in Switzerland and King Henry VIII of England brought their own interests and concerns to bear on the question of religion. As a result, by the second half of the sixteenth century there were numerous ways for Europeans to practice Christianity.

I n 1500, one Church united Europe—and almost defined it. Within fifty years, this was no longer so and that might be taken as the end of the Middle Ages. This was the result of a great upheaval, later called the Protestant Reformation. It marked a new era of European civilization and was to be of outstanding

Excerpted from *A Concise History of the World*, by J.M. Roberts. Copyright © 1993 by J.M. Roberts. Reprinted by permission of Sterling Lord Literistic, Inc.

importance in world history. Yet, like so many great changes, few could have foreseen the Reformation and those who launched it would have been horrified had they been able to glimpse the final outcome of what they were doing. They were men with what we should now think of as medieval minds, but they broke a tradition of respect for religious authority going back a thousand years. They ended the unity of Christendom which they deeply believed in. They created new political conflicts though they often thought they were concerned only with unworldly matters. Looking back, we can see too that they were taking the first and most important steps towards greater individual freedom of conduct, more tolerance of different opinions and much more separation between the secular and religious sides of life. All these things would have appalled them. In short, they launched much of modern history.

In theory, Europe had been wholly Christian since the Dark Age conversions of the barbarians. Only in Spain did Christian kings in 1500 rule any large number of non-Christian subjects; in other countries a few Jews lived apart from Christians, segregated in their ghettos, taxed and not usually enjoying the same legal protection as Christians. Apart from these special cases, all Europeans were Christians: the words almost mean the same thing in the Middle Ages. Religion was the one Europe-wide tie and Christendom was an undivided whole, held together by a common faith and the work of the Church, Europe's only continent-wide legal institution. Church law operated in every land through courts alongside and separate from the lay system. All universities were governed and directed by churchmen. Finally, in every country the same sacraments were administered and imposed the same pattern on the great events of people's lives—birth, marriage and death.

EARLY REFORMERS

In spite of its unrivalled position, there had always been plenty of criticism of the Church. There was nothing new about it. Evils which were still worrying critics when the sixteenth century began had been much denounced in the Middle Ages—the ignorance of clergymen, for example, or their misuse of power for personal gain, or their worldly lives. Many such ills—and others—had long been attacked, often by clergymen themselves, and writers had long poked plenty of fun at priests who liked drinking and chasing girls more than attending to their spiritual duties, and had contrasted poor priests devoted to their flocks with their rich, self-indulgent superiors. Yet anti-clericalism—that is, attacking the clergy—did not mean that people wished to forsake the Church itself or doubted the truth of Christianity.

There had long been efforts made by the clergy to put their house in order. As the fifteenth century went on, some critics—many priests among them—began to suggest that it might be necessary to turn back to the Bible for guidance about the way to live a Christian life, since so many of the clergy were obviously not making a very good job of it. They were often labelled heretics and the Church had powerful arms to deal with them. Some of these men, the Oxford scholar Wyclif or the Czech John Hus (who was burnt), for example, had strong popular support, and appealed to the patriotic feelings of fellow-countrymen who felt that the papacy was a foreign and unfriendly institution. Some heretics could draw also on social unrest; no Christian could easily forget what the Bible had to say about the injustices of life.

The followers of Wyclif and Hus, 'Lollards' and 'Hussites' as they were called, were harried and chased by the authorities. It was not they who were to pull down the Church they often criticized. It was still very strong in 1500 and by no means in much worse shape then than at earlier times, even if we seem suddenly to hear more about what is going wrong. Its influence was still taken for granted at every level of society, controlling, moulding, setting in familiar grooves and patterns the accidents of each individual's life, watching over him or her from the cradle to the grave. Religion was so tangled with everyday life that their separation was almost unthinkable. In most villages and little towns, for instance, there was no other public building than the church; it is not surprising that people met in it for community business, and for amusement, at 'church-ales' and on feast days (when even dances were held in it).

PROBLEMS IN THE CHURCH

Being mixed up in the everyday world was not always good for the Church. Bishops who played a prominent part in the affairs of their rulers had always been in danger of being too busy to be good shepherds of their flocks. The great Cardinal Wolsey, archbishop of York and favourite of the English Henry VIII, never visited his see until sent there in disgrace after falling from favour and power. At the very centre of the Church, the popes themselves often seemed to worry too much about their position as temporal princes. Because the papal throne and the papal bureaucracy had both fallen more or less entirely into Italian hands, foreigners especially felt this. Pluralism—holding many offices and neglecting their duties while drawing the pay for them—was another problem the Church had long faced and did not seem to be able to put right. One reason was that for all the grandeur of the way many bishops and abbots lived, for all the extravagance of the papal court at Rome ('Since God has given us the papacy', one pope is supposed to have said, 'let us enjoy it'), there never seemed to be enough money to go round and, as a result, jobs had to be dished out to reward services. Poverty created other difficulties too. It was unusual for a pope to have to go so far as Sixtus IV, who was finally reduced to pawning the papal tiara, but using juridical and spiritual power to increase papal revenues was an old complaint, and it had its roots in the need to find revenue.

Money was short in the parishes, too. Priests became more rigorous about collecting tithes—the portion of the parishioners' produce (usually a tenth or twelfth) to which they were entitled. This led to resentment and resistance which then tempted churchmen into trying to secure their rights by threatening to refuse people the sacraments—to excommunicate them—if they did not pay up. This was a serious business when men believed they might burn in hell for ever as a result. Finally, poverty was also a cause of clerical ignorance (though not the only one). The standard of education among the clergy had improved since the twelfth century (this owed much to the universities) but many parish priests in 1500 were hardly less ignorant or superstitious than their parishioners.

Against this background, when the papacy began to build a great new cathedral in Rome—the St Peter's which still stands there—it had to find new ways to raise money. One of these ways was licensing more salesmen of 'indulgences'. These were preachers who, in return for a contribution to the funds needed for St Peter's, gave the pope's assurance that subscribers would be let off a certain amount of time in Purgatory, that part of the after-world in which the soul was believed to be purged and cleansed of its worldly wickedness before passing to heaven.

LUTHER AND THE PROTESTANT REVOLT

It was the unexpected spark for a religious revolution. In 1517 a German monk, Martin Luther, decided to protest against indulgences as well as several other papal practices. Like the old-fashioned scholar he was, he followed tradition by posting his arguments in a set of ninety-five 'theses' for debate on the door of the castle church in Wittenberg, where he was a professor at the university. Here began the Protestant Reformation. Soon his arguments were translated from their original Latin into German. They ran through Germany like wildfire—printing gave them a wider audience than that for earlier criticisms of the papacy. Unknowingly, Luther was becoming a maker of world history, but he had the temperament for the task. He was a Saxon, the son of peasants, impulsive and passionate, who at the age of twenty-one had become a monk after an emotional upheaval set off by a thunderstorm which broke on him as he was trudging along the highway. Overcome by terror and a feeling of his own sinfulness which made him sure he was fit only to go to hell if he was struck by lightning and killed, Luther suddenly felt the conviction that God cared for him and would save him. It was rather like St. Paul's conversion on the road to Damascus in its suddenness and violence. Luther's first celebration of Mass was another overwhelming experience, so convinced was he of his personal unworthiness to be a priest. Later he was to believe Satan appeared to him—and he even threw his ink-pot at him. Luther's nature was such that, when convinced he was right, he was immovable and this explains his impact. Germany may have been ripe for Luther, but the Reformation would not have been what it was without him.

An enormous dislike of the Italian papacy waited to be tapped in Germany. Luther turned to writing and preaching with a will when the primate of Germany, the archbishop of Mainz, tried to silence him. His fellow-monks abandoned him, but his university stood by him and so did the ruler of Saxony, the state he lived in. Eventually his writings divided Germans into those who came to be called 'Lutherans' (though he was first called a 'Hussite') and those who stood by the pope and the emperor. Support came to him not only from clergy who disapproved of the teaching and practice of the Roman clergy, but from humble folk with grievances against tithe-gatherers and church courts, from greedy princes who coveted the wealth of the Church, and from others who simply took his side because their traditional or habitual rivals came out against him.

Luther in the end set out his views in the form of new theological doctrines—that is to say, statements about the beliefs a Christian ought to hold in order to be sure that he really was a Christian and that he would be saved from Hell after death. He said that the Church itself and even attendance at the sacraments was not absolutely necessary to salvation, but that men might be saved if they had faith in Jesus Christ. This was very important. He was teaching that in the last resort it was possible to hope to be saved even without the Church, by simply relying on your own private relationship with God. It has been said that he dethroned the pope and enthroned the Bible, God's Word, which every believer could consult without the Church coming between him and it. A view putting such stress on the individual conscience was revolutionary. Not surprisingly, Luther was excommunicated, but he went on preaching and won wider and wider support.

The political quarrels Luther's teaching aroused between Germany's rulers broke out in wars and revolts. After a long period of turmoil, a general settlement had to be made. By the peace of Augsburg of 1555 (nine years after Luther's death) it was agreed that Germany should be divided between Catholic and Protestant (the word had come into use after the signing of a 'Protestation' against the papacy in 1529). Which religion prevailed in each state was to be decided by its ruler. Thus yet another set of divisions was introduced into that divided land. The emperor Charles V had to accept this; it was the only way of getting peace in Germany, though he had struggled against the Reformers. For the

In 1517, Martin Luther sparked the Protestant Reformation by detailing abuse and corruption within the Roman Catholic Church.

first time Christian princes and churchmen acknowledged that there might be more than one source of religious authority and more than one recognized Church inside western Christendom.

Something else, of which Luther himself disapproved, had already begun to happen by then. Protestantism tended to fragment, as more and more people began to make up their own minds about religious questions. Other Protestants had soon appeared who did not share his views. The most important were to be found in Switzerland, where a Frenchman, John Calvin, who had broken with Catholicism, began to preach in the 1530s. He had great success at Geneva, and set up there a 'theocratic' state—that is, one governed by the godly where it had been born. The result in any case, was further division—there were now three Europes, two Protestant and one Catholic, as well as several minor Protestant sects.

One country where Protestantism was to be particularly important for the future was England. In that country many of the forces operating elsewhere in favour of throwing off allegiance to the papacy were at work, and so was a very personal one, the wish of Henry VIII to get rid of his queen who was not able to give him a son and heir. Yet Henry was a loyal son of the Church; he had actually written a book against Luther which earned him papal approbation as 'Defender of the Faith', a title still borne by his descendant today. It is very likely that he would have been able to get his marriage to his queen 'annulled'—that is, deemed not to have been a valid marriage—by the pope, had she not been aunt to the emperor Charles V, whose support was needed by the Church against the German heretics. So, as the papacy would not help, Henry quarrelled with the pope, England broke away from allegiance to Rome, and the lands of the English monasteries were seized by the Crown. Some Englishmen also hoped to make the English Church Lutheran, but that did not happen.

Protestantism's successes forced change on Rome. Whatever hopes Roman Catholics might have of returning to the former state of affairs, they would have to live for the foreseeable future in a Europe where there were other claimants to the name of Christian. One effect was that Roman Catholicism became more rigid and intransigent—or, to put it in a different way, better disciplined and more orderly. This was the 'Counter-Reformation'. Several forces helped but the most important of them was a general Council of the Church which opened at Trent in north Italy in 1545 and sat, on and off, until 1563. It redefined much of the Church's doctrine, laid down new regulations for the training of priests and asserted papal authority. Putting its decisions into practice was made a little easier by the work of a remarkable

Spaniard, Ignatius Loyola, who had founded a new order of clergy to serve the papacy, the Society of Jesus, or 'Jesuits'. Sanctioned in 1540 and bound by a special vow of obedience to the pope himself, the Jesuits were carefully trained as an elite corps of teachers and missionaries (Loyola was especially concerned to evangelize the newly discovered pagan lands). More than any other clergy they embodied the combative, unyielding spirit of the Counter-Reformation. This matched Loyola's heroic temper, for he had been a soldier and always seems to have seen his Society in very military terms; Jesuits were sometimes spoken of as the militia of the Church. Together with the Inquisition, a medieval institution for the pursuit of heresy which became the final court of appeal in heresy trials in 1542, and the 'Index' of prohibited books first issued in 1557, the Jesuits were part of a new armoury of weapons for the papacy.

Reformation and Counter-Reformation divided Europeans bitterly. The Orthodox world of the east was little affected, but everywhere in what had been Catholic Europe there were for more than a century religious struggles [and] political struggles envenomed by religion. Some countries successfully persecuted minorities out of existence: Spain and (in large measure) Italy thus remained strongholds of the Counter-Reformation. Rulers usually made up their minds for themselves and their subjects often fell in with their decisions. Foreigners occasionally tried to intervene; Protestant England had the Channel to protect her, and was in less danger than Germany or France. Yet religion was not the only explanation of the so-called 'religious wars' which devastated so much of Europe between 1550 and 1648. Sometimes, as in France, what was really going on was a struggle for dominance between great aristocratic families who identified themselves with different religious parties. . . .

Although even then many people still thought of religion as well-worth fighting over and certainly as something which justified murdering or torturing your errant neighbours, statesmen for the most part began to take more account of other matters in dealing with one another. The world became a tiny bit more civilized when they turned their attention back to arguments about trade and territory, and away from religion. Europe by then, in the second half of the seventeenth century, was divided into states, most of which did not officially tolerate more than one dominant religion, but in some of which—in particular, England and the United Provinces—a fair degree of tolerance was practised.

THE REFORMATION INSPIRED POLITICAL CONFLICT IN EUROPE

H.G. KOENIGSBERGER

By the early 1500s, many Europeans had grown weary and resentful of the corruption and worldliness of the Roman Catholic Church, which appeared to be just as interested in politics, finance, and humanism as it was in salvation. In the following selection, H.G. Koenigsberger examines how a movement to reform the church, begun by a German monk named Martin Luther in 1517, resulted in a new form of Christian worship: Reformed or Protestant Christianity. Koenigsberger also discusses how Roman Catholic leaders responded to this "Protestant Reformation" with a Catholic Reformation of their own. The Catholic Reformation, or Counter-Reformation, curbed some of the earlier abuses of the church but also made the church more militant.

These religious struggles, Koenigsberger notes, frequently became political struggles as well. Martin Luther, for instance, had the support of many German nobles with various disagreements with the papacy. The Germans were joined by the powerful English and wealthy Dutch in the Protestant camp. Likewise, the driving forces behind the Catholic Reformation were often the kings of France and Spain rather than the church itself. By 1550, in fact, the age of religious wars in Europe had begun.

H.G. Koenigsberger was professor of history at King's College, London.

Excerpted from *Early Modern Europe, 1500–1789*, by H.G. Koenigsberger. Copyright © H.G. Koenigsberger 1987. Reprinted by permission of Pearson Education Limited.

In 1517, Martin Luther, an Augustinian monk and a star-professor at the new Saxon university of Wittenberg, attacked the practice of the sale of indulgences. Originally, indulgences had been remissions of church penalties for religious transgressions granted to those going on crusades. Gradually they had come to mean a remission of punishment by God, such as the period of time spent in purgatory, by means of the Church's 'power of the keys,' to be purchased by payment of a sum of money. The practice was evidently open to abuse, and in 1517 the money which was being collected in Germany through the exploitation of people's fear of God's punishment for their sins was being channelled to Rome to pay for the building of St. Peter's.

LUTHER CLAIMS THE CHURCH IS UNNECESSARY FOR SALVATION

Luther's attack, however, questioned not so much the morality as the theological basis of indulgences. In the theological controversies which followed the terms of conflict widened rapidly as the implications of Luther's position became clear, both to the defenders of orthodoxy and to himself. They amounted to nothing less than the claim that salvation was due to the Christian's faith alone, and not to good works, and this in turn meant the end of the position of the Church and the papacy as necessary mediators between the individual and God.

Normally, the papacy would have acted rapidly and effectively against such heresy. But the politics of the imperial election of 1519, in which the pope supported Francis I, forbade the appearance of too obvious papal interference in Germany. In the meantime Luther found himself the champion of a varied religious, anticlerical and xenophobic movement. Through preaching and writing it spread throughout Germany and beyond. For the first time in history, the printing press played a vital role in affecting, and indeed in creating, mass opinion.

On 20 April 1521, at the imperial diet at Worms, Luther finally defied pope and emperor by refusing to retract his opinions: 'Here I stand. I can do no other. God help me. Amen.' These words, or perhaps supposed words, have come to stand in the Protestant tradition as one of the great dramatic moments of the human mind. But what did they signify? Were they a declaration of the freedom of the human mind in the face of venerable tradition grown tyrannical, or were they only the affirmation of a private obstinacy raised to spurious universality by their theatrical setting and the irreverent political aims of most of those present?

To most Catholics, then and since, (and that was and is the majority of Europeans), Luther and the other reformers were simply heretics. Their specific doctrines remained utterly unimportant, for it simply made no sense to choose to be a heretic. But at the time Luther's very personal convictions and his unsurpassed ability to express them found echoes among thousands who had been left unmoved by the arguments of Erasmus and the Christian humanists. The reformed Churches which were set up in parts of Germany and in Denmark and Sweden developed very much as 'Lutheran' churches, in spite of their mutual differences and in spite of the reformer's own unwillingness to become involved in the founding and organization of new Churches.

RELIGIOUS REFORM SUPPORTS POLITICAL CHANGE

Luther did not continue to occupy the centre of the stage. After 1521 his finest achievements were the translation of the bible and, by this translation, the virtual creation of the modern literary German language, together with the elaboration of his religious beliefs and, especially, his placing of music into the very centre of the church service. Many of those who were willing to accept his theology were nevertheless not convinced that this meant an irreparable breach with Rome; and there were those on the Catholic side, including for many years the emperor Charles V himself, who agreed with them and, who, for the sake of reuniting the Church, were willing to meet the Lutherans at least part of the way.

From the beginning, however, the spread of the Reformation was closely linked with political and economic interests. It suited many German princes and cities, to break with Rome in order to secularize church property or to defeat political opponents. In 1524–25 the peasants of southern and central Germany claimed justification for their movement in Luther's doctrines of Christian freedom. The reformer was horrified to see his views distorted for purely secular ends and exhorted the princes to massacre their rebellious subjects. This the princes duly did; but who was to recall the princes themselves, or the great fortified cities, to their Catholic duty? . . .

THE CATHOLIC CHURCH RESPONDS TO LUTHERANISM

The Reformation totally changed the problem of Catholic reformation, and it did so in three ways. In the first place, it suddenly created an urgency in the work of moral reform of the clergy and of their pastoral work which had hardly been perceived before. A number of new orders were founded, both for men and for women, whose members set a new tone in strictly observed religious life. More effective still were new orders whose members specialized in preaching. Important as the printing press had been in spreading the ideas of the reformers, their success with the masses was primarily due to the excellence of their preaching. Now the Capuchins, an autonomous branch of the Franciscan Order founded in Italy in 1525, began to match the reformers in preaching. More important still were the Jesuits. Ignatius Loyola (1491–1556), a Spanish soldier, founded the Society of Jesus, originally to convert the heathen outside Europe. Summoned to Rome (1534) the Order became the most effective intellectual champion of the Catholic Church against the Protestants. Sworn to unconditional obedience to the pope, organized with military discipline, thoroughly trained in the liberal arts and in theology, the Jesuits became advisers of popes, professors at Catholic universities, confessors to princes and, perhaps even more effectively, to princely ladies, and the most fearless and imaginative of the Catholic overseas missionaries. The Jesuits' ideas of education, derived largely from Erasmus and the Christian humanists but now applied in a much more authoritarian manner, were implemented in schools all over Catholic Europe and were influential, although rarely acknowledged, even in Protestant countries.

CATHOLIC KINGS DEFEND THE CHURCH

The second change wrought by the Reformation was the active involvement of the European states in the problem of church reform. Since the Council of Constance, a hundred years earlier, the monarchies had taken little interest in this problem but had, on the contrary, striven to extend their control over the churches of their own countries, often as we have seen, at the expense of papal authority. Now it was precisely those monarchies which had been most successful in their anti-papal policy, Spain, France and some of the German princes, such as the archdukes of Austria and the dukes of Bavaria, who came to the defence of the old Church. Having achieved the degree of control which they wanted they preferred not to let loose the perhaps uncontrollable social, intellectual and emotional forces set in motion by Luther and the other reformers. More and more insistently they also demanded the reform of the Church 'in head and members'. It was constant pressure by the emperor Charles V and later also by the French government which played the major role in persuading the reluctant papacy to summon the reforming Council of Trent (1545–47, 1551–52, 1562–63).

The third change which the Reformation forced on the Catholic Church was a thorough reconsideration of a number of basic Catholic doctrines. It was a recognition that the Reformation movement was more than an individual man's heresy. For some three decades there were theologians on both sides who hoped that a general council would find a doctrinal compromise acceptable to all Christians, except perhaps the far-out prophets. The three sessions of the Council of Trent put an end to such hopes by reinforcing papal authority, and by reaffirming and clearly defining the Catholic doctrine of salvation by both faith and works (against the Protestants' insistence on salvation by faith alone), the seven sacraments (baptism, confirmation, penance, eucharist, marriage, holy orders and extreme unction), transubstantiation (the real change of the bread and wine into the body and blood of Christ in the eucharist), the denial of the cup to the laity in the eucharist and the confirmation of the Catholic Church's position as the sole interpreter of the word of God. Within the church, the authority of the pope remained supreme.

THE INQUISITION AND THE INDEX

These definitions were supplemented by resolutions on the better education of the clergy, the obligation for bishops to be resident in their dioceses and by other administrative and moral reforms. As early as 1542 the papal inquisition, first established at the time of the Albigensian 'crusade' was reorganized and reintroduced in many parts of Europe where it had all but disappeared. After the closure of the council the popes set up a special commission to implement its decrees. In 1574 the first index of prohibited books was issued by the papacy. From then on, no good Catholic was allowed without special dispensation to read the works of Machiavelli, Luther and the other reformers or any other works held to be harmful to salvation.

RELIGIOUS WARS IN FRANCE RESULT IN A MASSACRE

FILIPPO CAVRIANI

Wars between Catholics and Protestants were particularly bitter in France, which was in a state of virtual civil war from 1559 to 1593. French Protestants, known as Huguenots, enjoyed the support of many of France's most powerful nobles, including Henry Bourbon, king of Navarre. Arrayed against them was the French royal family, the Valois, and its supporters. Although the king of France was Charles IX, real power lay with his mother, Catherine de Medici, granddaughter of the Florentine despot Lorenzo.

In 1572, Catherine agreed to a marriage between Henry and her daughter Marguerite, seeking to smooth over disputes between Protestants and Catholics. Hundreds of leading Protestants traveled to Paris for the wedding. Among them was Admiral Coligny, a close adviser to Charles IX. Convinced by one of her supporters, the duke of Guise, that Coligny was a threat to the Catholic monarchy, Catherine agreed to have him and thousands of other Protestants killed in an event known as the Saint Bartholomew's Day Massacre.

In the following selection, Catherine's physician Filippo Cavriani gives his account of the massacre.

Without waiting any longer, the king sent for the King of Navarre and the Prince of Condé; and at this extraordinary hour they came to the king's chamber, accompanied by the men of their train. When these wished to come in—

and among them were Monin and Piles—they were stopped at the door by the soldiers of the guard. Then the King of Navarre, turning towards his people with a sorrowful face, said to them, 'Adieu, my friends: God knows whether I shall see you again.'

At the same moment Guise left the palace and went to find the captain of the citizens to give him the order to arm two thousand of his men and to surround the Faubourg Saint-Germain, where more than fifteen hundred Huguenots were living, so that the massacre might take place on both banks of the river at the same time.

Nevers, Montpensier and the other lords at once armed themselves, and together with their people, some on foot, some mounted, went to the various posts that had been allotted to them, all prepared to act in concert.

The king and his brothers did not leave the Louvre [the residence of the royal family].

Cossein, the Gascon commander, the German Besme, a former page to Monsieur de Guise, Hautefort, the Italians Pierre Paul Tossinghi and Petrucci, went with a numerous troop to the house of the Admiral, whom they had orders to kill. They broke down the door and went up the stairs. At the top of it they found a kind of makeshift barricade, made of chests and benches hurriedly heaped together. They thrust their way into the room, found eight or ten servants, whom they killed, and saw the Admiral, standing at the foot of his bed and dressed in a furred gown. The day was only just dawning and things could barely be made out. They asked him, 'Are you the Admiral?' He replied that he was. They rushed at him and covered him with insults. Besme grasped his sword and made to plunge it into his bosom. But he cried out, 'Ah, young soldier, have pity upon old age!' Vain words. With one stroke Besme laid him at his feet: they fired two pistols straight into his face and left him lying there lifeless. The whole house was given over to pillage. Meanwhile some of these men appeared on the balcony and said, 'He is dead.' Those below, Guise and the others, would not believe it. They asked him to be thrown out of the window, which was done. The corpse was stripped, and when it was naked pieces were cut off it. . . .

Everywhere there were people who fled and others who ran after them, crying 'Kill! Kill!' There were men and women who, with the knife at their throats, were called upon to recant to save their lives, but they would not, and so lost both soul and body. There was no mercy either for age or for sex. It was in very truth a massacre. The streets were strewn with naked, mutilated corpses; the river was covered with them.

The murderers wore the sleeve of a shirt on their left arms. Their watchword was 'Glory to God and the king!'

When it was day, Monseigneur d'Anjou [the king's brother] took horse and went through the city and the suburbs with eight hundred cavalry, a thousand foot and four pieces of artillery to beat down the houses that resisted. There was no need for them. The Huguenots, attacked without warning, thought only of flight.

There was no laughter among the shouts. The victors did not shout with joy, as victors usually do, for the spectacle before them was so heart-breaking and hideous. . . .

The Louvre remained closed: everything there was in silence and terror. The king stayed in his chamber: he looked cheerful, laughed and joked. It was a long while before the court could recover and take on something of the appearance of calmness again. Today everyone is eagerly seeking to profit by the situation, soliciting either places or privileges. Up to the present nothing has been done except to give the Marquis de Villars the office of Admiral. The king is feared, and it is seen that he means to be obeyed.

It is said that Coligny, talking to his son-in-law Téligny a week ago about the prediction of an astrologer who had said that he would be hanged, made game of it and said, 'Consider whether there is any likelihood of such a thing happening—unless indeed it means that I shall be hanged in effigy, as I was some months ago.' Now the astrologer had told the truth, for his body, dragged about the streets and the object of the vilest insults, was beheaded and hanged by the feet from the gibbet of Montfaucon, there to become meat for crows.

Such was the miserable end of the man who not long before was the master of half France. Upon him there was found a medal with these words engraved, *Either a complete victory, or an assured peace, or an honourable death.* None of these wishes was to come true.

The tragedy has lasted three whole days, amid raging fury. It is only just beginning to die down. The booty has been enormous: it is reckoned at a million and a half gold crowns. More than four hundred of the bravest gentlemen and the best captains of the party have perished. Most of them had come well provided with clothes, jewels and money, to make a good show at the wedding of the King of Navarre. The mob has enriched itself with their spoils.

The Parisians are pleased; they feel relieved and assuaged. Yesterday they hated the queen; today they proclaim her 'The mother of the kingdom and the preserver of the Christian name'.

INTERNAL CONFLICTS DESTROY JAPAN'S ASHIKAGA SHOGUNATE

MARY ELIZABETH BERRY

During the Renaissance, Japan fell into a state of prolonged civil war. Until 1467 the country had been stabilized by a ruling institution known as the Ashikaga Shogunate. The Ashikaga were one of Japan's important landowning families. They supplied the shoguns, who ruled Japan in the name of its semidivine emperor; the word *shogun* means "the emperor's military adviser." Conflicts both inside the Ashikaga clan and with other powerful families tore the country apart after 1467.

In the following selection, Mary Elizabeth Berry describes the political instability that gradually transformed Japan in 1467 and 1550. As Japan became a nation of competing warlords equipped with private armies, Berry notes, military power and control of land became closely intertwined.

Mary Elizabeth Berry is professor of history at the University of California, Berkeley.

I n 1467, a quarrel over succession in the Ashikaga house, fueled by similar quarrels in two major *shugo* [military governors] houses, deeply divided shogunal officials. Tens of thousands of soldiers recruited by *shugo* across Japan gathered in the streets of Kyoto to support rival factions. Fighting finally dissi-

Reprinted by permission of the publisher from *Hideyoshi*, by Mary Elizabeth Berry (Cambridge, MA: Harvard University Press). Copyright © 1982 by the President and Fellows of Harvard College.

pated there ten years later, leaving the capital in ruins, the ninth
Ashikaga shogun uneasily installed in office, and much of the nation in rebellion. Military proprietors abjured the authority of the
shogunate in order to declare autonomous control over their
holdings and to expand their dominion to neighboring areas.

This widespread rebellion of military men had been prefigured
in regional uprisings earlier in the century, in attempts by shogunal officials in the Kantō to separate themselves from Kyoto, and
in the military's antipathy toward some Ashikaga leaders that
led to the murder of the sixth shogun in 1441. The rebellion was
given license, however, by the long and bitter succession quarrels that testified to profound rifts within the governing class and
a common willingness to revert to armed confrontation. The
specter of the Ashikaga and the *shugo* at war with one another
for a decade in the Capital of Peace and Tranquillity (Heian-kyō)
established lawlessness as the norm.

A LAWLESS JAPAN

In the early decades after 1467, the illusion of political continu-
ity was sustained by the survival of the shogun and some of his
shugo. The local contests between neighboring proprietors that
characterized the first stages of civil war could be perceived by
men of the day as passing disturbances that would effect a new
balance of power. Yet by the time Hideyoshi [a future leader of
Japan] left home to seek his fortune in the 1550s, all the com-
monplaces of an earlier day had been discarded: the emperor and
his shogunal surrogates had been denied practical authority over
the nation; the state was atomized by competing warlords who
created their own autonomous domains; land was distributed by
local powers in exchange for military service; and law was
rewritten by individual lords to declare their primacy and the
eclipse of higher tribunals.

In effect, the principles that had undergirded government until 1467 were repudiated as the dichotomy between official, centralized authority over land resources and private management
was shattered. Private management of land was the sole certainty
by 1550. Accompanying this change was the rise of two assumptions of rule that, though not new to the sixteenth century,
had never before been confronted so clearly or to the exclusion
of loftier views: that power over land devolved upon those able
to muster and control military force, and that the control of military force depended upon stern and independent administration of the lands a lord could take.

Despite Civil War, Japanese Civilization Flourished

NOEL PERRIN

In the following selection, Noel Perrin asserts that Japan had a vibrant, creative civilization in the era from 1490 to 1600, the "Age of the Country at War." The Japanese economy and population were growing, the arts enjoyed patronage and popular appreciation, and Buddhist scholarship thrived. Moreover, Japanese craftsmen produced, Perrin claims, the best weapons on earth.

The dominant force in society was, however, war. Competing landlord clans fought one another using private armies of samurai, or military retainers. The samurai were reared and trained according to a complex military code combining the arts of war with loyalty, self-discipline, and proper etiquette, even toward one's enemies. Samurai traditionally considered fighting with firearms dishonorable, preferring the face-to-face combat required by swordplay. Although, as Perrin notes, the Japanese made high-quality firearms, only peasant rebels and, surprisingly, Buddhist monks, used them in battle.

Noel Perrin taught history at Dartmouth College.

By 1560, the use of firearms in large battles had begun (a general in full armor died of a bullet wound that year), and fifteen years after that they were the decisive weapon in one of the great battles of Japanese history.

All this represents what would now be called a technological

Excerpted from *Giving Up the Gun: Japan's Reversion to the Sword, 1543–1879*, by Noel Perrin. Copyright © 1979 by Noel Perrin. Reprinted by permission of David R. Godine, Publisher, Inc.

breakthrough. As present-day Japanese writers like to point out, the Arabs, the Indians, and the Chinese all gave firearms a try well ahead of the Japanese, but only the Japanese mastered the manufacturing process on a large scale, and really made the weapon their own.

There were good reasons for Japan's special success. The country was a soldierly one to begin with. As St. Francis Xavier wrote in 1552, after a two-year stay in Japan, 'They prize and honor all that has to do with war, and there is nothing of which they are so proud as of weapons adorned with gold and silver. They always wear swords and daggers, both in and out of the house, and when they go to sleep they hang them at the bed's head. In short, they value arms more than any people I have ever seen.' St. Francis had seen a good many, beginning with his own warlike relatives in Spain. It is probably fair to say that military glory was the goal of every well-bred male in sixteenth-century Japan, except a handful of court nobles in Kyoto. *Their* goal was literary glory.

JAPAN'S CONFLICTS CREATED A DEMAND FOR FIREARMS

Furthermore, at the moment when firearms arrived, Japan happened to be in the middle of a century-long power struggle. The Japanese name for the period from 1490 to 1600 is *Sengoku Jidai*, or Age of the Country at War. Several dozen major feudal lords were vying to get military control of the country, make a puppet of the shogun (the emperor was already the shogun's puppet), and rule. Naturally, such men were interested in new weapons and in anything else that would give them an advantage. . . .

The thing Japan manufactured most of was weapons. For two hundred years she had been the world's leading exporter of arms. The whole Far East used Japanese equipment. In 1483, admittedly an exceptional year, 67,000 swords were shipped to China alone. A hundred and fourteen years later, a visiting Italian merchant named Francesco Carletti noted a brisk export trade in 'weapons of all kinds, both offensive and defensive, of which this country has, I suppose, a more abundant supply than any other country in the world.' Even as late as 1614, when things were about to change, a single trading vessel from the small port of Hirado sailed to Siam with the following principal items of cargo: fifteen suits of export armor at four and a half taels the suit, eighteen short swords at half a tael each, twenty-eight short swords at a fifth of a tael, ten guns at four taels, ten guns at three taels, and fifteen guns at two and a half taels.

These were top-quality weapons, too. Especially the swords. A Japanese sword blade is about the sharpest thing there is. It is designed to cut through tempered steel, and it can. Tolerably thick mails don't even make an interesting challenge. In the 1560s one of the Jesuit fathers visited a particularly militant Buddhist temple—the Monastery of the Original Vow, at Ishiyama. He had expected to find the monks all wearing swords, but he had not expected to find the swords quite so formidable. They could cut through armor, he reported, 'as easily as a sharp knife cuts a tender rump.' Another early observer, the Dutchman Arnold Montanus, wrote that 'Their Faulchions or Scimeters are so well wrought, and excellently temper'd, that they will cut our *European* blades asunder, like Flags or Rushes. . . .'

A REFINED CULTURE DESPITE CIVIL WAR

Finally, Age of the Country at War or not, Japan was in booming good health. During the sixteenth century it had a larger population than any European country: twenty-five million people, compared to sixteen million in France, seven million in Spain, four and a half million in England, and maybe a million in what is now the United States. Agriculture was flourishing. So was the building industry. A Jesuit named Luis Frois saw Lord Oda Nobunaga's newly built castle at Gifu in 1569, and reacted the way his colleague Gaspar Vilela did to the monks' swords. 'I wish I was a good architect, or had the gift of being able to describe places well,' Father Frois wrote his superior, 'because I assure you emphatically, that among all the palaces and houses which I have seen in Portugal, India, and Japan, I never yet saw anything comparable to this in freshness, elegance, sumptuousness, and cleanliness.'

As for education, the Buddhist monks maintained five 'universities,' the smallest of them larger than the Oxford or Cambridge of the time. And while no exact statistics are available, there is every reason to believe that the general literacy rate was higher in Japan in 1543 than in any European country whatsoever.

Interest in the arts ran high, too. Career military officers—that is to say, members of the *bushi* class—were expected to read and quote the classics between battles, while in 1588 the senior military commander in the whole country gave a series of poem parties. A timely poem could sometimes even save a man's life. During a suspected rebellion, for example, a court noble named Lord Tameakira was being held for questioning by the military governor of Suruga, a tough samurai. It was believed that Lord Tameakira knew the whole plot, and that a little judicious torture would make him reveal it. While they were building the fire, Lord Tameakira requested an inkstone and paper. Everybody supposed that he was going to write out a confession, and the paper was promptly brought. Instead he composed a poem.

It is beyond belief!
I am questioned not on the art of poetry
But on the things of this transient world!

The military governor and his staff were so impressed by the elegance of this response that they released Lord Tameakira unharmed.

WORLD HISTORY BY ERA

The International Exchange of People, Ideas, Products, and Diseases

CHAPTER 6

EUROPEAN DISEASES DEVASTATE THE AMERICAS

RONALD WRIGHT

According to Ronald Wright, author of the following selection, the Spanish were able to conquer and colonize the Americas in the 1500s because Native American (Amerindian) peoples were devastated by European diseases. Smallpox, malaria, measles, and other Old World afflictions killed, Wright notes, as many as 90 million people in the New World between 1500 and 1600. Among the dead were political and spiritual leaders who, Wright suggests, may have helped Native American peoples better cope with their Spanish overlords.

Over many centuries of exposure, the peoples of Europe, Africa, and Asia had built up a degree of immunity to indigenous diseases such as smallpox. Though smallpox outbreaks were a constant threat, most Old World peoples were able to survive smallpox attacks because their bodies had developed resistance to the disease. Native Americans, however, had never been exposed to Old World diseases. Consequently, their immune systems could offer little resistance. Though unintentional, the importation of Old World microbes into the Americas acted, Wright points out, as a sort of biological warfare.

Ronald Wright is the author of many books of travel and history, including *Cut Stones and Crossroads: A Journey in Peru*, and *Time Among the Maya*.

Excerpted from *Stolen Continents*, by Ronald Wright. Copyright © 1992 by Ronald Wright. Reprinted by permission of Houghton Mifflin Co. All rights reserved.

W hy were Amerindians so vulnerable? Why was America so overwhelmed by Europe that, unlike Asia and Africa, it has never been decolonized? Why are the modern countries of America not really American at all, but imitation Europes built on American soil? Why does none use an American language at the diplomatic level? Why isn't there a single president, prime minister, or monarch with an Amerindian name?

The usual answers . . . are self-serving and grounded in assumptions of superiority: the Indians lost because they were primitive, because their societies were weak, because they were few, because they were superstitious, and so forth. Such explanations explain nothing, even by their own false premises. The rolling back of colonialism in the present century has little to do with how "primitive" the natives were upon first contact. Places as diverse as Guinea [in Africa] and New Guinea [in Southeast Asia] are today governed by descendants of their original inhabitants. Many parts of ancient America were more advanced (in Western terms) than those. Yet Africans and Papuans have reclaimed a qualified autonomy, while the word *American* does not even mean a native of the continent.

Why was America different? The short answer is disease. As in H.G. Wells's *War of the Worlds,* Europe possessed biological weapons that fate had been stacking against America for thousands of years. Among these were smallpox, measles, influenza, bubonic plague, yellow fever, cholera, and malaria—all unknown in the Western Hemisphere before 1492. Somehow they had not made the journey to the New World with the remote ancestors of the American Indians during the last Ice Age. Perhaps they were frozen to death on the way; perhaps they had not yet evolved. Whatever the reason, Native Americans, having had no exposure, had little or no immunity; they caught the new sicknesses quickly, and infection was extremely virulent. "The Indians die so easily that the bare look and smell of a Spaniard causes them to give up the ghost," one eyewitness wrote. Even today, isolated tribes can be decimated by something as "minor" as the common cold on first contact with missionaries or prospectors. In just two years—1988 to 1990—the Yanomami of Brazil lost 15 percent of their people, mainly to malaria and influenza.

The New World did have some diseases all its own—perhaps syphilis, for one, which appeared in Europe in 1498—but they were few and not mass killers.

THE EFFECTS OF EUROPEAN DISEASES

It is now clear that Old World plagues killed at least half the population of the Aztec, Maya, and Inca civilizations shortly before their overthrow. The sheer loss of people was devastating enough (Europe reeled for a century after the Black Death, which was less severe), but disease was also a political assassination squad, removing kings, generals, and seasoned advisers at the very time they were needed most.

The great death raged for more than a century. By 1600, after some twenty waves of pestilence had swept through the Americas, less than a tenth of the original population remained. Perhaps 90 million died, the equivalent, in today's terms, to the loss of a billion. It was the greatest mortality in history. To conquered and conqueror alike, it seemed as though God really was on the white man's side.

Survivors of this apocalypse looked back on the pre-Columbian world as an uncontaminated paradise. From a sixteenth-century Maya book:

> There was then no sickness;
> They had then no aching bones;
> They had then no high fever;
> They had then no smallpox;
> They had then no burning chest . . .
> They had then no consumption . . .
> At that time the course of humanity was orderly.
> The foreigners made it otherwise when they arrived here.

SUGAR BECOMES THE NEW WORLD'S FIRST CASH CROP

SIDNEY W. MINTZ

In the following passage, anthropologist Sidney W. Mintz examines the development of the sugar business in the New World in the 1500s. He traces its origin to sugar-refining practices begun by the Spanish and Portuguese on central Atlantic island groups such as the Canaries, which lay close to the African coast, in the 1400s. Once Spanish colonists on the island of Santo Domingo (now Haiti and the Dominican Republic) mastered the techniques of producing sugar from sugar cane, they sold sugar to a European market where the commodity was still a luxury available only to the rich. Mintz also notes that, as in the Canaries, Caribbean sugar producers began very early to use African slaves as laborers.

By the end of the Renaissance, Mintz asserts, control of the sugar industry had passed to the English, Dutch, and French. All three began to serve an ever-expanding market as sugar became cheaper and more popular in Europe. The expansion of sugar production meant an expansion in the "need" for African slave labor to produce it, and thus in the transatlantic slave trade.

Sidney W. Mintz is a professor of anthropology at Johns Hopkins University in Baltimore.

A t the time that the Portuguese and the Spaniards set out to establish a sugar industry on the Atlantic islands they controlled, sugar was still a luxury, a medicine, and a spice in western Europe. The peoples of Greece, Italy, Spain, and North Africa were familiar with sugar cane as a crop and, to some extent, with sugar itself as a sweetener. But as sugar production in the Mediterranean waned, knowledge of sugar and the desire for it waxed in Europe. The movement of the industry to the Atlantic islands occurred when European demand was probably growing. Individual entrepreneurs were encouraged to establish sugar-cane (and other) plantations on the Atlantic islands, manned with African slaves and destined to produce sugar for Portugal and other European markets, because their presence safeguarded the extension of Portuguese trade routes around Africa and toward the Orient. . . .

There were intimate links between the Atlantic-island experiments of the Portuguese, especially São Tomé, and west European centers of commercial and technical power, especially Antwerp. It is of particular significance that from the thirteenth century onward, the refining center for European sugar was Antwerp, followed later by other great port cities such as Bristol, Bordeaux, and even London. Control of the final product moved into European hands—but not, it bears noting, into those of the same Europeans (in this instance, the Portuguese) who pioneered the production of sugar overseas. The increasing differentiation of sugars, in line with the growing differentiation of demand, was another cause of growth. The descriptive lexicon for sugars expanded, as more and more sorts became familiar to the Europeans.

SUGAR WAS A LUXURY ITEM

Sugar itself was now known throughout western Europe, even though it was still a product *de luxe,* rather than a common commodity or necessity. No longer so precious a good as musk or pearls, shipped to the courts of Europe via intermediary countries and their luxury traders, sugar was becoming a raw material whose supply and refining were managed more and more by European powers, as European populations consumed it in larger and larger quantities. The political differentiation of the western states interested in sugar proceeded apace after the fifteenth century. To a surprising degree, the way sugar figured in national policies indicated—perhaps even exercised some influence over—political futures.

Portugal's and Spain's sugar experiments in the Atlantic islands had many parallels, though later they diverged sharply. In the fifteenth century both powers looked for favorable locales for sugar production: while Portugal seized São Tomé and other islands, Spain captured the Canaries. After about 1450, Madeira was the leading supplier, followed by São Tomé; by the 1500s, the

Canary Islands had also become important. And both powers experienced a growing demand for sugar (suggested, for instance,
by the household accounts of Isabella the Catholic, queen of
Castile from 1474 to 1504).

The sugar industries in the Spanish and Portuguese Atlantic islands were characterized by slave labor, a tradition supposedly
transferred from the Mediterranean sugar plantations of the Arabs
and Crusaders. But the Spanish scholar Fernández-Armesto tells
us that the striking feature of the Canarian industry was its use of
both free and enslaved labor, a combination that resembled more
the pioneering mixed-labor systems of a later era: the seventeenth-
century British and French Caribbean plantations, on which enslaved and indentured laborers would work alongside one another. Slaves were decidedly important, perhaps crucial; but a
substantial amount of the labor was actually done by free wage
earners paid partly in kind—some of them specialists, others tem-
porary laborers. This system was probably not quite so atypical
as it seems. But it is true that free wage earners hardly figure in
sugar's history between the Atlantic island phase and the epoch
of revolution and emancipation in the New World, from the start
of the Haitian Revolution until emancipation in Brazil. "The Canarian system," Fernández-Armesto tells us, "evokes far more the
methods of the Old World, and the equal sharing of produce between owners and workers is most akin to the farming a *mezzadria*
[by sharecropping], which developed in late medieval northern
Italy and in some parts is still practised today."

SUGAR AND SLAVE LABOR IN THE AMERICAS

Sugar cane was first carried to the New World by Columbus on
his second voyage, in 1493; he brought it there from the Spanish
Canary Islands. Cane was first grown in the New World in Spanish Santo Domingo; it was from that point that sugar was first
shipped back to Europe, beginning around 1516. Santo Domingo's
pristine sugar industry was worked by enslaved Africans, the first
slaves having been imported there soon after the sugar cane.
Hence it was Spain that pioneered sugar cane, sugar making,
African slave labor, and the plantation form in the Americas. Some
scholars agree with Fernando Ortiz that these plantations were
"the favored child of capitalism," and other historians quarrel with
this assessment. But even if Spain's achievements in sugar production did not rival those of the Portuguese until centuries later,
their pioneering nature has never been in doubt, though scholars
of New World sugar have sometimes neglected Spain's early Caribbean accomplishments in the sugar trade because their global
significance was slight. Wallerstein and Braudel are cavalier in

their disregard; Braudel has sugar cane and sugar mills not reaching Santo Domingo until after 1654, for instance.

By 1526, Brazil was shipping sugar to Lisbon in commercial quantities, and soon the sixteenth century was the Brazilian century for sugar. Within the Spanish New World, the early achievements in Santo Domingo and the rest of the Caribbean were outstripped by developments on the mainland. In Mexico, Paraguay, the Pacific coast of South America, and in fertile valleys everywhere, sugar cane prospered.

Yet the very first experiments with sugar-cane growing and sugar making on Santo Domingo had been doomed to failure. When two planters there tried to make sugar—Aguilón in 1505–6 and Ballester in 1512—Spain was not yet ready to support their ambitions, nor were the skills extant in Santo Domingo able to sustain them. The only available milling techniques were probably modeled on tenth-century Egyptian edge-roller mill designs, originally intended for use as olive presses. Such devices were inefficient and wasteful of labor. Another serious problem was the labor supply itself. The rapid destruction of the indigenous Arawakan-speaking Taino Indians of Santo Domingo had left too little manpower even for the gold mines, let alone for the experimental sugar plantations. The first African slaves were imported before 1503, and in spite of local fears of depredations by slave runaways (cimarrones), the importations continued. By 1509 enslaved Africans were being imported to work the royal mines; others soon followed to power the sugar industry.

SUGAR BECOMES COST-EFFECTIVE

When the surgeon Gonzalo de Vellosa—perhaps taking note of the rising prices of sugar in Europe—imported skilled sugar masters from the Canary Islands in 1515, he took the first step toward creating an authentic sugar industry in the Caribbean. With the Canary Island technicians, he (and his new partners, the Tapia brothers) imported a mill with two vertical rollers, usable with either animal or water power and "patterned on that developed in 1449 by Pietro Speciale." The gold deposits in Santo Domingo were soon nearly exhausted; labor was more and more likely to be African, as the vertiginous decline of the aboriginal population continued. But the price of sugar had become high enough in Europe to compensate partly for cost of transporting it, and to encourage additional risks in production, perhaps especially in Spain's settled Caribbean colonies, where alternative opportunities (such as mining) were shrinking.

One scholar has estimated that the mill fabricated by the Canary Island engineers in Santo Domingo could grind enough cane in one season to produce 125 tons of sugar a year if water-powered, and "perhaps a third of that" if powered by animals. Vellosa and his associates lacked the capital to develop the infant industry by themselves. But they took advantage of the presence of three Jeronymite fathers, sent to Santo Domingo to supervise Indian labor policy, who eventually became the de facto governors of the colony. At first the Jeronymites merely endorsed the pleas of the planters for royal support. Soon, however, they made loans of state revenues they had collected to the planters. When the new king, Charles I, ordered the replacement of the Jeronymites by the royal judge Rodrigo de Figueroa, the policy of state assistance continued and expanded. By the 1530s, the island had a "fairly stable total" of thirty-four mills; and by 1568, "plantations owning a hundred-fifty to two hundred slaves were not uncommon. A few of the more magnificent estates possessed up to five hundred slaves, with production figures correspondingly high." One interesting feature of this development was the part played by the state and, indeed, by civil servants, who owned, administered, bought, and sold plantations. Not only was there no private and separate "planter class" at the outset; the commission merchants and other intermediaries who emerge in the Caribbean sugar colonies of other, rival powers were absent.

THE SUGAR INDUSTRY IN SPANISH AMERICA FADES

In the other Greater Antilles—Cuba, Puerto Rico, and Jamaica—Spanish settlers eventually brought in sugar cane, the methods for its cultivation, the technology of water- and animal-powered mills, enslaved labor, and the process for grinding, boiling, and fabricating sugars and molasses from extracted juice, as well as for distilling rum from the molasses. And yet this burgeoning Spanish American industry came to almost nothing—in spite of royal support, much intelligent experimentation, and successful production. The Portuguese planters in Brazil succeeded where the Spaniards in the Antilles failed. Within only a century, the French, and even more the British (though with Dutch help from the outset), became the western world's great sugar makers and exporters. One wonders why the early phase of the Hispanic sugar industry stagnated so swiftly after such promising beginnings, and the explanations we have are not entirely satisfactory. The flight of island colonists to the Mexican mainland after the conquest of Tenochtitlán (1519–21); the Spaniards' obsession with metallic riches; the excessively authoritarian controls imposed by the crown on all productive private enterprise in the

New World; the chronic lack of capital for investment; the so-called *deshonor del trabajo* (ignobility of [manual] labor) supposedly typical of the Spanish colonists—these factors seem reasonable, but are not entirely convincing. Probably we will not learn why such important early experiments failed until we better understand the nature of the Spanish market for Caribbean sugars, and Spain's ability or inability to export a sugar surplus. With Spain's conquests of Mexico and the Andes, a basic shift was created in policy: for more than two centuries thereafter, the Caribbean possessions served primarily as way stations and fortresses along the trade routes, signaling Spain's unproductive, tribute-taking, labor-squandering role in the Americas. The pioneering opportunity was soon lost from about 1580 in the Greater Antilles, until the French and the English began sugar-cane planting on the smaller islands (particularly Barbados and Martinique); after 1650, the Caribbean region produced little sugar for export. By that time the European market situation had modified, and the momentum of production had passed out of Spanish hands.

Whereas the Spaniards (and, to a lesser extent, the Portuguese) concentrated their colonizing efforts in the New World on the extraction of precious metals, for their North European rivals trade and the production of marketable commodities mattered more, and plantation products figured importantly—cotton, indigo, and, soon enough, two beverage crops: cacao, a New World cultigen and more an indigenous food than a drink, and coffee, of African origin. The costs of labor and the lack of capital held down New World plantation production at first, and gains were made at the cost of production elsewhere. "To thrive, the colonists had to catch better or cheaper fish than the Dutch in the Baltic or the North Sea, to trap or persuade the Indians to trap better or cheaper furs than the Russians, to grow better or cheaper sugar than the Javanese or Bengalis." The first crop in the New World to win a market for itself was tobacco, an American domesticate, swiftly transformed from a rare upper-class luxury into a working-class necessity. Tobacco made headway even against royal disapproval, and became part of the consumption of ordinary folk by the seventeenth century. But by the end of that century, sugar was outpacing tobacco in both the British and the French West Indies; by 1700, the value of sugar reaching England and Wales was double that of tobacco. The shift from tobacco to sugar was initially even more pronounced in the French Caribbean colonies than in the British, though in the long term the French market for sugar never attained the scale of the British market.

OPPORTUNITIES FOR BRITAIN, FRANCE, AND THE NETHERLANDS

Certain facts stand out in the history of sugar between the early decades of the seventeenth century, when the British, Dutch, and French established Caribbean plantations, and the middle of the nineteenth century, by which time Cuba and Brazil were the major centers of New World production. Over this long period, sugar production grew steadily, as more westerners consumed sugar and each consumer used it more heavily. Yet technological changes in the field, in grinding, and even in refining itself were relatively minor. Generally speaking, the enlarged market for sugar was satisfied by a steady extension of production rather than by sharp increases in yield per acre of land or ton of cane, or in productivity per worker.

But the impulse to produce sugar, as well as to trade in it and consume it, can be traced further back in the record. Soon after Sir Walter Raleigh's first voyage to the Guianas in 1595, the English explorer Captain Charles Leigh attempted to start a settlement on the Waiapoco (Oyapock) River (now the border between Brazil and French Guiana). Though neither effort succeeded, both were connected with an interest in sugar and other tropical products. In 1607 Jamestown—the first English colony in the New World— was founded. Sugar cane was brought there in 1619—as were the first enslaved Africans to reach an English colony—but the cane would not grow. Three years earlier, sugar cane had been planted in Bermuda, but this tiny, arid island never produced sugar. These facts indicate that even before the seventeenth century there was a lively awareness of the desirability of sugar, and of at least some of its potential market—in short, of its long-term profitability as a commodity. The aim of acquiring colonies that could produce sugar (among other things) for the metropolis hence predates the seventeenth century. And before she was able to produce sugar in her own colonies, England was not above stealing it. In 1591 a Spanish spy reported that "English booty in West India [American] produce is so great that sugar is cheaper in London than it is in Lisbon or the Indies themselves."

AN ENGLISH SLAVE TRADER'S FIRST VOYAGE

RICHARD HAKLUYT

African slaves first came to the New World in the 1510s to work on Spanish sugar plantations in the Caribbean. Slaves were already performing similar work in North Africa, and in such Atlantic island groups as the Canaries. The Spanish and Portuguese who controlled the New World, however, hoped that Native Americans rather than Africans would provide the bulk of their cheap labor.

Beginning in the mid-1500s, English merchants seeking to interfere and compete with Spanish shipping and commerce brought slave cargoes from Africa to the Caribbean, thus inaugurating the Atlantic slave trade. The following selection is from a contemporary account of the first voyage of John Hawkins, the first Englishman to engage in the trade. The account traces Hawkins's journey from England to the Guinea coast in Africa, then to the island of Hispaniola (modern-day Haiti and the Dominican Republic). Spanish traders, enemies to England, were initially hesitant to do business with Hawkins. Yet Hawkins was ultimately able to demonstrate that the slave trade offered huge profits.

Richard Hakluyt published the first histories of England's overseas exploits in the 1580s.

Excerpted from *Voyages of the Elizabethan Seamen: Select Narratives from the "Principal Navigations" of Richard Hakluyt*, edited by Edward John Payne (Oxford: Clarendon Press, 1907).

The FIRST VOYAGE of the Right Worshipful and Valiant Knight SIR JOHN HAWKINS, sometimes Treasurer of Her Majesty's Navy Royal, made to the WEST INDIES, 1562.

Master John Hawkins having made divers voyages to the isles of the Canaries, and there by his good and upright dealing being grown in love and favour with the people, informed himself amongst them, by diligent inquisition, of the state of the West India, whereof he had received some knowledge by the instructions of his father, but increased the same by the advertisements and reports of that people. And being amongst other particulars assured that Negros were very good merchandise in Hispaniola, and that store of Negros might easily be had upon the coast of Guinea, resolved with himself to make trial thereof, and communicated that device with his worshipful friends of London. . . . All which persons liked so well of his intention, that they became liberal contributors and adventurers in the action. For which purpose there were three good ships immediately provided: the one called the *Solomon*, of the burden of 120 tons, wherein Master Hawkins himself went as General: the second the *Swallow*, of 100 tons, wherein went for captain Master Thomas Hampton: and the third the *Jonas*, a bark of 40 tons, wherein the master supplied the captain's room: in which small fleet Master Hawkins took with him not above 100 men, for fear of sickness and other inconveniences, whereunto men in long voyages are commonly subject.

With this company he put off and departed from the coast of England in the month of October, 1562, and in his course touched first at Teneriffe, where he received friendly entertainment. From thence he passed to Sierra Leona, upon the coast of Guinea, which place by the people of the country is called Tagarin, where he stayed some good time, and got into his possession, partly by the sword and partly by other means, to the number of 300 Negros at the least, besides other merchandises which that country yieldeth. With this prey he sailed over the ocean sea unto the island of Hispaniola, and arrived first at the port of Isabella: and there he had reasonable utterance of his English commodities, as also of some part of his Negros, trusting the Spaniards no further, than that by his own strength he was able still to master them. From the port of Isabella he went to Puerto de Plata, where he made like sales, standing always upon his guard: from thence also he sailed to Monte Christi, another port on the north side of Hispaniola, and the last place of his touching, where he had peaceable traffic, and made vent of the

whole number of his Negros: for which he received in those
three places, by way of exchange, such a quantity of merchandise that he did not only lade his own three ships with hides,
ginger, sugars, and some quantity of pearls, but he freighted also
two other hulks with hides and other like commodities, which
he sent into Spain. And thus, leaving the island, he returned and
disembogued, passing out by the islands of the Caicos, without
further entering into the Bay of Mexico, in this his first voyage
to the West India. And so, with prosperous success and much
gain to himself and the aforesaid adventurers, he came home,
and arrived in the month of September, 1563.

THE CHILI PEPPER TRAVELS THE GLOBE

JEAN ANDREWS

The New World of the Americas offered the Old World of Africa, Europe, and Asia a huge variety of new food products. Corn, beans, peanuts, pumpkins, squash, tomatoes, and potatoes are only a few of the foods that explorers and settlers took home to Europe, and from there to the rest of the world. Other substances, cocoa and tobacco in particular, offered Old World peoples new sweets and stimulants. Foods, indeed, form a major component of what scholars call the Columbian Exchange—the exchange of goods, ideas, people, and diseases across the Atlantic Ocean.

In the following selection, Jean Andrews describes how the chili pepper, a product originally from Brazil, entered world cuisines. Peppers, which belong to the genus *Capsicum* and of which there are dozens of varieties, quickly became a rival to the more well known black pepper of India and Southeast Asia. By the 1600s, peoples from Japan to India, Turkey to Mexico were using various chili peppers to add spice to their meals.

Jean Andrews is a naturalist, writer, and gourmet chef. She is the author of *Peppers: The Domesticated Capsicums*.

I t is the New World chili pepper that gives the characteristic bite to many Old World cuisines. What would the food of India be without curry—or curry powder without peppers? Indonesia's sambals without their distinctive fire? Hungary's goulash without paprika? Italy's antipasto without pepperoni? Five hundred years ago, none of the people in these countries

Adapted from "The Peripatetic Chili Pepper: Diffusion of the Domesticated Capsicums Since Columbus," by Jean Andrews, in *Chilies to Chocolate: Food the Americans Gave the World*, edited by Nelson Foster and Linda Cordell. Copyright © 1992 The Arizona Board of Regents. Reprinted by permission of the University of Arizona Press.

had ever seen or heard of a chili pepper. No Old World language had a word for chili peppers before 1492.

For Christopher Columbus, reaching the New World constituted a failure to achieve his objective, which was to find a route to the spice lands of the Far East, and he died thinking that he had found the fabled Orient instead of the New World with its vastly different kinds of riches. One of these treasures was the pungent flavoring widely used in the Americas and, on the islands of the Caribbean, referred to as *ají*. Columbus called the unfamiliar spice "pepper" (*pimiento*) after the black pepper (*pimienta*) he was seeking.

Columbus carried specimens of the new pepper, which belongs to the genus Capsicum, back to the Iberian Peninsula, and from there it spread rapidly around the globe, changing and enhancing the cuisines of every land it touched. Today it may be the most widely used spice in the world. Certainly it ranks high on the list, alongside black pepper (*Piper nigrum*), which is derived from an unrelated plant.

CHILI PEPPERS CAME FROM THE NEW WORLD

So swiftly and thoroughly did the chili pepper disperse that botanists long held it to be native to India or Indochina, but all scholars now concur that it is a New World plant with origins in South America. Researchers still disagree, however, about just where the capsicums arose. One group, led by [botany professor] W. Hardy Eshbaugh, says its place of origin was central Bolivia, while another, whose chief proponent is Barbara Pickersgill [British botanist], claims that it was the area east of Bolivia in the mountains of southern Brazil. It seems safe to say that chili peppers originated in the area south of the wet forests of Amazonia and the semiarid cerrado of Brazil. . . .

The Portuguese part of this saga of exploration and trade began more than half a century before Columbus reached the Americas. Under the guidance of Prince Henry the Navigator, the Portuguese began their imperial quest on the western coast of Africa, and by 1460 they had traversed the bulge extending from Cape Bojador to Cape Verde and Sierra Leone. They continued down the coast, bit by bit, until in 1488 Bartholomeu Dias rounded the Cape of Good Hope and sighted the Indian Ocean.

During these years the Portuguese began trading in slaves and African goods while continuing their search for spices, gold, and additional sources of slaves. Six years after the discovery of America, Vasco da Gama arrived in India via the Cape of Good Hope and the Indian Ocean, thereby establishing the Portuguese trade monopoly earlier guaranteed by the Treaty of Tordesillas [signed in 1494, which divided the globe into Portuguese and Spanish zones of trade and exploration]. During the following century of unchallenged dominion, Portuguese vessels transported New World plants and goods, including chili peppers, along this route to Africa and the Far East. . . .

THE CHILI PEPPER REACHES ASIA

Portuguese traders introduced the capsicums to India with equal speed, and three varieties of chili peppers were seen there by 1542. According to the early European botanist Carolus Clusius, *Capsicum* was known in Goa [a Portuguese colony in India] by the middle of the sixteenth century as "Pernambuco pepper." Apparently, Brazilian chili peppers were loaded aboard ships bound for Lisbon, where they were transferred to the huge carracks of the India fleet that annually made the long voyage around Africa to Goa, and some of the peppers carried with them to the Malabar Coast the name of their supposed place of origin in Brazil. . . .

New World capsicums reached the East Indies (Indonesia) by 1540, according to [British botanist] Henry N. Ridley. They were introduced either by the Portuguese or by Arab and Gujarati traders, who had been active in Southeast Asia for a thousand years. Since 1511, Malacca had served as a forward base for Portuguese trading and missionary expansion into China (1513), Japan (1542), and eastern Melanesia, and by 1550 the Portuguese had a permanent foothold on Macao. Their trading galleon, the *Nao da Macao*, ran from Goa via Malacca to Macao and thence to Nagasaki, Japan, until the mid–seventeenth century. From any of these Portuguese ports of call, local seagoing craft—Malaccan, Javanese, Siamese (Thai), Cambodian, and Chinese, as well as Indian and Arabic—could easily have carried American peppers throughout the East Indies and the Spice Islands (the Moluccas) and even to the Philippines and China. The chili peppers may also have been disseminated by traders with Arab and Persian colonies that had been established during the seventh and eighth centuries in Canton and Hangchow, on China's southeast coast. . . .

It is probable that the new spice reached China by one or more sea routes. In their southern ports the Chinese maintained intimate trade relations with the Portuguese, particularly after the founding of the Portuguese trading colony in Macao. Chinese merchants also dealt with the Portuguese in the Spice Islands and with the Spanish in the Philippines, and either of these places may have served as their source of the hot little fruits from America. During that early period there was no regular overland trade to carry capsicums between the coastal cities and interior provinces like Yunnan or Szechuan.

TRADE ACROSS THE PACIFIC

The Portuguese reached Japan in 1542, and from then until 1636, when Japan closed its doors to all except the Dutch, there was ample time for the trading galleon from Goa to bring Japan its first capsicums. On the other hand, the Japanese may have come in contact with chili peppers through trading missions of their own, as Japanese vessels were already plying the waters of Southeast Asia by the time the Portuguese arrived in Japan. Using ships built from Spanish designs, the Japanese also had some direct trade with the west coast of New Spain, in what is now Mexico, until access was denied in 1611.

Portugal put the Philippines on European maps in 1512, but it was Spain that colonized the archipelago after Ferdinand Magellan claimed it for Spain in 1521. The first settlers were sent out from New Spain in 1542, and the first capsicums may have come with them. In 1564, after the Spanish navigator Andres de Urdaneta showed that it was possible to sail to Mexico from the Far East by following prevailing westerlies, a Manila-Acapulco galleon route was established, providing regular contacts between the two ports for the next two and a half centuries and thus expediting the introduction of American food plants not only to the Philippines but also to Micronesia and eastern Melanesia. To this day, Filipinos refer to many of these plants by names adapted from Native American languages. . . .

PEPPERS WERE UNPOPULAR IN EUROPE

Curiously, Europe itself proved to be slow when it came to accepting the New World peppers. In an epistle dated 1493, Peter Martyr wrote that Columbus had brought Spain "pepper more pungent than that from the Caucasus," and although we are told by Oviedo (1526) that in the New World "Christians"—meaning the Spanish colonists—were quick to eat the new spice in as great a quantity as the natives did, stay-at-home Spaniards seem to have been less culinarily adventurous. We can safely assume that chili peppers were being grown on the Iberian Peninsula as early as 1493, but they were favored more as curiosities and ornamentals than as seasoning. Unlike their creole and mestizo relations in the New World, Iberians even today have not acquired a taste for the fiery fruit. . . .

Like the Portuguese and Spanish, other western Europeans were slow to take to chili peppers. Eastern Europeans integrated them more readily into local food patterns, but Europeans as a whole did not widely appreciate their value as a spice until the first decade of the nineteenth century, when capsicums were reintroduced from the Balkans during the Napoleonic blockade of European ports and won acceptance as a substitute for other imported seasonings.

Ironically, the capsicums came very late to North America. Except for the two Spanish colonies of Santa Fe and Saint Augustine, chili peppers were to be found nowhere north of modern-day Mexico until after colonization by northern Europeans. About 1600 the Dutch, English, and French broke the Iberian trade monopoly in the Far East, and the spice market became a free-for-all. Thus, both the British and the Dutch had ample sources of peppers by the time they began to colonize North America early in the seventeenth century, but peppers did not take hold there until later, when the plantation system and African slavery were instituted. Southern plantations had a climate suitable to the cultivation of peppers, and the African slaves, both from the West Indies and directly from Africa, had already developed eating patterns that demanded hot peppers.

Thus capsicums traveled from the New World to the Old and back again to Europe by way of the Orient—all before the arrival of the Pilgrims at Plymouth Rock. During the time required for that journey, peoples of Africa, India, the Middle East, and the Far East so completely incorporated the new spices into their cookery that each area had developed not only a unique cuisine based on capsicums but also unique peppers not to be found in the Americas today.

CATHOLIC MISSIONARIES MOVED AGGRESSIVELY IN INDIA

J.M. RICHARDS

Beginning with Vasco da Gama in 1498, Portuguese explorers were the first Europeans to reach the trade centers of Asia. Their colonies, however, were limited to a few coastal outposts. The most important of these were Goa in India and Macao in China. Portugal was not satisfied, however, with mere trade. They hoped to bring Roman Catholic Christianity to Asia, and Goa and Macao became centers of missionary activity as well as commerce.

In the following selection, J.M. Richards describes the attempts by Roman Catholic missionaries to convert the Hindu inhabitants of Goa to Christianity. Their efforts ranged from building cathedrals and schools to training Indian priests. As Richards points out, Catholics grew less tolerant after the Counter-Reformation began in Europe. They destroyed Hindu temples, banned certain Hindu rituals, and brought the Inquisition to Goa. The Inquisition, the Church's legal arm, did not hesitate to use intimidation and torture in this small Portuguese corner of India.

J.M. Richards was a writer and journalist who wrote for the London *Times* for over twenty years.

Since to the Portuguese the extension of their military and mercantile power was inseparable from the spread of their religion—as indeed it was to the Mughal empire, which was establishing itself at the same date further north—the Catholic Church played an increasingly dominant role. The first missionaries were Dominican friars who came out as chaplains in [conqueror of Goa] Albuquerque's fleet. The first conversions of the native Goans to Christianity were made by the Franciscans, who came out in 1517. And then in 1542 Jesuit missionaries from Portugal reached Goa, led by St Francis Xavier who travelled all over the East but remained Provincial [the top Church official] of Goa until his death ten years later. He was canonized in 1622. He established schools and universities and brought out the first printing-press, which was not however set up until 1556. All education, as was customary throughout Europe at that time, was in the hands of the Church, from the College of the Holy Faith in Goa down to the parish schools which St Francis founded. He ordained Goan converts as secular priests and, in pursuit of large-scale conversion, fostered the work of the religious orders whose special task this was: the Jesuits and Dominicans —and later the Augustinians—in the island of Goa, the Jesuits also in neighbouring Salsete, the Franciscans in Bardez across the Mandovi River. The first seminary for the teaching of theology was founded in 1541 and three others during the following hundred years. The Jesuits, too, as well as acquiring land in Goa encouraged cultivation, especially the planting of coconut trees.

PORTUGUESE CATHOLICS OPPOSED HINDUISM

Many of the bishops, priests and missionaries sent out from Portugal spent the rest of their lives in the East, and therefore had more influence than the viceroys and lay officials who were normally appointed for a three-year term; and the Church's intolerance soon made itself felt. This was especially so after one of the viceroys, Constantino de Braganza, under whom the diocese of Goa was raised to an archdiocese and Metropolitan See of the East, brought out the Inquisition in 1560.

Albuquerque had not interfered with Hindu religious practices nor had he destroyed Hindu temples. But from about 1540 onwards, under the influence of the Counter Reformation in Europe and with the arrival of the Inquisition in Goa, this liberal policy was reversed. A strict censorship of literature was imposed. New laws forbade the public profession of any but the Christian religion—indeed of any but the Roman Catholic, for even the Syrian Christians, who had been in India since long before the arrival of the Portuguese, were treated as heretics and their forcible conversion to the Roman rite attempted. Although the activities of the Inquisition were directed against Christian heretics, especially Protestants, and Jews, and not against [Hindus], in Goa the Hindus were also its target, being accused of "disrespect for Christianity".

A viceregal decree of 1567 required the destruction of all [Hindu] temples in Portuguese-controlled areas, the banning of ritual ablutions—an essential element of Hinduism—and the expulsion of non-Christian priests, holy men and teachers. Hindus were forbidden to visit their temples in adjoining lands and were compelled in some cases to attend at churches and convents to listen to the Christian gospel. Social intercourse between Christians and non-Christians was discouraged. Christian converts were favoured in the appointment of Goans to public office, and some offices were reserved for converts. The conversion of Hindus may have been facilitated by the fact that for generations the Hindus had been harassed by the Muslims, and felt that the religion of their new Christian masters might give them some protection.

HINDUS WERE FORCED TO ADOPT CHRISTIANITY

The law still laid down that the conversion of those of other religions should be by persuasion and not by force—a law that was not very effective in practice since persuasion, as the enactments described above suggest, included methods little short of force. Moreover an exception to this law was made, in Goa at least, in the case of Hindu orphans, and an orphan was defined for this purpose as a boy under 14 years or a girl under 12 who had lost his or her father, even if the mother or grandparents were still alive. All such "children of heathen in the city and islands of Goa", said a decree published in Lisbon in 1559, "should forthwith be taken and handed over to the College of Sao Paulo of the Company of Jesus in the said city of Goa, in order that they may be baptized, educated and catechized by the Fathers of the said College." A later decree specifically authorized the use of force in removing such orphans from their families and the punishment of families who tried to smuggle their children away into Hindu territory.

MATTEO RICCI: A BRIDGE BETWEEN EUROPE AND CHINA

JONATHAN D. SPENCE

During the sixteenth century, Roman Catholic missionaries aggressively introduced Christianity to the new areas settled by European explorers. One of their greatest targets was China, which offered a huge population of potential converts. To that end, the Portuguese base at Macao, in southern China, offered missionaries a convenient, permanent base from which to work. Missionaries to China, however, quickly learned that conversion might go both ways.

In the following selection, Jonathan D. Spence summarizes the life and activities of Matteo Ricci, an Italian Jesuit who spent much of his life in China. Ricci acquired such expertise in the Chinese language and Chinese philosophy that local officials invited him to be the first European to visit the Chinese emperor in Beijing. Ricci took pains to demonstrate to the Chinese that European culture was advanced in such fields as astronomy, geometry, and mathematics. However, Spence notes, Ricci found the Chinese slow to accept Christianity. Indeed, Ricci had to modify certain aspects of the Christian message to make it understandable and palatable to the Chinese. He understood the Chinese emphasis on order and tradition, and contrasted it favorably to the disorder of Europe. Yet Ricci remained frustrated by what he thought was China's adherence to "primitive superstitions."

Jonathan D. Spence is Sterling Professor of History at Yale University and the author of a number of books on Chinese history.

Ricci's account of his labors in China was to give European readers a new level of insight into the realities of Chinese society, even if one tinged with exaggeration and nostalgia. Born in the Italian city of Macerata in 1552, Matteo Ricci was educated in the Jesuit College of Rome, which at the time was probably the best school in Europe for science and mathematics. There he also received a broad training in Latin and theology, in geography, and in the then important field of mnemonic training—one of Ricci's memory teachers, Panigarola, could allegedly recall as many as a hundred thousand mental images by using the memory placement and storage theories then in vogue. After formally joining the Society of Jesus, Ricci was posted to Goa, on the West Indian coast, where a Catholic enclave was ensconced in the recently established Portuguese base. By 1582 he was transferred to Macao, on the tip of southern China, and after intensive Chinese language training in Macao, he entered China in 1583 and established a small residence near Canton.

INTRODUCING THE WEST TO CHINA

Ricci was to live the remainder of his life in China, first in the south, then in Nanjing on the Yangzi River, and finally in Peking, where he died in 1610. No Westerner had ever come near to attaining his levels of knowledge of Chinese culture, language, and society. Within a year of settling in China, Ricci realized that if he was to convert the Chinese to Christianity, he must do it by proving the advanced level of Western culture to the Chinese elite. In pursuit of this goal, as soon as his language was good enough he produced a global map, with commentary, to show the advanced levels of Western geography and astronomy; a book on friendship, to demonstrate the high levels of intrapersonal morality in the West; a manual on memory theory, to show the Chinese how the Westerners organized their knowledge; and a translation—completed with the aid of a highly educated Chinese collaborator—of the opening chapters of Euclid's *Geometry*. He also carefully crafted a complex series of religious dialogues between a Catholic priest and a Chinese scholar, designed to show the superiority of the Western spiritual tradition and the balance of logic and faith that lay at its heart.

Ricci's early views on China are known only through his letters home and to his superiors in the order, but after his death his colleagues found that he had left two lengthy manuscripts, one analyzing and describing Chinese culture and society, and one summarizing the history of the Jesuit mission in China, and his own role in the conversion process. (He destroyed a third manuscript, his own spiritual diary, on his deathbed.) When edited by his fellow Jesuits, translated into Latin, and published in Europe in 1616, the two surviving manuscripts at once established a new benchmark for the study and description of China.

Like those that had come before, Ricci's portrait of China was strongly favorable. In contrast to the fragmented states of post-Reformation Europe—the murderous Thirty Years War erupted in 1618, following hard on the heels of the bitter religious wars in France and the Netherlands—China offered a picture of a vast, unified, well-ordered country, held together by a central controlling orthodoxy, that of Confucianism. Of Confucius himself, Ricci wrote that "if we critically examine his actions and sayings as they are recorded in history, we shall be forced to admit that he was the equal of the pagan philosophers and superior to most of them." Ricci wrote that though directed at a distance by reclusive emperors, the daily administration of the country was in the hands of a professional bureaucracy selected by a complex hierarchical examination based on merit. Social life was regulated by complex laws of ritual and deportment that induced social harmony. The working classes knew their place, marriages were harmoniously arranged by the young people's parents, and the practice of footbinding kept the women chastely at home. The classical Chinese language itself was so difficult that the years spent in mastering it curbed the "youthful licentiousness" to which China's young men might otherwise have been prone. China's patent distrust of foreigners could be easily explained by their worries over national security and the unsettling effect of newcomers and merchants on their long-established ways. Even the Chinese mode of drinking alcohol was so well controlled that hangovers were virtually unknown.

RICCI ADJUSTS CHRISTIANITY TO SUIT CHINA

Given this generally favorable depiction of Chinese moral and social life, Ricci was at some pains to point out why the Chinese were resistant to the appeals of Christianity. He explained this by a number of factors: one was the dominant role of Buddhism in China, which Ricci described harshly as a mass of primitive superstitions, fostered by uneducated and often immoral monks and priests. Another was the deeply entrenched belief in astrology, which had replaced scientific astronomy as the primal mode for studying the heavens, and had come to dominate many levels of Chinese decisions over private and public life. Overlapping in some ways with both these aspects, but also raising new elements and problems, was the system of Chinese ancestor worship. Ricci spent many years pondering these ceremonies, and their relationship to the conversion procedure. Since it became clear that most Chinese could not be persuaded to embrace Christianity if they were also told to give up the homage they paid to their ancestors, Ricci redefined ancestral worship. He concluded that the Chinese rites to ancestors were acts of homage to the departed rather than religious invocations designed to obtain favors or benefit. The same in essence was true of Chinese ritual ceremonies in the name of Confucius. Accordingly, Chinese might continue to observe such ceremonies even after they had been converted to Christianity. (They should, however, be persuaded to give up their concubines before conversion.)

In choosing the Chinese characters that should be used to translate the Christian monotheistic concept of God, Ricci took another characteristically ingenious yet compromising stance. He decided that the two Chinese characters *Shang-di*, connoting something approximating the "Lord-of-all" or "Highest Ruler," could be retained for use in the new context. This was partly because current Chinese use of *Shang-di* was not religious in the Christian spiritual sense. Ricci also argued that in the far recesses of the Chinese past such a concept of the one true God had existed, although the knowledge of that God had subsequently faded from Chinese consciousness with the reediting of the cultural past by the Buddhist-influenced neo-Confucians of the twelfth century. Yet to balance these interpretations, Ricci suggested that a new coinage—*Tian-zhu* or "Heaven's Lord"—might also be used by missionaries and their Chinese converts to avoid the confusing cultural overlays of *Shang-di*.

Ricci made few criticisms of the Chinese in his lengthy manuscript. He did suggest—and this was later to become a fateful argument—that Chinese science had somehow fallen behind that of the West by failing to develop its full potentials, once so strongly part of Chinese culture. The Chinese, wrote Ricci, "have no conception of the rules of logic," and consequently "the science of ethics with them is a series of confused maxims and deductions." Similarly, though "at one time they were quite proficient in arithmetic and geometry, in the study and teaching of these branches of learning they labored with more or less confusion." The implication was clearly that with a more rigorous system of logic, and a renewed concentration on mathematics and science, which the West was in a position to offer, China would become a better place.

The Renaissance Closes with an Era of Great Leaders

CHAPTER 7

AKBAR THE GREAT CREATED A NEW INDIA

WALDEMAR HANSEN

Akbar was the third of the Mughal emperors, reigning from 1556 until 1605. His grandfather Babur began the Mughal conquest of India early in the sixteenth century, but Akbar was the emperor who managed to bring together India's diverse political, religious, and cultural components to create what many historians describe as modern India. In the following selection, Waldemar Hansen, an author and playwright based in New York City, examines some of Akbar's accomplishments.

India has always been inhabited by diverse peoples, and its borders have shifted constantly over the course of history. When Akbar took the throne, much of India was still divided among various kings, or rajas. While most were Hindu, many were Muslim or Sikh, and frequent warfare plagued India. In addition, large populations of Christians, Buddhists, and followers of other religions added more complexity to a region best described as an ever-changing patchwork of castes, cultures, and languages. According to Hansen, Akbar's genius lay in inspiring the peoples of India to follow a single ruler above all others. In addition, Akbar demonstrated that Indian civilization transcended religious, cultural, or geographic boundaries.

I t was Akbar who first displayed imaginative Mughal genius. In 1556, at the age of thirteen, he acceded to what was left of [the first Mughal conqueror] Babur's domains; by 1560 he had seized the reins of government from a regent, and within forty-five years achieved the impossible feat of welding together

Excerpted from *The Peacock Throne: The Drama of Mogul India*, by Waldemar Hansen (New York: Holt, Rinehart & Winston, 1972). Copyright © 1972 by Waldemar Hansen. Reprinted by permission of the author.

two-thirds of India (including all of today's Pakistan). Short and stocky with a lucky wart on the left side of his nose, indefatigable Akbar literally mesmerized the subcontinent. By war and persuasion he won over those proud rajahs who ruled enormous desert realms in Rajputana. His tolerant harem blended Indian and Mughal, Persian, and even Armenian women. He abolished Islam's hated religious poll tax, established an effective reform of land levy, and inaugurated a daring liberalism which placed Hindu on a par with Moslem. In that momentary exotic capital at Fatehpur Sikri he even concocted his own weirdly eclectic religion—really a spiritual syncretism far in advance of its time. Akbar flouted orthodox Moslem bigotry by making himself virtual pope of India. All these innovations went side by side with hard-pressed military campaigns enlarging the empire: Gujarat and Bengal were conquered, quarrelsome Afghans took heed, Kashmir found itself annexed along with fortresses on the very borders of Persia's domains. Akbar seized hitherto unseizable areas in a stubbornly resistant mid-India.

These achievements were quite untypical of either his progenitors or descendants: no esthetics, no cunning, only a majestic elemental force—"like handling ducks' eggs after hens'." Akbar's physical prowess exceeded Babur's. His passions could terrify: flaring up at the treachery of a foster-brother caught in palace intrigue, he stunned the man with a blow of his fist and then had him thrown from a parapet with the judgment "son of a bitch" punctuating his fall. Yet though steeped in violence and war, Akbar could also be deeply humane. Virtually untutored, he sparked intellectual curiosity and surrounded himself with eminent scholars. Akbar the Great, third of the Mughal emperors, compared favorably with any European monarch of his period.

AKBAR CEMENTED MUGHAL AUTHORITY

Perhaps he was even greater than they: to unify seventeenth-century India required more than ruthless Oriental tyranny, while charitable humanism would have been laughed at. Yet this Hercules had combined authority with stunning broadmindedness, exerting such powers of conciliation that he was able to unite India's disparate religious and ethnic components at a time when abstract national concepts were totally unknown (at least to India). Then, to ensure respect for himself and his descendants, the miracle worker had hypnotized Hindu and Moslem alike into accepting holy monarchic transcendence: both religions must obey the Mughal emperor, and any opposition was sacrilege. Abruptly, haloes began to appear behind the royal head in Mughal court painting. Akbar's strange pantheistic religion may have died with him, but the imperial sanctity he created would linger until 1857—long after the cessation of effective Mughal power.

Akbar's son Jahangir and grandson Shah Jahan could literally coast on all his glory. In the tradition created for them, they were nothing less than semi-divine; tinged with mystique, they ruled a Moslem church and a Hindu-Moslem state.

Hindus hoped that their interference might be limited to the collection of revenues. And revenues were indeed great: the wealth of the Mughal Empire was by now so enormous that all attempts at inventory would be given up after four hundred pairs of treasury scales oscillated day and night for five months. . . .

INDIA'S ETHNIC DIVERSITY

Pullulating [teeming] within these cells of empire, a hundred million subjects fell under Mughal hegemony—the Moslems an ironic minority amid a mass of Hindus whose potential for rebellion against alien rule seemed for the moment neutralized by regional division, jealousy, and mistrust. It was all an ethnic beehive: heroic Rajput clans, fierce tribes swarming over Afghanistan plateaus, sturdy Jats, bearded Sikhs of the Punjab with combs gathering together the woman's-length hair which their religion forbade them to cut, and white-garbed Jains who considered all life so holy that they wore masks to avoid killing even a gnat by breathing. Islam alone bristled with sects and intra-religious frictions, to say nothing of the enormous complexities of a coexisting Hinduism with its rigid caste system and stubborn village autonomy. In addition, a heterogeneous assortment of adventurers—Turks, Persians, Tartars, Uzbeks, Circassians, and Georgians, even Africans and Europeans—made their way to the Mughal court. . . .

Helping his descendants to rule such huge domains, Akbar had refined a practical realm based on familiar sources. No one could fail to recognize its affinity to old Baghdad and Ispahan and the whole fairy-tale East: a quasi-Arab, quasi-Persian hierarchy had simply been adapted to an Indian setting. The emperor presided over his typically opulent Oriental court; he enjoyed an exclusive harem, where mysterious ladies were strictly veiled by jealous laws of purdah—the very word referred to screens of state behind which they viewed the spectacle of durbar [official meetings]. Most of these women would be hidden from history in this candidly masculine Mughal world, though a few empresses and princesses asserted their vivid characters. . . .

In any event, such a whirligig of Moslems and Hindus perpetually threatened to shatter into pieces through the accelerations of hatred, jealousy, and religious strife. Their centripetal bond was the powerful personality of the emperor himself—exactly what Akbar had in mind. It was all really a variation on knights in armor, an Oriental round table imported from the steppes of central Asia. Refined by India, the system intermittently worked in its own bizarre way; not a few nobles even proved loyal.

A Detached Emperor Presided over a Vigorous China

Ann Paludan

China's Ming dynasty began in 1368. By the time the emperor Wanli took the throne in 1573, China was the richest and most populous nation on earth. Its population numbered over 100 million, and Chinese craftsmen, industrialists, and merchants found their goods in demand throughout the world. Moreover, the Ming period saw a flowering of Chinese culture and building; two of its legacies, the Forbidden City in Beijing and the Great Wall, still stand as testimonies to China's dynastic tradition. During Wanli's reign, Europeans such as the Jesuit missionary Matteo Ricci reported on China's relative peace and order as well as its many technological advances.

However, as Ann Paludan points out in the following selection, later Ming emperors such as Wanli remained aloof from the vitality and creativity of the Chinese people. While China enjoyed unprecedented economic and intellectual activity, Wanli chose to leave administration and government to councillors and court eunuchs. Moreover, Wanli's extravagance grew to be a drain on the state treasury.

Ann Paludan, a former British Foreign Service officer, has written a number of books on Chinese history and culture.

W anli (1573–1620) ruled for 47 years, the longest reign since Han Wudi in the 2nd century BC. Third (but eldest surviving) son of Longqing, he was 10 years old on accession.

Excerpted from *Chronicle of the Chinese Emperors*, by Ann Paludan. Copyright © 1998 Thames & Hudson Ltd., London. Reprinted by permission of Thames & Hudson Ltd.

During Wanli's reign the social and economic transformation of China into a modern state which had begun in the early 16th century continued. New crops from America such as maize [corn], sweet potatoes and peanuts increased food production and the population reached over 100 million, double that of the early Ming. The 'Single Whip' [which made taxes payable in money rather than land] tax reforms and the spread of silver currency produced an economic boom. Wealth shifted from land to commercial and manufacturing enterprises: the growing of industrial crops like cotton, sugar-cane and tobacco with mills and factories centred in special regions—silk wares in Suzhou, paper factories and the Jingdezhen porcelain kilns in Jiangxi. Technical advances improved the standard of manufactured goods, and with the general expansion of maritime trade in east Asia the demand for Chinese exports of luxury products rocketed, leading to the rise of a new class of extremely wealthy merchants, bankers and businessmen. The new rich class vied with the nobility in conspicuous consumption, building elaborate mansions and gardens and acquiring *objets d'art*, thus further stimulating production. It was a vigorous, creative and productive age and the great cities like Beijing, Nanjing, Suzhou and Hangzhou became centres of intellectual activity. Private academies promoted education and there was a blossoming of popular literature, novels and encyclopedias. This activity took place in spite of government policies, for politically it was a period of decline. After the first decade, Wanli's inaction led to a creeping paralysis of the administration and an inner decay which was to prove fatal.

POLITICAL INSTABILITY AND GOVERNMENT EXTRAVAGANCE

The reign had started well. Under the leadership of the most able of all Ming ministers, Zhang Zhuzheng, supported by Wanli's mother, Lishi, discipline and efficiency in the administration were restored, border attacks repelled and the financial situation stabilized. Wanli became restless under Zhang's strict control, however, and on his death, increasingly withdrew from state affairs. From the age of 25 onwards he blatantly neglected state duties and for the next quarter century, from 1589 to 1615, never appeared at imperial audiences, leaving ministers and foreign envoys to kowtow and pay respects to an empty throne. After 1591, Wanli ceased to perform public ceremonies, refusing even to attend his mother's funeral in 1614. The entire Ming administrative system revolved round the emperor and when he refused to act responsibility fell on the Grand Secretaries or was usurped by the eunuchs. The Grand Secretaries, however, were held at a distance. In 30 years (from 1590 to 1620) Wanli only saw them five times, and it was left to the eunuchs to transmit memorials to the emperor who steadily ignored displeasing subjects, finally refusing to consider all but the most urgent matters of finance and defense. . . .

Financial problems were compounded by the emperor's extravagance. Greedy—he suffered from dizzy spells, his feet and legs hurt and he grew so fat that he could no longer stand unaided—and sensually self-indulgent, he spent vast sums on his tomb and palaces, ordering expensive materials from the outermost parts of the empire. The Jesuit, Matteo Ricci (the first European ever to set foot in the Forbidden City), records seeing a convoy of wood two miles long on the Grand Canal, pulled by tens of thousands of workers, which he was told was being brought from the southwest to Beijing to rebuild two palaces which had burned down; the journey was going to take four years. Inordinately vain, Wanli spent a fortune on his family, clothing, jewellery and other luxuries: his wedding clothes cost 90,000 oz of silver, those for two daughters' weddings over one million, and the investiture of five sons in 1601, 21 million oz. These expenses were all taken from state money, leaving his private purse intact. (The contents of his tomb confirm his interest in clothes.) In addition, there was the cost of supporting the imperial family. [The first Ming emperor] Hongwu's decision to send his sons to the provinces proved an expensive one, for these princes enjoyed huge estates and salaries, keeping personal guards of many thousands; under Jiajing the court was supporting over 33,000 not including wives, concubines, female staff and sons-in-law; under Wanli, there were 45 princes of the first rank and over 23,000 lesser nobility. In some provinces half the revenue went on their support.

THREE STRONGMEN UNIFIED AND STABILIZED JAPAN

EDWIN O. REISCHAUER

Japan spent much of the late 1400s and 1500s in a state of chronic civil war. Competing landlords, often using armies of samurai retainers, competed with one another for superiority. Uprisings among peasants and Buddhist monks added to the instability. In the following selection, Edwin O. Reischauer describes how three men—Oda Nobunaga, Toyotomi Hideyoshi, and Tokugawa Ieyasu—in turn ended the civil wars and returned stability to Japan between 1568 and 1610.

Reischauer examines the accomplishments of each man; among their common strengths was the ability to command the loyalty of subordinate landlords and their clans. The decades of chronic warfare, however, had created an atmosphere in which the powerful knew nothing else. Hideyoshi, as Reischauer points out, tried to divert Japan's warriors' attentions with an invasion of Korea and China, but it was called off due to his death in 1598. It fell to Tokugawa, who took the title of shogun, or "the emperor's military adviser" in 1600, to create a system in which social order and peace were maintained by rigid controls.

Edwin O. Reischauer, who was born in Japan, taught Japanese history at Harvard University.

With their military heritage, most of the Daimyo [feudal landlords] were intent upon developing the military strength of their domains. Some of the more powerful

Daimyo, who ruled over several provinces, built up efficient fighting machines, with the peasantry as the backbone of the economic life of the realm and as the reservoir for military manpower, with the feudal aristocracy furnishing administrators and officers for the army, and with the merchants providing a transport corps in time of war.

THE REUNIFICATION BEGINS

The natural tendency was for the larger and stronger realms to swallow up or win dominance over weaker neighbors. In the second half of the sixteenth century, this process resulted in the creation of a single paramount power in Japan. The first great figure in the reunification of the country was Oda Nobunaga, a Daimyo who ruled over three provinces around the modern city of Nagoya east of Kyoto [Japan's capital]. By seizing the capital in 1568, he became the virtual dictator of central Japan, and he proceeded to consolidate his power by breaking the military might of the powerful central monasteries and by capturing the great temple-castle of the True Pure Land Sect in Osaka after a ten-year siege. But Nobunaga never achieved his goal of winning hegemony over all Japan. His career was cut short when a treacherous vassal murdered him in 1582.

Nobunaga's place as undisputed ruler of central Japan was soon assumed by his ablest general, Hideyoshi, a man of lowly birth who had risen to power by sheer ability. Within a few years of Nobunaga's death, Hideyoshi had eliminated the remnants of the Oda family and had established his supremacy over the remaining vassals of Nobunaga. He reconstructed the great castle at Osaka as the seat of his military government, but he gave evidence of a reviving interest in the imperial court at Kyoto by taking for himself the old Fujiwara posts of Prime Minister and Civil Dictator.

In 1587 Hideyoshi crushed the power of the great Satsuma realm of southern Kyushu and thereby won control over all western Japan. Three years later, all of eastern and northern Japan submitted to him after he had eliminated the chief Daimyo realm in the Kanto area. The restoration of political unity in Japan had at last been completed, and peace came to the land suddenly after more than a hundred years of incessant civil war.

A MILITARY ADVENTURE IN KOREA

Hideyoshi found himself in control of a superabundance of professional warriors who knew nothing but warfare. Possibly in order to drain off some of their excess fighting spirit, and probably because he himself, like many successful generals before him, fell victim to the world conqueror complex, Hideyoshi decided to embark on a program of world conquest, which for him meant the conquest of China. To do this he needed passage through Korea, and when the Koreans refused, he invaded the peninsula from the south in 1592. The Japanese armies rapidly overran almost all of Korea, but were eventually checked when they overextended their lines of communication and met the armies of China, which had come to the aid of its Korean satellite. The Japanese were forced back to southern Korea, where they held on for several years despite a gradually deteriorating situation and difficulties in maintaining their communications by sea. The death of Hideyoshi in 1598 gave them a welcome excuse for abandoning the whole venture, and their armies streamed home. Japan's first organized attempt at overseas conquest had ended in complete failure.

The political vacuum created by the death of Hideyoshi was soon filled by one of his foremost vassals, Tokugawa Ieyasu, who had been Hideyoshi's chief deputy in eastern Japan, where he had built himself a castle headquarters at the small village of Edo, the future Tokyo. In 1600, Ieyasu decisively defeated a coalition of rivals, and fifteen years later he destroyed the remnants of Hideyoshi's family when he captured the great Osaka castle by trickery and overwhelming might.

TOKUGAWA BRINGS STABILITY TO JAPAN

Ieyasu, impressed by the inability of the heirs of Nobunaga and Hideyoshi to keep the reins of government in their own hands, was obsessed with the idea of building up a political system strong enough to survive his death. Political stability became his primary goal, and it was equally sought and maintained by his successors. There is no doubt that the Tokugawa created political stability. During the first half of the seventeenth century they created a political system which was to endure almost unchanged for two and a half centuries, and which was to establish a state of domestic peace as complete as that enjoyed by any people at any time. Unfortunately, they secured peace and stability by a series of rigid controls over society, by ruthless suppression of many of the most creative tendencies in the Japan of that day, and by a return to many of the outmoded forms of feudalism—in short, by resorting to what was essentially a reactionary policy even in the early decades of the seventeenth century.

The Tokugawa, like the Minamoto before them, rejected the idea of rule from the old central district around Kyoto and established their new military capital at their castle in Edo, which they expanded into one of the greatest fortresses man has ever created. It was protected by wide moats, high embankments, and massive castle walls, arranged in a series of concentric circles with an overall diameter of slightly more than two miles. Today, the inner circles of the great castle form the beautiful imperial palace grounds in the heart of Tokyo.

KING PHILIP OF SPAIN TRIES TO PRESERVE HIS EMPIRE

David Howarth

In the late 1500s Philip II, king of Spain, controlled an empire that stretched from Europe to Mexico and South America to the Philippines. Gold and silver from American mines flowed into his treasury, and Spanish ships commanded the world's oceans. Moreover, Spain had taken the leading role in the Catholic Counter-Reformation, which tried to invigorate Catholicism as it curbed the spread of Protestant Christianity.

David Howarth, author of the following selection, points out that despite Philip's appearance of great power, his empire was tenuous. The Spanish had never managed to establish control over England, which was governed by Elizabeth, Philip's half-sister by marriage. Not only was England staunchly Protestant, but English ships constantly interfered with Spanish vessels in the Atlantic. Philip failed to solve the English problem in 1588 with the Spanish Armada, a huge fleet organized to invade England. Moreover, Howarth points out, Spain's riches were also illusory, as royal expenditures and inflation reduced the value of America's gold and silver. Nonetheless, Howarth claims, Philip tried valiantly to maintain his role as the greatest Catholic monarch.

David Howarth, a popular historian, is the author of thirteen books of English and world history.

Excerpted from *The Voyage of the Armada: The Spanish Story*, by David Howarth (New York: Viking, 1981). Copyright © 1981 by David Howarth. Originally published by Cassell & Co., London.

In 1583 Philip was sixty-one and had been king for over thirty years. From the Escorial [his palace near Madrid] he ruled, or hoped to rule, a world of almost infinite complexity. Geographically his empire was the biggest any king in history had controlled: in Europe there was Spain and Portugal, Sicily, Naples and Milan, and parts of the Netherlands and France; and overseas the Spanish and Portuguese dominions in America, Africa, India and the East. Right on the other side of the world the Philippine Islands were named after him. And for two years in his youth his marriage to Mary Tudor had also made him titular King of England.

Only the Spanish possessions overseas had come to him purely by conquest; those in Europe had fallen into his hands by tricks of inheritance, through the tangled branches of royal family trees. Royal marriages, like the duke's, were always political. Babies could be betrothed before they were born, laws against incest could be cast aside, doddering palsied old men could be married to teenage girls in last-minute hope of producing an heir to combine the power of two royal houses. All princes and princesses had to expect this calculated, unromantic mating: Queen Elizabeth [of England] alone refused it, and played the inheritance game by keeping her suitors guessing. Philip himself had been married four times, to heiresses of Portugal, England, France and Austria, and had not seen any of his brides before the ceremonies started. All of them had died. One way and another he could prove he was related to almost everyone with royal blood, and could lay some kind of a claim to every throne. Sometimes he had supported a shaky claim with the threat of the Spanish army.

PHILIP WAS THE PROTECTOR OF THE CATHOLIC CHURCH

But it was not only a political empire; it was also a religious entity, and that was what made it so complex. King Philip was His Most Catholic Majesty. He believed he was appointed by God to defend the truth against infidels and heretics. The pope was Vicar of Christ: Philip, in his own eyes, was Champion of God, the equal of the pope in God's designs. In this sense, his boundaries were vague. There were people all over Europe, caught in the ebb and flow of Reformation and Counter-Reformation, whose loyalties were divided between their country and their church. In almost all of Philip's Catholic domains, Protestants had been exterminated, or pushed far under ground, by the Inquisition [the Roman Catholic law court]. The only exception was the Netherlands. All through his reign they had been in revolt, partly against the shame of foreign rule and partly to protect their Protestant creed: he had to keep an immensely expensive army there, and it had never succeeded in putting the rebels down. But he was not only concerned with his own domains. It was his personal duty, divinely imposed as he believed, to punish Protestants everywhere and rescue Catholics who lived under Protestant rule.

He was a strange crusader. By inclination, he was not a man of action: he had never been any good at the martial arts, and had never tried to inspire or lead an army. He had only once in his life been present at a battle and then, although his own side won, the whole thing had disgusted him. Luckily, there were excellent generals in Spain, among them his own much younger illegitimate brother Don Juan, his nephew Alexander Farnese, Duke of Parma, the ageing Duke of Alba, and at sea the Marquis of Santa Cruz. These men directed his battles—God's battles, he would have said—while he stayed at home and decided whom they should fight against.

But neither was he a man of much intellect. The brain he applied to God's problems and his own was quite remarkably slow. He dreaded quick decisions; it always took him days, and sometimes years, to make up his mind about anything. His people called him Philip the Prudent, and he made rather a virtue of his chronic hesitation. 'Time and I are one,' he would say while he procrastinated, expecting—and sometimes rightly—that problems would disappear if he waited long enough. He was also extremely slow to learn, either from his own experience or from the much more brilliant men of his court. The mixture of mediocrity and power made him immovably self-righteous and obstinate. . . .

A SICKLY AND SOLITARY KING

He led an unhealthy life, immured in the Escorial. It was said he spent three or four hours of every day at his prayers. No doubt that was a solace, but it was also a penance: he suffered from very painful and swollen knees. His physicians said it was gout, and perhaps they were right; but perhaps it was an early symptom of the disease which led him at last, ten years after the armada, to a death of slow disgusting agony, when his body decomposed while there was still life in it. Whatever it was, those hours of kneeling on marble floors must have made it worse; so must the physicians, who treated it by frequent bleeding, drawing off the blood from his feet. By the age when he had to apply his mind to planning the armada his knees were so grossly swollen that he could hardly hobble the yards from his bed to the desk where he worked, and he lived in such pain that he could never sleep soundly. Instead, he often sat at his desk until dawn, working his ponderous, industrious way through the mountains of papers that never grew any less. The armada was created, an act of immense will-power, by a man distracted by insomnia and pain.

King Philip II

King Philip loved his children, except Don Carlos the eldest, who was too warped in mind and body for anyone to love. His letters to them were gentle and even mildly humorous in a paternal way. He had also loved at least one of his wives, and was said to be kind to his servants. But outside that little circle he was seldom moved by pity— and he once said, to a man condemned to the stake for heresy, that he would carry the wood to burn his own son for such an awful crime. He was far from being alone in this lack of pity; it was an era when churches, especially the Spanish Church, disregarded the virtues of charity and mercy. The God that Philip served was all-powerful, all-knowing and unforgiving. He could and did take part by miracles in men's affairs. Yet paradoxically He depended on His servants to do His will. He demanded worship absolutely exactly in the forms the Catholic Church proclaimed, and not in any other. He also demanded the most cruel and terrible punishments men could devise for anyone who deviated in the least degree. Especially, He demanded this service from the man to whom He had given the highest earthly power: King Philip. It was truly an awful burden for a man to carry.

THE SPANISH EMPIRE WAS UNWIELDY

It was also a burden for a human empire. Saddled with that primitive belief, the Spanish empire was doomed to fall to pieces, and during Philip's reign the cracks had begun. In an age when reports and orders were carried by horsemen and sailing ships, the empire was too big for any kind of central control—and far too big for the clerkly bureaucratic control he tried to impose on it. He hated to delegate an atom of his power: among the heaps of papers momentous questions waited his decisions while he struggled with trivialities. The empire was choking to death on paper.

Also it was bankrupt. Vast treasures flowed into it from dominions in east and west, but nobody understood that continually creating new money only led to inflation. Philip had mortgaged all the empire's revenues for years ahead, mainly to foreign bankers. He always hoped some windfall would pay off his debts; but the bankers knew he would never be solvent again, and he began to find he could not even borrow. Trite though it might seem, the designs of God cost an awful lot of money.

It would be quite absurd to say that Philip, or the Spanish people or anyone else, were to blame for having this difficult concept of the Christian God. It had grown through generations, and they had inherited it. For a century past the Inquisition had very strictly imposed on them the Catholic forms of worship, and they wore their conformity as a soldier wears a uniform. Few Spaniards ever met a heretic, and those who did, in the Netherlands for example, met them only as political and warlike enemies. Inevitably, military and religious affairs were mixed in their minds. The mixture was made more profound by St Ignatius of Loyola, a Spanish soldier himself, who founded the Society of Jesus in 1540. The Jesuits became an international organization with a frankly military structure, which demanded, like an army, unquestioning obedience to its senior officers, and oaths which overrode mere national loyalty. This kind of religious institution had an immense appeal for Spaniards, especially soldiers; in them, religious and national loyalty coincided.

But in Philip's simple mind the mixture of military and religious thought became an insoluble muddle. The God he conceived had the vices and ambitions of an earthly tyrant, which has always been a philosophical impossibility, suited only to primitive people in elementary societies. Yet the society Philip ruled was highly complex. In all his problems as a ruler, how could he ever distinguish his own will from the will of a God who was so much like himself? He never could and never did. In all his projects he explained to everyone that he was pursuing God's design, as if it were just a happy coincidence that God's purpose happened to add to Philip's power. Foreigners, fearful or envious of the dominance of Spain, thought this was hypocrisy, but it was not. Reading Philip's letters in the twentieth century and judging him by twentieth-century standards—which of course has the inherent unfairness of history—one has to say he was bigoted, dogmatic, self-righteous, illogical, ruthless and hopelessly confused; but also, he was appallingly sincere.

Elizabeth I, Queen of England

Lytton Strachey

During the reign of Elizabeth I, from 1558 to 1603, England became one of the world's great powers. When the young queen, the daughter of Henry VIII, took the throne, England was a pawn of France and Spain and the site of bloody conflicts between Catholics and Protestants. By the early 1600s England had disentangled itself from European power struggles and become staunchly Protestant. In addition, English ships and English adventurers, such as Sir Francis Drake and Sir Walter Raleigh, had begun the process by which England was to take control of the world's seas.

In the following selection, Lytton Strachey examines the personality and accomplishments of Elizabeth and asserts that she created an atmosphere that encouraged greatness. He argues that the queen's apparent indecisiveness masked a strong and determined will. In addition, her energy and common touch presented a strong contrast to her great rival, the dour Philip II of Spain. Moreover, Strachey claims, Elizabeth understood that her role was to bring the cultivation and secularism of the Renaissance to England and thereby create a truly unique English civilization.

Lytton Strachey is one of the great English biographers of the twentieth century. His books include *Queen Victoria* and *Eminent Victorians* as well as *Elizabeth and Essex*.

T he lion heart, the splendid gestures—such heroic things were there, no doubt—visible to everybody; but their true significance in the general scheme of her character was remote and complicated. The sharp and hostile eyes of the Spanish ambassadors saw something different; in their opinion, the outstanding characteristic of Elizabeth was pusillanimity [timidity]. They were wrong; but they perceived more of the truth than the idle onlooker. They had come into contact with those forces in the Queen's mind which proved, incidentally, fatal to themselves, and brought her, in the end, her enormous triumph. That triumph was not the result of heroism. The very contrary was the case: the grand policy which dominated Elizabeth's life was the most unheroic conceivable; and her true history remains a standing lesson for melodramatists in statecraft. In reality, she succeeded by virtue of all the qualities which every hero should be without— dissimulation, pliability, indecision, procrastination, parsimony. It might almost be said that the heroic element chiefly appeared in the unparalleled lengths to which she allowed those qualities to carry her. It needed a lion heart indeed to spend twelve years in convincing the world that she was in love with the [French] Duke of Anjou, and to stint the victuals of the men who defeated the Armada; but in such directions she was in very truth capable of everything. She found herself a sane woman in a universe of violent maniacs, between contending forces of terrific intensity— the rival nationalisms of France and Spain, the rival religions of Rome and Calvin; for years it had seemed inevitable that she should be crushed by one or other of them, and she had survived because she had been able to meet the extremes around her with her own extremes of cunning and prevarication. . . .

Religious persons at the time were distressed by her conduct, and imperialist historians have wrung their hands over her since. Why could she not suppress her hesitations and chicaneries and take a noble risk? Why did she not step forth, boldly and frankly, as the leader of Protestant Europe, accept the sovereignty of Holland, and fight the good fight to destroy Catholicism and transfer the Spanish Empire to the rule of England? The answer is that she cared for none of those things. She understood her true nature and her true mission better than her critics. It was only by an accident of birth that she was a Protestant leader; at heart she was profoundly secular; and it was her destiny to be the champion, not of the Reformation, but of something greater—the Renaissance. When she had finished her strange doings, there was civilisation in England. . . .

Elizabeth Was Complex, Vigorous, and Cultivated

Undoubtedly there was a touch of the sinister about her. One saw it in the movements of her extraordinarily long hands. But it was

During her reign, Queen Elizabeth encouraged literary and artistic activities that helped England develop its cultural voice.

a touch and no more—just enough to remind one that there was Italian blood in her veins—the blood of the subtle and cruel Visconti [the despots of Renaissance Milan]. On the whole, she was English. On the whole, though she was infinitely subtle, she was not cruel; she was almost humane for her times; and her occasional bursts of savagery were the results of fear or temper. In spite of superficial resemblances, she was the very opposite of her most dangerous enemy—the weaving spider of the Escorial. Both were masters of dissimulation and lovers of delay; but the leaden foot of Philip [king of Spain] was the symptom of a dying organism, while Elizabeth temporised for the contrary reason—because vitality can afford to wait. The fierce old hen sat still, brooding over the English nation, whose pullulating energies were coming swiftly to ripeness and unity under her wings. She sat still; but every feather bristled; she was tremendously alive. Her super-abundant vigour was at once alarming and delightful. While the Spanish ambassador declared that ten thousand devils possessed her, the ordinary Englishman saw in King Hal's [Henry VIII] full-blooded daughter a Queen after his own heart. She swore; she spat; she struck with her fist when she was angry; she roared with laughter when she was amused. And she was often amused. A radiant atmosphere of humour coloured and softened the harsh lines of her destiny, and buoyed her up along the zigzags of her dreadful path. Her response to every stimulus was immediate and rich: to the folly of the moment, to the clash and horror of great events, her soul leapt out with a vivacity, an abandonment, a complete awareness of the situation, which made her, which makes her still, a fascinating spectacle. She could play with life as with an equal, wrestling with it, making fun of it, admiring it, watching its drama, intimately relishing the strangeness of circumstance, the sudden freaks of fortune, the perpetual unexpectedness of things. "Per molto variare la natura è bella" [the many variations of nature are beautiful] was one of her favourite aphorisms.

The variations in her own behaviour were hardly less frequent than nature's. The rough hectoring dame with her practical jokes, her out-of-doors manners, her passion for hunting, would suddenly become a stern-faced woman of business, closeted for long hours with secretaries, reading and dictating despatches, and examining with sharp exactitude the minutiae of accounts. Then, as suddenly, the cultivated lady of the Renaissance would shine forth. For Elizabeth's accomplishments were many and dazzling. She was mistress of six languages besides her own, a student of Greek, a superb calligraphist, an excellent musician. She was a connoisseur of painting and poetry. She danced, after the Florentine style, with a high magnificence that astonished beholders. Her conversation, full, not only of humour, but of elegance and wit, revealed an unerring social sense, a charming delicacy of personal perception. It was this spiritual versatility which made her one of the supreme diplomatists of history. . . .

Nor was it only in her mind that these complicated contrasts were apparent; they dominated her physical being too. The tall and bony frame was subject to strange weaknesses. Rheumatisms racked her; intolerable headaches laid her prone in agony; a hideous ulcer poisoned her existence for years. Though her serious illnesses were few, a long succession of minor maladies, a host of morbid symptoms, held her contemporaries in alarmed suspense and have led some modern searchers to suspect that she received from her father an hereditary taint. Our knowledge, both of the laws of medicine and of the actual details of her disorders, is too limited to allow a definite conclusion; but at least it seems certain that, in spite of her prolonged and varied sufferings, Elizabeth was fundamentally strong. She lived to be seventy—a great age in those days—discharging to the end the laborious duties of government.

Shakespeare Commemorates Elizabeth's Reign

William Shakespeare

William Shakespeare is the best-known product of the Elizabethan age of English literature and culture. But he is only one of many illustrious artists of the age. The playwright Christopher Marlowe, the poets John Donne and Edmund Spenser, and the philosopher Francis Bacon also created some of their greatest works during the reign of Elizabeth I (1558–1603). Indeed, Elizabeth's reign inspired a uniquely creative atmosphere for not only writers and philosophers, but also businessmen, explorers, and adventurers.

The following selection is from act 5 of Shakespeare's *Henry VIII*, the last of his history plays to be staged, probably in 1613. The play tells the story of Henry VIII, Elizabeth's father and king of England from 1509 to 1547, who separated England from the Roman Catholic Church to legalize his marriage to Anne Boleyn, Elizabeth's mother. The play closes with the christening of the Princess Elizabeth by Archbishop Cranmer, the head of the new Church of England. Shakespeare took the opportunity to have his characters predict greatness for Elizabeth and for her people, a greatness that he saw played out in his own lifetime and memorialized in one of his last plays.

G ARTER (royal servant). Heaven, from thy endless goodness, send prosperous life, long, and ever happy, to the high and mighty princess of England, Elizabeth!

From *Henry VIII*, by William Shakespeare, act 5, scene 5, in *The Complete Works of Shakespeare*, edited by Hardin Craig (Chicago: Scott, Foresman, 1951).

FLOURISH. *Enter* KING *and Guard.*

CRANMER. [*Kneeling*] And to your royal grace, and the good
    queen,
My noble partners, and myself, thus pray:
All comfort, joy, in this most gracious lady,
Heaven ever laid up to make parents happy,
May hourly fall upon ye!

KING HENRY. Thank you, good lord archbishop:
What is her name?

CRANMER.   Elizabeth.

KING HENRY.   Stand up, lord.

[*The King kisses the child.*]

With this kiss take my blessing: God protect thee!
Into whose hand I give thy life.

CRANMER.   Amen.

KING HENRY. My noble gossips, ye have been too prodigal: I
    thank ye heartily; so shall this lady, When she has so much
    English.

CRANMER.   Let me speak, sir,
For heaven now bids me; and the words I utter
Let none think flattery, for they'll find 'em truth.
This royal infant—heaven still move about her!—
Though in her cradle, yet now promises
Upon this land a thousand thousand blessings,
Which time shall bring to ripeness: she shall be—
But few now living can behold that goodness—
A pattern to all princes living with her,
And all that shall succeed: Saba [the Queen of Sheba] was never
More covetous of wisdom and fair virtue
Than this pure soul shall be: all princely graces,
That mould up such a mighty piece as this is,
With all the virtues that attend the good,
Shall still be doubled on her: truth shall nurse her,
Holy and heavenly thoughts still counsel her:
She shall be loved and fear'd: her own shall bless her;
Her foes shake like a field of beaten corn,
And hang their heads with sorrow: good grows with her:
In her days every man shall eat in safety,
Under his own vine, what he plants; and sing
The merry songs of peace to all his neighbours:
God shall be truly known; and those about her
From her shall read the perfect ways of honour,
And by those claim their greatness, not by blood.
Nor shall this peace sleep with her: but as when
The bird of wonder dies, the maiden phoenix,

Her ashes new create another heir,
As great in admiration as herself;
So shall she leave her blessedness to one,
When heaven shall call her from this cloud of darkness,
Who from the sacred ashes of her honour
Shall star-like rise, as great in fame as she was,
And so stand fix'd: peace, plenty, love, truth, terror,
That were the servants to this chosen infant,
Shall then be his, and like a vine grow to him:
Wherever the bright sun of heaven shall shine,
His honour and the greatness of his name
Shall be, and make new nations: he shall flourish,
And, like a mountain cedar, reach his branches
To all the plains about him: our children's children
Shall see this, and bless heaven.
 KING HENRY.   Thou speakest wonders.
 CRANMER. She shall be, to the happiness of England,
An aged princess; many days shall see her,
And yet no day without a deed to crown it.
Would I had known no more! but she must die,
She must, the saints must have her; yet a virgin,
A most unspotted lily shall she pass
To the ground, and all the world shall mourn her.
 KING HENRY. O lord archbishop,
Thou hast made me now a man! never, before
This happy child, did I get any thing:
This oracle of comfort has so pleased me,
That when I am in heaven I shall desire
To see what this child does, and praise my Maker.
I thank ye all. To you, my good lord mayor,
And your good brethren, I am much beholding;
I have received much honour by your presence,
And ye shall find me thankful. Lead the way, lords:
Ye must all see the queen, and she must thank ye,
She will be sick else. This day, no man think
Has business at his house; for all shall stay:
This little one shall make it holiday.

1368

The Ming dynasty takes control of China.

1420s

Ming emperors construct the Forbidden City in Beijing.

1454

The Turkish Ottoman Empire conquers Constantinople, marking the end of the thousand-year-old Byzantine Empire; the end of the Hundred Years' War between England and France.

1455

German craftsman Johann Gutenberg prints a section of the Bible using moveable type on the first printing press in Europe; by the early 1500s over one thousand print shops operate in Europe.

1460s

Portuguese merchants trade regularly on the west coast of Africa.

1464

The Songhay Empire establishes control over much of inland West Africa, dominating the region until 1591.

1467

The beginning of over a century of civil war in Japan; competing landlords, or daimyos, fight one another using samurai retainers, while peasant uprisings and Buddhist revolts add to the violence.

1469

Ferdinand, king of Aragon, marries Isabella, queen of Castile; their marriage sets the stage for the unification of Spain; Lorenzo de Medici inherits control of Florence.

1471

The death of the Inca emperor Pachacuti; under his rule the Inca Empire grew to dominate an empire that stretched over two thousand miles along the Pacific coast of South America.

1480s

Ming Chinese leaders begin to build the Great Wall of China to protect the Middle Kingdom of the warlike nomads of Central Asia.

1487

Under Bartolomeu Dias, Portuguese ships sail around the southern tip of Africa.

1492

Ferdinand and Isabella complete the reconquest of Spain by defeating Granada, the final Islamic kingdom on the Iberian Peninsula; Christopher Columbus, sailing in the name of Queen Isabella, guides three small ships from Spain to the New World; Columbus claims the territory for Spain.

1497

Vasco da Gama leads a Portuguese fleet around Africa and to the Indian port of Calicut; Portuguese ships go on to dominate Indian Ocean trade for much of the sixteenth century.

1502

Moctezuma (Montezuma) II becomes Aztec emperor; under his reign, which lasted until 1520, the empire reached its height, dominating a population of millions in central Mexico.

1503

Leonardo da Vinci paints the *Mona Lisa*.

1506

Construction of the vast basilica of St. Peter in Rome begins; the great Renaissance artists Michelangelo and Raphael aid in its design.

1510

The Portuguese take control of Goa in India, establishing it as a base for both trade and missionary activity.

1511

Raphael paints *The School of Athens*.

1512

Michelangelo completes the painting of the Sistine Chapel ceiling.

1513

Niccolò Machiavelli, humanist and Florentine diplomat, publishes *The Prince*.

1517

Martin Luther, a German monk, begins the Protestant Reformation by issuing his Ninety-five Theses, a list of "points of dispute" concerned with corruption in the Roman Catholic Church; by the 1520s, Protestant, or "protest," Christianity is sweeping Europe; Spain legalizes the slavery of Africans in the New World.

1519

Ferdinand Magellan begins a voyage around South America and into the Pacific Ocean; members of his crew become the first to circumnavigate the globe, returning to Spain in 1521; King Charles I of Spain is elected Holy Roman Emperor and takes the title of Charles V.

1521

The Spanish conquistador Hernán Cortés completes the conquest of Tenochtitlán, the capital of the Aztec Empire in Mexico; European diseases such as smallpox help the Spanish take control as millions of Native Americans die.

1523

Babur the Tiger, the first Mughal, begins to make military raids into India from Afghanistan; by 1529 Babur's armies control much of northern India.

1526

At the Battle of Mohacs, the Ottoman Empire under Suleiman II defeats the Christian kingdom of Hungary.

1527

Imperial troops under Charles V sack the city of Rome and bring much of Italy under Spanish control.

1529

Ottoman troops mount a siege of Vienna; although the siege fails the Turks remain a threat to central and western Europe for the next 150 years.

1531

Under the conquistador Francisco Pizarro, Spanish troops encounter the Inca Empire of Peru; by 1533 they control it, thanks to disunity among the Incas as well as European diseases and firearms.

1533

Henry VIII, king of England, takes control of the Church of England and divorces Catherine of Aragon, his first wife and the aunt of Charles V; he then marries his mistress Anne Boleyn, mother of the future Queen Elizabeth I.

1534

The Ottoman Empire conquers Baghdad.

1543

Portuguese merchants reach Japan, introducing both Catholicism and gunpowder weapons.

1545

The first meeting of the Council of Trent begins the Catholic Counter-Reformation; by 1563, the final meeting, church officials determine to root out corruption and defend the church using both peaceful and violent means.

1556

Akbar the Great becomes the third Mughal emperor; Akbar introduces an Indian golden age by encouraging religious toleration, sponsoring artistic and architectural works, and constructing roads, ports, and a competent bureaucracy; Philip II succeeds Charles V as king of Spain; his domains include much of western Europe, the Americas, and the Philippine Islands of Southeast Asia. Philip sees himself as the primary earthly defender of the Roman Catholic Church.

1558

Elizabeth I becomes queen of England; she soon brings to England a reasonably tolerant Protestantism and actively encourages foreign trade and cultural accomplishment.

1562

The English sea captain John Hawkins takes a cargo of slaves from Africa to the Caribbean, inaugurating the large-scale Atlantic slave trade.

1570

Oda Nobunaga, a minor daimyo, begins the process of reuni-
fying and pacifying Japan.

1571

At the Battle of Lepanto, a Catholic coalition defeats a Turkish
fleet, stopping the Ottoman advance into the Mediterranean.

1572

Following a wedding between the Protestant Henry of
Navarre and the Catholic Princess Marguerite of France,
Catholic nobles and mobs massacre thousands of French
Protestants; the event is known as the St. Bartholomew's
Day Massacre; Wanli becomes the emperor of the Ming dy-
nasty.

1588

Philip II's Spanish Armada fails to invade England and replace
Elizabeth I with a Catholic monarch; the event reflects England's growing power at sea; the warlord Hideyoshi con-
tinues to pacify Japan by declaring it illegal for peasants or
monks to possess weapons.

1590s

The plays of William Shakespeare, born in 1564, are performed
regularly at Elizabeth's court.

1598

Philip II of Spain dies.

1600

Tokugawa Ieyasu completes the reunification of Japan and begins the Tokugawa Shogunate.

1601

Matteo Ricci, a Catholic missionary, visits the Chinese emperor
Wanli in the Forbidden City; he impresses the emperor
with products of European culture and technology.

1603

Elizabeth I of England dies.

1605

Akbar the Great in Mughal India dies.

1607

English colonists settle at Jamestown in Virginia.

FOR FURTHER RESEARCH

PRIMARY SOURCES

Babur, Emperor of Hindustan, *Memoirs*. Trans. Annette Suzanna Beveridge. New Delhi: Oriental Books, 1971.

Christopher Columbus, *Journal of First Voyage to America*. Trans. Van Wyck Brooks. New York: Albert and Charles Boni, 1924.

Hernando Cortés, *The Despatches of Hernando Cortés*. Trans. George Folsom. New York: Wiley and Putnam, 1843.

Bernal Diaz del Castillo, *The True History of the Conquest of Mexico*. Trans. Maurice Keatinge. New York: Robert M. McBride, 1927.

Felipe Guaman Poma de Ayala, *Letter to a King: A Picture History of the Inca Empire*. Trans. and ed. Christopher Dilke. London: Allen and Unwin, 1978.

Richard Hakluyt, *Voyages of the Elizabethan Seamen*. Ed. Edward John Payne. Oxford, England: Clarendon, 1907.

Martin Luther, *Christian Liberty*. Ed. Harold J. Grimm. Philadelphia: Fortress Press, 1957.

Niccolò Machiavelli, *The Prince*. Trans. George Bull. Middlesex, England: Penguin Classics, 1961.

Christopher Marlowe, *Complete Works*. Ed. Roma Gill. Oxford, England: Clarendon, 1987.

Sir Thomas More, *Utopia*. Trans. Peter K. Marshall. New York: Washington Square Press, 1965.

Giovanni Pico della Mirandola, *Oration on the Dignity of Man*. Trans. Elizabeth Freeman Forbes. Lexington, KY: Anvil Press, 1953.

The Notebooks of Leonardo da Vinci. Trans. and ed. Edward Mac-Curdy. New York: George Braziller, 1954.

William Shakespeare, *The Complete Works of Shakespeare*. Ed. Hardin Craig. Chicago: Scott, Foresman, 1951.

"The Twenty-One Precepts of Hojo Soun," in *Ideals of the Samurai: Writings of Japanese Warriors*. Trans. William Scott Wilson. Burbank, CA: Ohara, 1982.

EMPIRES AND CIVILIZATIONS

Barr C. Brundage, *Empire of the Inca*. Norman: University of Oklahoma Press, 1963.

Geoffrey W. Conrad and Arthur A. Demarest, *Religion and Empire: The Dynamics of Aztec and Inca Expansion*. Cambridge, England: Cambridge University Press, 1984.

R. Trevor Davies, *The Golden Century of Spain, 1501–1621*. New York: St. Martin's Press, 1937.

Richard S. Dunn, *The Age of Religious Wars, 1559–1715*. New York: Norton, 1978.

Philippe Erlanger, *Saint Bartholomew's Night*. Trans. Patrick O'Brian. New York: Pantheon, 1962.

Jason Goodwin, *Lords of the Horizon*. New York: Henry Holt, 1998.

Thomas A. Hale, *Scribe, Griot, and Novelist: Narrative Interpreters of the Songhay Empire*. Gainesville: University of Florida Press, 1990.

Harry Hearder, *Italy: A Short History*. Cambridge, England: Cambridge University Press, 1990.

David Howarth, *The Voyage of the Armada: The Spanish Story*. New York: Viking, 1981.

Ray Huang, *1587, A Year of No Significance: The Ming Dynasty in Decline*. New Haven, CT: Yale University Press, 1981.

H.G. Koenigsberger, *Early Modern Europe 1500–1789*. London: Longman Group UK, 1987.

Franz Michael, *China Through the Ages*. Boulder, CO: Westview, 1986.

H.P. Nicholson, *Art of Aztec Mexico: Treasures of Tenochtitlán*. Washington, DC: National Gallery of Art, 1983.

Roland Oliver and Anthony Atmore, *The African Middle Ages 1400–1800*. Cambridge, England: Cambridge University Press, 1981.

Noel Perrin, *Giving Up the Gun: Japan's Reversion to the Sword*. Boston: David R. Godine, 1979.

Edwin O. Reischauer, *Japan: Past and Present*. 2nd ed. Tokyo: Charles E. Tuttle, 1946.

Percival Spear, *A History of India*. Vol. 2. Middlesex, England: Penguin Books, 1965.

Stuart Cary Welch et al., *The Emperor's Album: Images of Mughal India*. New York: Metropolitan Museum of Art, 1987.

Andrew Wheatcroft, *The Ottomans*. London: Viking, 1993.

GREAT LEADERS

Mary Elizabeth Berry, *Hideyoshi*. Cambridge, MA: Harvard University Press, 1982.

Maurice Collis, *Cortés and Montezuma*. New York: New Directions, 1999.

Felipe Fernandez-Armesto, *Ferdinand and Isabella*. London: Weidenfeld and Nicolson, 1975.

Waldemar Hansen, *The Peacock Throne*. New York: Holt, Rinehart, and Winston, 1972.

Harold Lamb, *Suleiman the Magnificent: Sultan of the East*. Garden City, NY: Doubleday, 1951.

Jean Hippolyte Mariejol, *The Spain of Ferdinand and Isabella*. Trans. Benjamin Keen. Brunswick, NJ: Rutgers University Press, 1961.

Ann Paludan, *Chronicle of the Chinese Emperors*. London: Thames and Hudson, 1998.

Alison Plowden, *Elizabeth Regina: The Age of Triumph, 1588–1603*. New York: Times Books, 1980.

Lytton Strachey, *Elizabeth and Essex*. New York: Harcourt, Brace, and World, 1928.

EXPLORATION, TRADE, AND EXCHANGE

Jean Andrews, "The Peripatetic Chili Pepper: Diffusion of the Domesticated Capiscum Since Columbus," in *Chilies to*

Chocolate: Food the Americas Gave the World. Ed. Nelson Foster and Linda S. Cordell. Tuscon: University of Arizona Press, 1992.

Alfred W. Crosby, *The Columbian Exchange: Biological and Cultural Consequences of 1492*. Westport, CT: Greenwood, 1972.

George Harold Dunne, *Generation of Giants: The Story of the Jesuits in China in the Last Decades of the Ming Dynasty*. Notre Dame, IN: University of Notre Dame Press, 1962.

Samuel Eliot Morison, *Christopher Columbus, Mariner*. Boston: Little, Brown, 1942.

Dan O'Sullivan, *The Age of Discovery 1400–1550*. London: Longman, 1984.

J.H. Parry, *The Establishment of the European Hegemony 1415–1715*. 3rd ed. New York: Harper Torchbooks, 1966.

Edward Reynolds, *Stand the Storm: A History of the Atlantic Slave Trade*. London: Allison and Busby, 1985.

Paul William Roberts, *Empire of the Sun*. New York: Riverhead, 1994.

Jonathan D. Spence, *The Chan's Great Continent: China in Western Minds*. New York: W.W. Norton, 1998.

Simon Winchester, *Pacific Rising*. New York: Touchstone/Simon & Schuster, 1991.

Ronald Wright, *Stolen Continents*. Boston: Houghton Mifflin, 1992.

RENAISSANCE ART AND THOUGHT

Bernard Berenson, *The Italian Painters of the Renaissance*. New York: Phaidon, 1952.

Selwyn Brinton, *The Golden Age of the Medici*. London: Methuen, 1925.

Jacob Burckhardt, *The Civilization of the Renaissance in Italy*. Trans. S.G.C. Middlemore. New York: Harper Colophon, 1929.

E.R. Chamberlin, *Everyday Life in Renaissance Times*. London: B.T. Batsford, 1965.

Hans J. Hillerbrand, *Christendom Divided: The Protestant Reformation*. New York: Corpus, 1971.

Vincenzo Labella, *A Season of Giants: 1492–1508*. Boston: Little, Brown, 1990.

William Manchester, *A World Lit Only by Fire*. Boston: Little, Brown, 1992.

Charles G. Nauert Jr., *Humanism and the Culture of Renaissance Europe*. Cambridge, England: Cambridge University Press, 1995.

J.M. Roberts, *A Concise History of the World*. New York: Oxford University Press, 1995.

S.H. Steinberg, *Five Hundred Years of Printing*. Rev. John Trevitt. London: British Library and Oak Knoll Press, 1996.

Jeff Hay received a Ph.D. in history from the University of California, San Diego, where he taught in the innovative Making of the Modern World program. He now teaches world history at San Diego State University. In addition to editing two volumes of Greenhaven Press's Turning Points in World History series, Hay is working on a three-volume encyclopedia on the history of the Third Reich.